Rosie's BAKERY

CHOCOLATE-
P·A·C·K·E·D
JAM-FILLED
BUTTER-RICH
NO-HOLDS-BARRED
COOKIE BOOK

Rosie's BAKERY

CHOCOLATE-
P • A • C • K • E • D
JAM - FILLED
BUTTER-RICH

NO - HOLDS - BARRED

COOKIE
BOOK

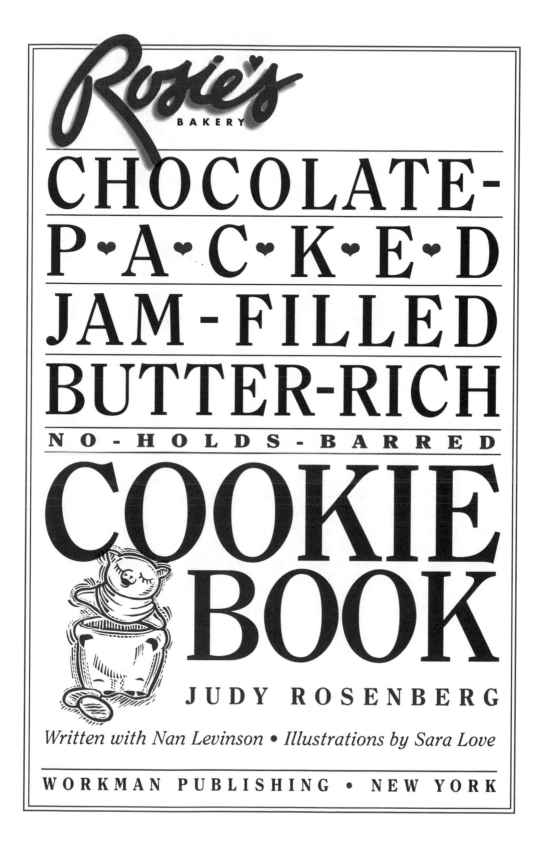

JUDY ROSENBERG

Written with Nan Levinson • Illustrations by Sara Love

WORKMAN PUBLISHING • NEW YORK

Library of Congress Cataloging-in-Publication Data
Rosenberg, Judy
Rosie's bakery chocolate-packed, jam-filled, butter-rich, no-holds-barred cookie book / by Judy Rosenberg.
p.   cm
Includes index.
ISBN 0–7611–0625–1 (alk. paper). — ISBN 1–56305–506–6
(pbk. alk. paper)
1. Cookies. I. Title
TX772.R655   1996

641.8'654—dc20
96–43823

CIP

Cover and book design by Janet Vicario
Cover photographs by Richard Feldman

Workman books are available at special discounts when purchased in bulk for premiums and sales promotions as well as for fund-raising or educational use. Special editions or book excerpts can be created to specification. For details, contact the Special Sales Director at the address below.

Workman Publishing Company, Inc.
708 Broadway
New York, NY 10003-9555

Manufactured in the United States of America

First printing October 1996
10 9 8 7 6 5 4 3 2 1

Dedication
♥ ♥ ♥ ♥ ♥ ♥ ♥

To my mother, and to my father
who is now
loving me from above

Acknowledgments

❤ ❤ ❤ ❤ ❤ ❤ ❤

To Nan Levinson, whose humor, wit, and mastery of words will never cease to amaze me.

❤ ❤

To Mimi Santini-Ritt, my dedicated recipe tester, who is a joy to work with, and who will hopefully be testing recipes for my next book in her brand new kitchen (that is, if she isn't touring the country playing bridge)!

❤ ❤

To Beverly Jones, whose creativity and mastery of baking is an inspiration.

❤ ❤

To Eliot Winograd, my business partner, for taking care of all the things that would drive me crazy if he wasn't there to do them.

❤ ❤

To my wonderful staff, without whom Rosie's would be merely a concept.

❤ ❤

To my agent, Doe Coover, my editor, Suzanne Rafer, and the book's designer, Janet Vicario, as well as the other members of the editorial and art staffs at Workman, who made this book a reality.

❤ ❤

To my children, Jake, Noah, and Maya, for eating all the leftover cookies in the freezer.

❤ ❤

Lastly and most importantly, to my husband, Richard, whose inner strength and enlightened perspective on life carry me through the most stressful of times.

Contents

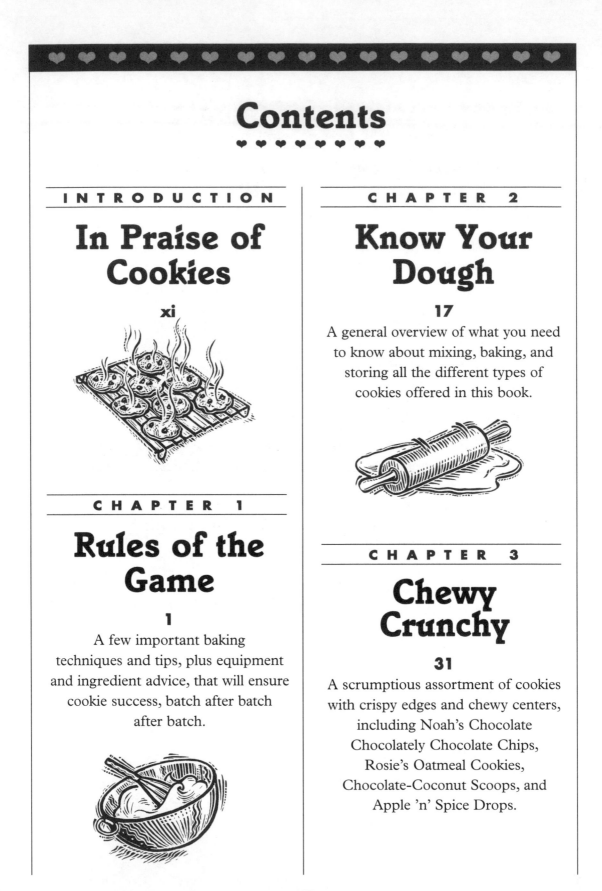

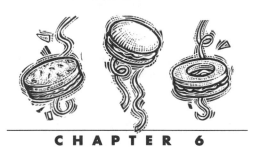

IN PRAISE

OF COOKIES

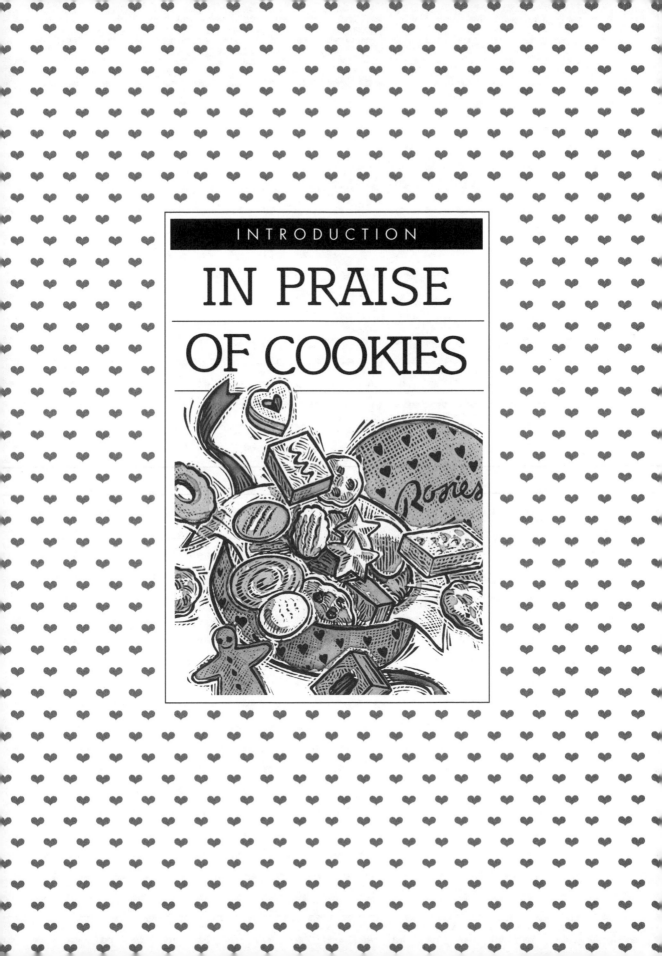

There's no getting around it: I love cookies. We go back a long way, after all, since I first made their acquaintance by way of a zwieback that my mother stuck in my eager hands around the time I got my first tooth. I like to think it was more than mere instinct that led me to insert it directly into my mouth and gum away to my heart's content, knowing with baby certainty that here was a thing of glory.

Call it a knowledge bred in the bone, or maybe an omen that one day I would switch from living *for* cookies to making my living *from* cookies. It's a big burden to put on a little cookie, I know, but the memory of zwieback's combination of crunch and light sweetness came flooding back when I became a professional baker years later, and it stayed with me as I opened each Rosie's Bakery, reminding me that there are few things in this world more deeply satisfying than a really good cookie.

Armed with that first taste of happiness, I became a toddler with a mission. It was cookies I craved, and cookies I demanded. As soon as my first tooth was joined by a few others, I moved on to arrowroots. Now *there* was a cookie: crisp, buttery, dainty, decidedly more big-girl than zwieback. I sucked on the arrowroots too, but when I was ready to take real bites, I graduated to Lorna Doones, which even grown-ups ate.

Hot on the Cookie Trail

After that, whole worlds opened up to me, and with those limitless possibilities, nothing would do but to try them all. From the store: Oreos, Vienna Fingers, Nutter Butters, gingersnaps, the wafers (sugar and vanilla), Fig Newtons, animal crackers, windmills, and chocolate chips. And then there were the bar cookies: the brownies and butterscotch bars and dream bars and lemon bars and Congo bars. I reveled in them all, Nabisco's best and those homemade blue-ribbon winners.

Obviously I didn't arrive home from school each day to batches of cookies freshly pulled from the oven. My mother's not exactly the Norman Rockwell type, but that didn't matter. She knew a good cookie when she met one, and since cookies had carved out a place for themselves in my pantheon of essential foods, I made sure I got my fix in lots of other places.

In my childhood, midtown Manhattan wasn't what you'd call Girl Scout country, but some enterprising little girl always made her way up to our apartment each spring, bearing boxes of mint chocolate wafers and peanut butter sandwiches, which I urged my parents to buy in bulk and squirrel away for emergencies. (My kids do the same thing with me now, thinking that they're urging me too, but the truth is that I'd never skip a year of doing my part for Girl Scout cookie sales.)

Then there were the cookies you could buy by the pound at William Greenberg, a New York bakery that's still going strong. They were bite-size, many-shaped, and just sweet enough to please—a classier version of the bakery cookies that were standard fare at every bar mitzvah and wedding reception throughout the 1950s (although I confess to a lingering fondness for the pink and green checkered ones that were part of that mix).

Come high school, I made a daily stop at a bakery on my way home to get a half moon, those chubby cakelike rounds iced with half chocolate, half vanilla. And on weekends there were all those old favorites on the grocery store shelves. I could spend a half-hour, easy, deciding which kind to buy.

Any time was cookie time, but it was mostly at night that I indulged. You know—a little milk, a few cookies to soak it up, the perfect ending to the day. I could still go through a bag in a sitting today, if I hadn't reached this age of stunning self-restraint. Now, at the end of a meal I often crave just a taste of something sweet, and I've often thought that restaurants would do well to offer a cookie or two as an alternative to elaborate desserts. Hold the tiramisù, the kumquat–passion fruit coulis, the chocolate mocha devil's food mud pie. Just give me a couple of cookies on a plate, stately and elegant in their simplicity.

Of course, part of the pleasure of cookies is that they *can* be eaten in moderation and can be moderate in themselves. I know this goes against the prevailing morality, but let me throw caution to the winds and state unequivocally that the road to uncertain virtue is not paved with cookies. You can eat one butter-and-sugar-filled cookie— hey, even two or three—without condemning yourself to a lifetime of fat or ill-health. I'm of the belief that attending to your desires from time to time is a lot healthier than denial, anyway.

The Sweetest of Times

My soft spot for cookies isn't based just on taste. Rosie's Bakery—my work and my pleasure—came into being by way of a batch of sugar cookies I decorated for a long-ago Valentine's Day. Overdecorated might be a more accurate description: with feathers, sugar pearls, food coloring, and flowers, I really went to town. Opening a bakery was the last thing on my mind, but there it was, Valentine's Day, and cookies straight from the heart seemed the proper way to celebrate. It didn't hurt that they sold out at the galleries and the cake shop that stocked them, nor that customers clamored for more.

I figure that zweiback epiphany had something to do with it too, since there weren't a lot of other signs that I was destined to become a baker. I had never been one to play house or throw tea parties for my dolls, and until I began baking for public consumption, my repertoire consisted chiefly of a dynamite brownie recipe and an occasional birthday cake when no one else could be roped into making one. But I had always gravitated to food. I liked eating it, of course, but I also liked talking about it, looking at pictures of it, just being around it. Other people get that buzz, that all's-right-with-the-world feeling from books or ballparks, fast cars or frequent-flyer miles. For me, it's food—preferably of the sweet, bite-size variety.

So Rosie's began in 1974 with that batch of cookies, and before I knew it, I was officially in business in Harvard Square. In those days Cambridge, Massachusetts, wasn't like anyplace else. It's still not Main Street, U.S.A., but in the early 1970s there was such a sense of possibility—the air was positively perfumed with it. Graduate students were ferreting out the discovery that would change the world, revolutionaries were crafting the ideal society, teachers instructed in peace and harmony, feminists claimed their place in the sun, artists opened galleries, musicians serenaded on street corners, and everyone was writing the great American novel. All that ferment needed to be fed, and Rosie's Bakery was on the scene to feed mind, body, and soul.

In those early days, there was only me. I was up before sunrise to order the ingredients, prepare the batters, scoop the cookies, bake the pies, cut the brownies, frost the cakes, set up the bakery cases, sell the cookies, brownies, pies, and cakes, then wash the dishes and mop the floor before going home to catch four hours of sleep so I could begin all over the next morning. You have to like cookies an awful lot to keep that up, but I too was caught up in the free-floating optimism. I marvel a little, even now as I say it, but I learned how to be a baker by being one. I gathered and tested recipes, experimented with flavors and textures, tried different taste combinations. I was on the trail of something new, and I was having a great time! What sweeter way to greet the brave new world, I reasoned, than surrounded by chocolate chip cookies and sour cherry cream cheese brownies?

Food for All Ages

♥ ♥ ♥ ♥ ♥ ♥ ♥ ♥ ♥ ♥ ♥ ♥ ♥ ♥

Now—two decades, three stores, and millions of cookies and brownies later—Rosie's still meets the needs of the artists, teachers, revolutionaries, novelists, graduate students who have become professors, feminists who are also parents, and a host of other people who remember the '70s fondly, skeptically, or not at all. Cookies, it seems, are something we can all agree on.

As kids, we nosh on them. Then we learn to bake by making them when Mom or our teacher lets us add the chocolate chips and, in time, crack the eggs and mix the batter. Later on, we binge on them while we pull all-nighters at college, whip up a batch to impress our lovers, sell them at bake sales to raise money for worthy causes. Eventually we come full circle to teach our children how to make them, and finally we offer them joyfully to our beloved grandchildren.

Given all that, it's clear that cookies aren't just for kids. There's the occasional ambivalence: we tsk-tsk over those caught with their hand in the cookie jar or imply that we must tuck cookies away with our ballerina and firefighter dreams in order to be serious adults. But twenty years of chocolate chip cookies on Rosie's best-seller list have convinced me that the craving for cookies doesn't lessen with age.

The Collective Cookie Consciousness

❤ ❤ ❤ ❤ ❤ ❤ ❤ ❤ ❤ ❤ ❤ ❤ ❤ ❤ ❤ ❤

Cookies are part of a shared American experience, but we can't claim them all for ourselves. They've been delighting people all over the world for centuries: shortbread from Scotland; gingerbread from England (rumor has it that the first Queen Elizabeth invented the gingerbread man when she ordered her cooks to make little ginger cakes to imitate her courtiers); macaroons, éclairs, meringues, and other delectables from France; biscotti from Italy; kipfel from Austria; all manner of butter and spice cookies from the Netherlands, Germany, Scandinavia, Russia, and Greece.

Cookies seem to have made their debut in the south of France about 400 years ago. As the story goes, cooks tested the heat of their ovens by dropping little cakes onto hot pans; when they were baked, they were given to children as treats, presumably because they weren't fit food for grown-ups.

We know they were wrong, of course, but the childhood joy in cookies is certainly part of their appeal for me. I bake cookies because I want to pass on to my children the taste memories I treasure—the butter crunch of real shortbread, the rich ooze of good chocolate. Sharing food and the making of it has always been a bond, tying generations together. I want to offer those resonant tastes to my customers too, which is another reason why I bake and the prime one behind my enthusiastic "yes!" when my editor asked if I would be interested in writing a cookie book.

I wasn't alone in my excitement. All I had to do was announce the project to my kids and their cookie reflex kicked in higher than a line of Rockettes. They're used to having a mother who's up to her elbows in desserts every day, but a seemingly endless supply of cookies just waiting to be tasted must have conjured up Charlie's chocolate factory *and* a convention of stove-happy grandmothers, all in their very own kitchen. On cookie-baking days (which became nearly every day while this book was in progress), their pleasure perfumed the air more strongly than any spice, until we all slept with visions of snickerdoodles dancing in our heads.

My husband, Richard, was happy too, since he and I are living proof of the old adage about the way to a man's heart. Richard was a customer in my Cambridge store when he fell in love . . . with my chocolate chip cookies. Sometime later, he decided to ask me out, and the rest, as they say, is history.

The neighbors didn't mind my cookie marathon, either, nor did my kids' teachers, their playmates, the parents who stopped by to pick them up, my friends, nor anyone staging a bake sale or reception during the past two

years. My freezer was stuffed with cookies of all manner, ensuring that there was never an occasion for which I was not prepared.

Though I was glad to be a community resource, preparing a cookbook is a serious and consuming enterprise. I was immersed in perfecting recipes and baking techniques, culling the best from all those that had crossed my path over the years. I wanted to create a cookbook that would provide the only recipes you'd ever need for old standbys while offering a generous heap of new possibilities as well. And I was determined to find ways to make baking cookies easy and enjoyable so that you too could be prepared for all occasions—and for some non-occasions as well. It's my hope that you'll use this gathering of cookies as a kind of workbook, one to be underlined, starred, and notated for repeated use and future reference. That's what a cookbook is meant to be, after all: a sharing of knowledge and a laying on of hands.

Which, of course, is a large part of the pleasure in baking and eating cookies—those sweet mouthfuls that are portable, palatable, individual, ornamental, neat to eat, and simple to make. All praise, and pass the cookie jar.

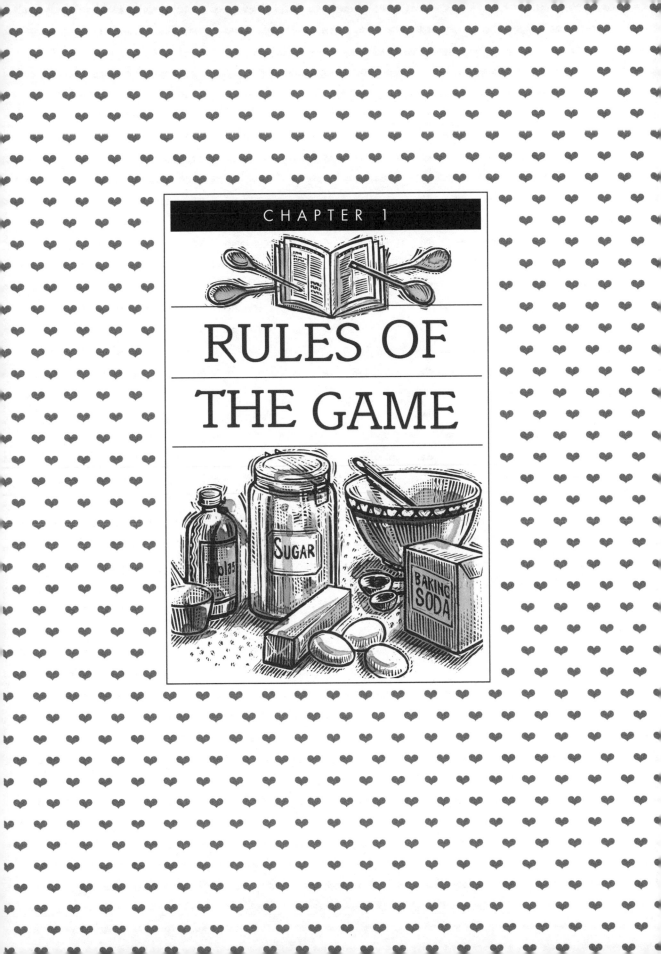

CHAPTER 1

RULES OF
THE GAME

It is true that cookies are a large part of the essence of childhood. "Cookie" is one of the first words babies learn and among the top ten they continue to use long after their vocabularies have expanded. Cookies are rewards, sneak treats, even bribes, I confess. And when kids try their hand at cooking, chances are that cookies will be one of the first things they make. That's because you learn to cook first what you like to eat best.

But cookies don't lose their appeal when we grow up—why should they? Cookies can be as sophisticated as we want them to be. Even those childhood favorites can be baked in smaller sizes and displayed elegantly, can be dipped in imported chocolate, cut in fancy shapes, studded with hazelnuts, accented with liqueurs . . . or eaten just as they were in the old days. Cookies are a sweet that we never tire of.

Into the Mouths of Babes

I love making cookies with my kids— with everybody's kids, in fact. Kids are great on quality control, and they're full of enthusiasm for the product—and usually for the process too, because it's wonderfully straightforward. I ask you: what could possibly cement the parent-child bond more solidly than a gob of cookie dough in common?

For me, a large part of the pleasure in baking cookies with kids comes in what they reveal about themselves as they contribute to the process. Before my children and I first made cookies together, I had perfect-mother fantasies that each of them would have their own kind of cookie, and I even named a few after them in encouragement. Then reality intervened. Now that they're old enough to help me bake when they want to, I spend much more time trying to keep everything even-steven than I do inventing toothsome new creations that they'll remember all their lives.

Still, each of the kids has carved out a role in the cookie baking process, though that happened more because of their personalities than because of my designs. My daughter, Maya, is meticulous by nature, so she's a natural at arranging the cookies. Her twin, Noah, is a sugar freak whose only goal in making cookies is to get as much batter into his mouth as possible. And their older brother, Jake, has reached the age of coolness, which means that he would never deign to take part in something so unhip as baking cookies. Funny, but coolness doesn't get in the way of his eating his share.

What you end up with when you bake with kids may look less than perfect, but with cookies, the making is so delectable and the eating is so satisfying that art is beside the point. Also, children aren't yet saddled with conventional wisdom about what a cookie *should* be, and more than once, the

3

freedom of their imagination has given me ideas for new combinations. After all, if chocolate and cherries go together in ice cream, why not in cookies too? And why *can't* cheesecake come in bars or Boston cream pie in cookies?

But, enough about baking with children. Rest assured cookies can be baked successfully even when you bake them alone!

Doughs and Don'ts

♥ ♥ ♥ ♥ ♥ ♥ ♥ ♥ ♥ ♥ ♥ ♥ ♥ ♥ ♥

After that paean to unbridled creativity, it seems pedestrian to return to do's and don'ts. But return I do, because there are techniques and hints that will make your cookie baking smoother—or chunkier, crispier, or whatever you're aiming for. A read-through of this chapter will set you in good stead for tackling any of the recipes that follow.

Good Bakers Praise Their Tools

♥ ♥ ♥ ♥ ♥ ♥ ♥ ♥ ♥ ♥ ♥ ♥ ♥ ♥ ♥

I don't know if it will come as a relief or a disappointment to know that baking cookies doesn't require much equipment. Some cooks I know spend as much time in kitchen stores as in the kitchen, which I admit is an excellent form of procrastination and certainly a boon to the economy. For the rest of us, though, most of the recipes in this book can be made with the following basic items.

❤ An *electric mixer* with paddle and whisk attachments and two mixing bowls. I prefer a mixer mounted on a base because it leaves your hands free to do other things while the batter is mixing. But a sturdy hand-held mixer does the trick as well, although it may take slightly longer.

❤ A *food processor.* This nearly all-purpose machine is excellent for grinding the nuts and fruits many cookies call for and for mixing shortbread dough and pastry crusts. I find myself using it more and more in my baking and can't remember how we got along without it in the old days.

❤ Three good-quality *baking sheets*. These should be flat, with slightly rolled edges. Shiny heavy-gauge aluminum is good, and so is a nonstick surface such as Silverstone. Air-cushion pans may now be all the rage, but I'm not crazy about them. Cookies baked on them don't get enough heat, so drop cookies don't crisp enough around the edges, cakey cookies spread too much, and shortbreads take forever.

• Several *mixing bowls* of various sizes.

• A set of *measuring scoops* for dry ingredients. (Glass measuring cups aren't accurate here.)

• A set of *measuring spoons*.

• A set of *measuring cups* for liquids.

• Two sturdy *rubber spatulas* for scraping bowls and folding in ingredients.

• Two *whisks:* one small, one medium.

• A medium-size *sifter* or *strainer* for sifting dry ingredients.

• A *wooden spoon* for custard fillings.

• A *metal spatula* for lifting the baked cookies off the baking sheet.

• *Parchment paper,* an absolute must for lining baking sheets, as I'll explain later (see "The Well-Tempered Pan," page 11).

• A *timer* to alert you when the cookies are ready.

• Two or three *wire cooling racks*.

• Two small *microwave-safe* or *Pyrex dishes* for softening butter and cream cheese and melting chocolate.

• A *double boiler* for melting chocolate on the stove.

• Several good-quality air-tight plastic *containers* for storage.

• A *butter knife* or *small spatula* for frosting and filling cookies.

Getting the Goods

I'm a great fan of experiments. On more than one occasion, that's how I've come up with a new or improved recipe or saved a less-than-stellar batch of cookies from oblivion. But when it comes to what goes into cookies, I become considerably less laissez-faire. The simple and commonsense truth is that good baking depends on good ingredients. That means that in most cases, the quality of your cookies will be in direct proportion to the quality of the ingredients you use.

Quality doesn't necessarily mean most expensive or hardest to find. In keeping with the trinity of cookiedom—convenience, availability, and yumminess—most of the ingredients in these recipes are available at your average grocery store and won't require you to leave an arm or leg in payment.

Flour

The recipes in this book usually call for either all-purpose or cake flour. I like to keep pre-sifted all-purpose flour on hand in case I'm feeling lazy and want to avoid extra steps. But because all flour settles as it sits, it's a good idea to sift even this flour along with the salt and leavening to make sure it's evenly incorporated.

Since cake flour is powdery and contains less gluten than all-purpose flour, it works better in certain cookies. But it *must* be sifted before or after it's measured or it will remain lumpy. When you sift it depends on the recipe. I'm told plain cake flour can be hard to find in some parts of the country, so if you run into that problem, you can substitute 1 cup minus 2 tablespoons of all-purpose flour for 1 cup of cake flour (you may find that you have to make some other adjustments too).

Formula:
1 cup – 2 tablespoons all-purpose flour=
1 cup cake flour

One note: Regular cake flour is *not* the same as self-rising cake flour. I had a call recently from a woman who had tried to make a couple of the cake recipes in *Rosie's All-Butter, Fresh Cream, Sugar-Packed, No-Holds-Barred Baking Book* and had created Mt. Vesuvius in her oven. Her kids declared it more fun than their chemistry set, but she was somewhat less pleased. Still, she was curious about what had gone wrong, and so was I. After we talked for a while, she mentioned that she had used self-rising cake flour, and the case was solved. Self-rising cake flour already contains leavening, so by adding the leavening the recipes called for, she had seriously overloaded the equation.

Butter

Since we seem to be living in an age where everything goes under the microscope, it was just a matter of time, I suppose, before bookstore shelves would be filled with books explaining the cultural and political significance of what we put into our mouths. The first time I came face to face with this phenomenon, my reaction was to reach for the nearest cookie jar as solace. But as soon as I was fortified with a handful of gingersnaps, I felt a rush of kindred warmth. I mean, what else could all these books mean but that there's a ton of people out there as fervent about food and flavor as I am?

The books are mines of food factoids, which won't make a dot of difference in how your cookies come out, but may entertain you while you're snacking on them. It was from one of these books, for instance, that I learned that a Frenchman invented margarine (*mon dieu!*) and that margarine used to be outlawed in Canada and New Zealand.

Strong butter lobbies, I guess. That got me thinking about the news flashes we get almost weekly, one insisting that banning butter from our kitchens will make us live forever, the next bringing word that margarine isn't so hot for us either. The problem is that I really like butter. I don't think there is a substitute for it in baking, particularly as a flavor enhancer. So my solution—imperfect, but most things are—is to use butter in my cookies, but to eat fewer of them than I might have before all the dispatches from the fat front.

I use only unsalted butter for baking because it gives me more control over the saltiness of a recipe. Salt was originally added to butter as a preservative, anyway, so it's unnecessary in these refrigerated days.

The temperature of the butter plays a role in baking, so I indicate in each recipe whether it should be cold, cool, or at room temperature. Room temperature works well for recipes such as chocolate chip cookies that require you to cream the butter and sugar. Cookies prepared in a food processor, such as Almond Raspberry Sandwiches, call for cold butter because the particles formed during processing leave air pockets when they melt during baking and create a crunchy texture.

To bring cold butter to room temperature, use a microwave oven set to the right time and power (on mine, it's 15 seconds at medium power), taking care not to melt the butter. Or leave the butter out of the fridge overnight or for 4 to 6 hours before you plan to bake (the time required depends on the temperature of the room, obviously).

Finally, remember that melted butter measures slightly differently from solid butter, so you're well advised to measure the butter *after* it is melted.

Brown Sugar

Brown sugar is white sugar with a dark syrup added. For dark brown sugar, the syrup is molasses; for light brown, it may be a smaller dose of molasses or another kind of syrup. What goes by the name of brown sugar today is a pale imitation of the stuff our foremothers used, which was full of calcium, iron, and a few other useful minerals. It's heartening to find that sugar has some healthful properties because of its bad rap in you-can-never-be-too-thin circles.

Dark brown sugar is less refined than its light cousin and contains more moisture, so it weighs more. The two types are often interchangeable, but they produce somewhat different outcomes: dark brown sugar tends to make a softer, moister cookie with a slightly sweeter taste.

Store brown sugar in an airtight container in the fridge or freezer to keep it from turning rock-hard. If this suggestion comes too late, you can soften brown sugar in the microwave.

Chocolate

If they asked me, I could write a book. Then again, maybe I have, since so many of the recipes in my first cookbook are chocolate-coated. I certainly have researched the stuff, believing first and foremost in mouth-on experimentation. I also collect chocolatiana, both by predilection and because once you become known for your chocolate obsession, the news comes in faster than an irate customer.

Chocolate has been around for a very long time. According to Aztec legend, the god of wisdom gave them the arts, the calendar, and chocolate. Not a bad legacy. Chocolate made its way to Spain and eventually to the rest of Europe (the French got hold of the recipe as part of the dowry of Louis XIII's Spanish bride), where it remained expensive and deliciously naughty for centuries. In England in the 17th century, a cup of chocolate cost nearly half its weight in gold and they say the English don't know the value of good food! Perhaps it's that aristocratic pedigree that accounts for competing claims of supremacy among chocolates, but what makes the difference is

the amount of cocoa butter, which is what gives chocolate its richness.

I have always stood firmly behind Baker's chocolate. That's where chocolate began on our shores—with a doctor named James Baker, who opened North America's first chocolate mill about five miles from where Rosie's home store now stands. Even a force as strong as chocolate can't buck the tide of history, though, and the mills were turned into condos several years ago. When they took the towers down, the air was chocolate perfumed for weeks. My kind of town.

When you come across chocolate in a recipe here, keep in mind that there are several types of chocolate, not just many brands, and the differences among the types matter. When a recipe specifies white chocolate—or unsweetened, or semisweet, or bittersweet chocolate—another kind won't do. The

types vary in flavor and in sugar content, and that can alter the chemistry of the recipe and the texture of the cookie.

For glazes, ganaches, and chopped chunks in cookies, I often use imported chocolates, such as Valrhona and Lindt, to mention just a couple of excellent brands. You'll find these and their cohorts in gourmet shops, upscale markets, and some cookware stores, such as Williams-Sonoma.

But because roundness is all, I come back to where I began: You can't go wrong with Baker's. Its quality is consistently good, you can find it in any grocery store in any part of the country, and it won't break the bank to keep it on hand for those I-can't-believe-it's-raining-again-we're-all-going-stir-crazy-so-the-only-possible-response-is-to-bake-a-batch-of-brownies days.

Eggs

The recipes in this book use large eggs, simply because that's what I chose to test them with. If you substitute other sizes, be aware that this will affect the result, though not necessarily drastically.

Occasionally I call for half an egg or egg yolk. Believe me, I've done this not to torment my readers, but because after many trials, I've found that it's the only solution to maintaining the texture or moistness for a reasonable-size batch of cookies.

❤ *To halve an egg,* crack it into a small bowl and whisk it vigorously until the yellow and white are as integrated as possible. Better yet, use a small electric chopper/grinder to do the work; it will blend the egg perfectly. A stirred large egg measures ¼ cup, so half an egg equals 2 tablespoons of egg. When a recipe calls for half an egg, simply pour out that amount.

Formula:
½ large egg = 2 tablespoons stirred egg

❤ *To divide a yolk in half,* hold a raw egg over a small bowl and crack its shell gently around the middle with a knife. Carefully separate the halves of the shell, and slide the yolk into the palm of your hand as you let the white run through your fingers into the bowl. With a sharp knife, slowly, carefully slice through the yolk's center (you can do this easily without also slicing your hand) and push half of it into the batter.

Oats

Those of us bred in cold northern climes have long been devotees of the humble oat, probably because it grows where other grains won't and it sticks to the ribs come those cold northern winters. None of which has much to do with the current cachet of oats in climes of all kinds, which seems to have come about because they're a health food that tastes good. I'm glad about the health and the heartiness, but I use oats for their taste and consistency.

These recipes call for either quick or rolled oats or sometimes a mixture of the two. Quick oats are rolled oats chopped smaller. They tend to absorb more liquid, so it's a good idea to use the kind a recipe calls for. If you have only rolled oats and need quick ones, chop them up in a food processor by pulsing several times. (Don't pulse more or you'll have oat flour.) For obvious reasons, you can't make the smaller quick oats into larger rolled ones, so in a pinch use the quick oats, but be aware that you may have to make other adjustments along the way, such as increasing the amount of flour slightly.

Raisins and Nuts

Whenever possible, I like to buy nuts in bulk at the health-food store. In any case, I always opt for nuts that are not chopped; they maintain their taste and freshness better. Store all nuts in an airtight container in the fridge—they'll stay fresher longer. In the event that they get the least bit soggy, they can always be recrisped in a 300°F oven for about 10 minutes. Raisins must be stored in an airtight container, in or out of the refrigerator. If they become dried out over time, just soak them in hot water for 10 minutes, drain off the water, and pat them dry.

Spices and Flavorings

Whenever possible, spices and flavorings should be fresh. Spices lose their punch over time and need to be re-placed periodically—some sources say as often as every six months, though that seems extreme to me. In the same vein, something like bottled lemon juice is a poor substitute for freshly squeezed, and there's really nothing equal to just-peeled lemon zest (the yellow layer of the rind).

You can cream a flavoring or spice in with the butter and sugar, or you can sift it into the flour. Opinions differ, and since I belong in neither camp, I'm very democratic in this book: I do it both ways to allow you to decide for yourself.

The Setup

I recommend reading through a recipe in its entirety and gathering all the necessary ingredients ahead of time. In fact, I recommend this to myself whenever I bake, which results in my following the advice at least half the time. The other half, I'm likely to find that I'm completely out of something I need—or a couple of ounces short, which isn't much better. Then I'm stuck with abandoning the effort to schlepping to the convenience store at some ungodly hour, all the time cursing myself for this false economy of time.

By taking out ingredients before you start, you can ensure that they're at room temperature, which they should be unless a recipe specifies otherwise (with butter, for instance). The truly organized baker not only lines up her ingredients beforehand but also sets each one aside as she uses it, so she doesn't get confused about which have gone in and which have yet to go.

May all my readers be truly organized, tranquil, and efficient bakers. For the rest, like me, I recommend that you pay attention and, more to the point, try to bake when you can concentrate on what you're doing. You'll enjoy it more.

The Well-Tempered Pan

❤ ❤ ❤ ❤ ❤ ❤ ❤ ❤ ❤ ❤ ❤ ❤ ❤ ❤ ❤

As far as I'm concerned, parchment paper is right up there with the invention of the dishwasher. I always use it to bake cookies and I've started using it for baking bars as well—shortbreads, brownies, crumb bars, the whole gang. With parchment, cookies don't stick and bars slide right out of the pan. It's economical too, because you can reuse it several times: In most cases, a quick wipe with a paper towel will remove any leftover crumbs and allow you to use the sheet for your next batch of cookies—even if it's a different type. As a fallback when you don't have parchment paper, grease your baking sheet with a thin coating of vegetable oil. Avoid butter as a grease; it tends to burn quickly.

At the Tone, the Time and Temperature Will Be . . .

❤ ❤ ❤ ❤ ❤ ❤ ❤ ❤

Mixers, food processors, ovens, and the strength of mixing arms vary greatly from kitchen to kitchen, so oven temperatures and lengths of baking time will vary too. That means that the specifications I offer here should be used as guides, not gospel. You'll learn what adjustments you need to make the first time you try a recipe. You may also discover that every recipe you try takes more or less time in your oven than in mine, which will help you to adjust your settings or times accordingly for all the other recipes in the book.

❤ Make sure that your oven is thoroughly preheated before you bake. This isn't just one of those things cookbook writers say because they're supposed to. If you put the cookies in before your oven has reached the right temperature, you can't count on their coming out as you expect, and why make unnecessary trouble for yourself? Preheating to the correct temperature can take anywhere from 5 to 10 minutes, depending on the oven, so plan that much ahead.

❤ Cookies bake more evenly when you make them the same size and space them at regular intervals on the baking sheet. The recipe will often specify how much space to leave between them. Leave a similar distance from the edge of the sheet too.

❤ I prefer to bake one sheet of cookies at a time. I place the baking sheet on a rack in the center of the oven so the air can circulate around it, baking the cookies evenly at the designated temperature. If you're pressed for time, you can place two sheets on two racks arranged as close to the center of the oven as possible. About two thirds of the way through, switch the top and bottom sheets and rotate them back to front. (Be careful to move them gently.) The baking time will be slightly longer with two sheets than with one.

❤ Even though it takes up time, wait until the baking sheet has cooled before putting more dough on it, or the cookies will spread too much. And the baked cookies need to cool, too: each recipe notes how to cool them, since this varies with type. For instance, when a batch of tender cakelike cookies

is done, slide the sheet of parchment off the hot baking sheet onto the counter (or, using a spatula, carefully transfer each cookie onto a sheet of foil or waxed paper on the counter), and let them cool further. Other types—chocolate chips are a prime example—get a little extra crunch around the edges from sitting on the hot baking sheet, so they should be allowed to cool there. Lining the sheets with parchment gives you another advantage here. You can just lift the paper off the baking sheet and slide all the cookies onto a cooling rack in one fell swoop.

A Storehouse of Freshness

❤ ❤ ❤ ❤ ❤ ❤ ❤ ❤ ❤ ❤ ❤ ❤ ❤ ❤ ❤

Freezing Dough

With the exception of cakelike cookies, most cookie doughs freeze well for up to three weeks, and some stay fresh in the refrigerator for three or four days. Doughs for drop cookies, shortbreads, rolled cookies, and brownies that don't contain leavening all do well in the refrigerator. Doughs for cakelike cookies don't last in the fridge, however, because their leavening and liquid become active over time and affect the cookies' flavor and texture. Doughs containing oats or oatmeal can be frozen, but they become a little drier because the oatmeal soaks up the liquid. To compensate, when I come to

Cookie Jars

A while ago, my husband, Richard, picked up about a dozen antique cookie jars at a garage sale, and I used them as decorations in our stores, where they were part of the furnishings and drew only the occasional comment. Then about eight years ago, I began to have more and more conversations about them. It turns out that Andy Warhol collected cookie jars, along with tons of other things, and when they were auctioned off after his death, they brought in nearly a quarter of a million dollars! That signaled the start of cookie jars as hot collector's items. Hotter than the cookies they held. So hot, in fact, that there are now cookie jar newsletters, a cookie jar encyclopedia, and even a cookie jar museum (it's in Lemont, Illinois, south of Chicago).

I myself prefer what's inside, but I do understand the appeal of this wonderfully whimsical pottery. I don't go quite as far as the old Betty Crocker cookbook that suggests tinting your cookies to match the color scheme of your tea party, but I like to use cookie jars as part of the presentation. My favorites tend to be from the 1930s and '40s, the heyday of cookie jar creation at midwestern potteries. I'm particularly fond of the quirky animal jars—pigs, cats, mice, a wise old owl, not exactly the fauna you'd want in your kitchen under other circumstances. I also love the red-nosed clown we named Baldy because of his wisp of hair, my fat little Dutch boy, and a jaunty sailor all in blue. Every time I look at him, I want to wink and say, "Can I buy you a cookie, sailor?"

baking them, I sometimes add a bit of water to the dough, or I flatten the mounds after I drop them onto the baking sheet so they will spread better.

Keeping Cookies

Wait until your cookies are completely cool before you put them in a container. This has many advantages, the most important being that it keeps them from getting soggy. The most immediate, though, is that you and everyone who wanders into the kitchen can snack on them in the meantime. Clear plastic containers are best for storing cookies and bars. The plastic preserves freshness; the clarity lets you see what's inside.

For soft cookies that are glazed or frosted (Maple Softies, Boston Cream

Pies) and delicate drop cookies (Banana-Nut Chocolate Chunks, Cranberry Orange Oatmeals), use the widest container available and put parchment paper between the layers. It's not a good idea to pile these cookies more than two deep because they get squashed. Shortbread cookies, such as Peanut Butter Shortbread, and hearty drop cookies, like Pecan Chocolate Chips, can be layered three or four times. Common sense should steer you through other quandaries.

Unless I plan to eat the cookies on baking day, I refrigerate or freeze them, even if they're on the menu for tomorrow. Freezing arrests things in time, so that if you take a newly baked cookie that has just cooled and freeze it, when you defrost it, it will come out as close to fresh as to make no difference. I don't recommend freezing baked goods for longer than two weeks, though. They tend to absorb a kind of freezer flavor or get freezer burn, a frost that forms in all freezers, frost-free or not.

When you're ready to eat frozen cookies, let them come to room temperature or pop them in the microwave on the correct setting (40 to 50 seconds on medium-high in mine). Or for those too impatient to wait for defrosting (need I note that this includes me?), there are always frozen chocolate chip cookie pops. Delicious!

Your second storage option is to put the cookies in a container in the fridge. Be sure to store cookies of similar textures together; if you mix crisp cookies with cakey ones, the softer ones will make the crisps go limp.

Option number three—leaving cookies sitting out at room temperature beyond the day they are baked—isn't often an option at all. Left to their own devices, some crisp cookies go soggy, chewy cookies dry out, and cakey cookies grow dry and heavy. (One exception to the rule is bar cookies containing fruit.) Cookie jars, enchanting as they are, don't protect cookies much from these forces of nature. Still, if you're like me and can't imagine a kitchen without one or two cookie jars on the counter, use them for crisp shortbread-type cookies, which will do just fine there for several days in most weather.

The Cookie's in the Mail

♥ ♥ ♥ ♥ ♥ ♥ ♥ ♥ ♥ ♥ ♥ ♥ ♥ ♥ ♥ ♥

When people talk about E-mail, they leave me far behind, but I bow to no one when it comes to b-mail. For the uninitiated, that's bakery mail. I speak from experience when I say that the best way to ship baked goods is in a sturdy tin lined with plain or decorative cellophane. For gifts, line the tin with a doily, then fit a piece of cellophane over the bottom and up the sides, leaving several inches extra to tuck over the top. Put your firmest, sturdiest, least gooey things on the bottom, cover them with cellophane, arrange another layer of goodies, follow with more cellophane, and continue until the tin is full but not too tightly packed.

When I send something moist, like a brownie, I usually wrap it in plastic before I put it in the tin to keep it from sticking to anything else. If there's a gap somewhere, fill it with a crinkled piece of cellophane or tissue paper to keep things from shifting around. When all the pieces are fitted in securely, fold the excess cellophane over them to keep them snug. Close the tin and freeze it overnight.

Just before shipping, pack the tin in a heavy cardboard box that is large enough for the tin to be surrounded by Styrofoam peanuts. Popcorn (the real thing) works too as a cushion, should you happen to have some sitting around the house. Or swathe the tin in bubble wrap and pack it securely enough to keep it from moving around. If you still have extra room, wad up newspaper or parchment paper to stuff the shipping box.

Overnight mail is best, of course, but that can get expensive; two-day mail is usually fine.

Mail Order

The best cookies for mailing are crispy or crunchy through and through: shortbreads, biscottis, and any cookies whose centers are as crisp as their edges, such as Thin Crisp Chocochips or Pecan Crisps. They will be just as fresh when they arrive as when you shipped them. Cookies with chewy centers and crispy edges, such as Rosie's Oatmeal Cookies and Dark Brown Sugar Chocolate Chips can certainly be shipped, but they will be just a step below what they were when you sent them out—their edges will be a bit soggier and their centers a bit drier. Macaroons, such as Hazelnut Macaroons and Chocolate-Dipped Almond Macaroons, actually ship quite well because of their moist and chewy nature, which becomes only more so when stored in a container for a day or two.

I do not recommend shipping cakey cookies; they get too moist. Any cookie with a soft or gooey top or a custard center, like the Lemon Meringues or the Boston Cream Pies, should not be shipped at all (any cookie with custard or a custard-like filling should not be left at room temperature for more than a day, lest the eggs spoil).

15

Showing Off

I think of cookies as the chameleons of pastries, since they can take on so many different appearances, depending on their size, shape, and presentation.

Is it elegance you want? Fan delicate, lacy cookies over a flowery antique dish.

Artistic plentitude? Create a mosaic using cookies of various shapes and sizes arranged in concentric circles, a checkerboard, or alternating rows or waves. Or give Motherwell and de Kooning a run for their money and try your hand at abstract expressionism.

Barbecue-hearty or picnic-casual more what you had in mind? Plump oatmeal cookies, stuffed with raisins and heaped to overflowing in a basket lined with a gingham cloth, ought to do the trick.

Or maybe what you're aiming for is a smorgasbord of the how-will-I-ever-choose-oh-I-guess-I'll-just-have-to-have-one-of-each variety. A pyramid of brownies and other bars, statuesque on a stoneware plate, is a good place to start. (As an aid to the decision making, you can cut the bars into smaller pieces, so it really is possible to taste everything.)

You can doll up a display of cookies with doilies, a starched white napkin folded to create a pocket, whole flowers, petals or buds, all manner of containers and pottery (I like to use platters of varying heights and sizes together), and table coverings of different colors and textures to create a backdrop. You can cast cookies as the star of your dinner table, as the pinnacle of a buffet, or as a complement for fruit, ice cream, or puddings.

There are limits, of course. I draw the line at floating cookies, wearable cookies, and any cookie too precious to eat. The purpose of display is to tantalize the senses, not torment them. So show off your cookies to their best advantage—then sit back and watch them disappear.

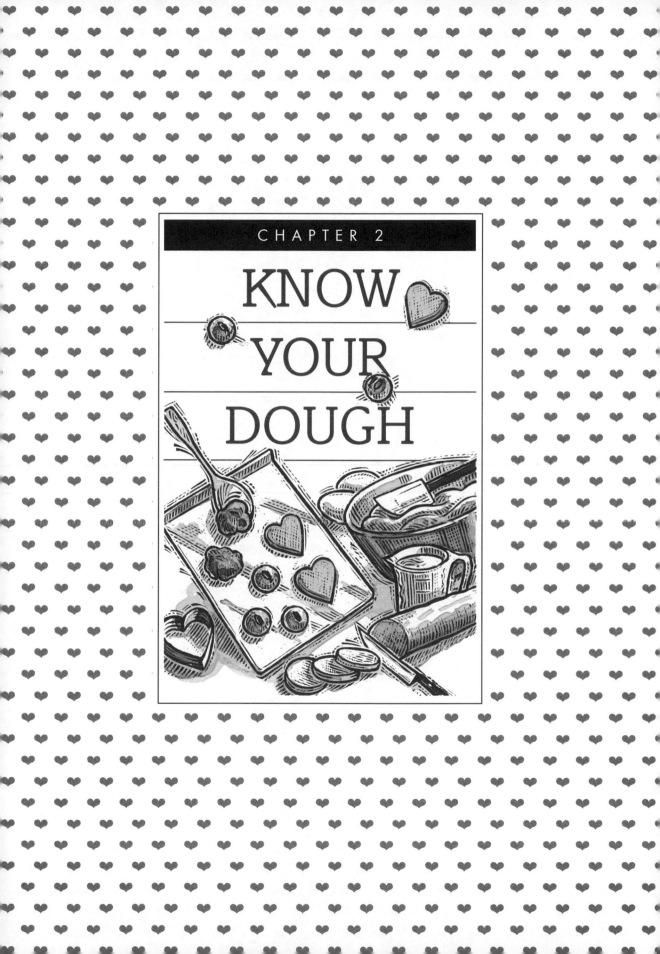

CHAPTER 2

KNOW
YOUR
DOUGH

The world, some say, can be divided into two kinds of people: those who feel the need to divide it into parts and those who don't. Baking books can also be divided into two kinds: those organized by baking methods and those organized by types of pastries. Most books fall into the first category, but never one to choose sides when I don't have to, I've organized this cookie book both ways.

The recipe chapters that make up the bulk of the book are designed around texture—how a cookie feels in your mouth or yields when you bite into it—since that's usually how we think about cookies. I mean, who sits down and says, "Gee, I'm really in the mood for a refrigerator cookie," or, "Couldn't you just sink your teeth into a rolled cookie right now?" Instead, when our taste buds tug at our neural circuits or hormones or whatever it is that sends feed-me messages to our brain, they say, "crunchy" or "melt on the tongue" or "make it sweet!" Gathering the recipes by texture should make it easier for you to find the right cookie for the right moment as well as a good mix of cookies for more elaborate baking projects.

Even those of us who don't care to divvy up the world need organizing principles from time to time, so I've ordered this how-to chapter along the more conventional line of baking techniques. Here you'll find mixing, baking, cutting, and storing tips for five categories of cookies: drop cookies, refrigerator cookies, rolled cookies, shortbreads, and bars.

Cookies are more forgiving than many other kinds of pastries, less fussy about the order you add the ingredients in, and flexible enough in their baking time and temperature to allow you to experiment to get the results you desire. It's only fairly recently, anyway, that recipes were carefully quantified and cooking was raised to a science governed by charts and rules. Before that, bakers worked by feel and by instructions passed down in appren-

ticeships and mothers' kitchens. I encourage you to do some of that too, finding the baking time, for instance, to give just the right crunch or butteriness that you seek in a specific cookie.

Even the most elaborate of systems has its limits, and you'll find some overlap of techniques and pointers among the categories. Conversely, some cookies and bars fit into a category only with a certain amount of prodding. Still, a read-through of this chapter and an occasional checking back will give you a good grounding for cookie baking of all kinds.

Drop Cookies

❤ ❤ ❤ ❤ ❤ ❤ ❤ ❤ ❤ ❤ ❤ ❤ ❤ ❤ ❤ ❤

The "drop" in drop cookies refers to the way they're made: by dropping scoops of dough (sometimes they're formed) onto the baking sheet. Drop cookies are kind of the five dwarfs of cookiedom: They can be chewy, crunchy, crispy, hearty, or cakey. This category is a large one. To make the appropriate instructions easier to find, I've divided drop cookies into three subcategories: chewy and crunchy drops, crispy drops, and cake-like drops.

Chewy and Crunchy Drops

Mixing: These are the most traditional drop cookies, including such favorite types as chocolate chip, oatmeal, and peanut butter. The method for mixing their dough is traditional, too: you cream the butter and sugar together, then add the eggs and, last, the dry ingredients.

Baking: Chewy drops and crunchy drops are essentially the same cookies, except for a difference in texture. Chewy cookies can be chewy through and through, as in Chocolate-Dipped Almond Macaroons and Hazelnut Macaroons; they can have chewy centers and a crunchy veneer, as with meringues; or they can have chewy centers and crunchy edges, as in many of the big drop cookies, like Rosie's

Oatmeal Cookies. Many of these cookies can also be baked until they are crunchy throughout. For instance, I like to make Noah's Chocolate Chocolatey Chocolate Chips and Pecan Oatmeal Chips that way. The beauty of this category is that you can control how chewy or crunchy your cookies are by how you form and bake them.

To get the soft centers that are the hallmark of chewy cookies, drop the batter in mounds onto a prepared baking sheet and bake the cookies at 375° to 400°F. Their edges will spread and become crunchier, but their centers will stay nice and soft. (The exception to this rule is the meringue, which is baked very slowly at a temperature as low as 200°F.) Remove chewy drop cookies from the oven when their edges are golden or crisp and their centers are a little lighter in color and still a bit puffy and tender.

Chilling the dough before you bake it is another way to get the center chewier than the edges. This works with all kinds of drop cookies, because chilling keeps the center set long into the baking process.

To create crunchier cookies, drop them onto the baking sheet as you would chewy drops, but then either press them flatter before baking so that the center doesn't puff up as they cook, or bake them a little longer. Sometimes you'll want to do both. Set the oven to 375° to 400°F, and bake the cookies long enough for the center to set and turn the same color and texture as the edges. Cooling these cookies on the baking sheet will make their bottom even crunchier, but they cool well on a rack too. Experiment with both methods to find the specifics that produce your ideal cookie.

Storing: These cookies are best eaten the first day. The crunchy edges become just a little less crunchy and the chewy centers just a little less chewy by the second day. However, as soon as you've decided that you just can't eat any more, you can place them in a plastic container in the freezer, where they'll hold for up to two weeks. When you're in the mood for a treat, remove a cookie (or three) from the freezer and bring it to room temperature or zap it in your microwave for between 30 to 50 seconds (depending on the size of the cookies) on medium-high power.

Crispy Drops

Mixing: Crispy drops, such as Orange Pecan Ginger Florentines and Fresh Ginger Crisps, take top honors for elegance and daintiness. They're the sort of sweet that Eloise might nibble when she goes down for tea at the Plaza's Palm Court. Or they're the

lacelike creations in the shop windows of the Place de la Madeleine that would entice Eloise's French counterpart, the irrepressible Madeline, as she and her schoolmates march by in two straight lines. This category also includes heartier cookies, such as Thin Crisp Chocochips and Chocolate Chip Pecan Mounds, which I suspect would please Eloise and Madeline too, because for all their grown-up grandeur, these cookies are among the most basic, appealing to spunky kids as well as more reserved adults.

Baking: Crispy drop cookies usually contain less flour than other drop cookies, so their dough is wetter and spreads more during baking. But because most of these delicacies are baked at 350° to 400°F, the higher heat caramelizes the sugar and butter and prevents the cookie from running all over the baking sheet. Some recipes call for the sugar and butter mixture to be cooked over a burner first, to speed up the caramelizing process. Others require the butter to be creamed with the sugar. No overarching guidelines here; crisps are individualists, each demanding its own instructions.

Storing: Although like most cookies, crispy cookies are best the first day, they can be kept in an airtight container at room temperature for a couple of days. After that I like to store the container in the freezer, in order to maintain their requisite crispness.

Cakelike Drops

Mixing: These gems, which include Sacher Tortes and Maple Softies, are miniature cakes you can have all to yourself with no need to share or to be modest in the slice you cut. Cakey drop cookies are mixed the same way as cakes: butter and sugar creamed together, eggs added, then liquid mixed in before or alternately with dry ingredients.

Baking: What you want here is a moist cookie, so scoop a good amount of batter onto the baking sheet for each one. I recommend a heaping tablespoonful, or at least a generously rounded one. Drop the cookies 2 inches apart, and if need be, run your index finger gently around their circumference to make perfect rounds.

Bake these cookies between 375° and 400°F until they rise. Be vigilant to catch them when they have just set but haven't yet formed a crust. At the right doneness, the cookies will spring back when you touch them. Don't wait until a crust has formed, or the drops will be slightly overbaked and drier than is optimal.

Storing: These cookies are great the first day, but if you wish to save them, freeze them in an airtight container for up to two weeks. Be sure to defrost them thoroughly before scarfing.

Refrigerator Cookies

♥ ♥ ♥ ♥ ♥ ♥ ♥ ♥ ♥ ♥ ♥ ♥ ♥ ♥ ♥

We used to call these icebox cookies, although I've never seen a real icebox in my life. I've heard stories about them, though. A friend's mother talks about dragging her red wooden wagon with its block of ice up a steep hill each week of her childhood, rushing against the heat to arrive home before the ice had melted away.

There's something appealing about that image, even if it was hard work, probably because it speaks of a friendlier time. I romanticize it, I'm sure, but for me just saying "icebox" evokes an era of neighbors chatting from their front stoops, waiting for the iceman to cometh, while kids play stickball and kick-the-can in the street until their mothers call them in to dinner and, half grumbling, half grateful, they comply.

"Refrigerator," on the other hand, sounds much more efficient, which is accurate when it comes to preparing these cookies. They are made from stiff dough that's formed into a log, chilled, sliced, and then baked. Some cooking column I read noted that refrigerator cookies are

convenient when you want to bake just a few cookies at a time. I have a little trouble imagining such a situation, but I suppose it's not inconceivable. Me, I damn the torpedoes and bake the whole batch in the following way.

Mixing and Molding: When the dough has been mixed, either with an electric mixer or in a food processor, mold it by hand into one or two logs. (You may need to dip your hands in flour to keep the dough from sticking.) Place the log along one edge of a piece of waxed paper or plastic wrap that is 3 to 4 inches longer than the log. Roll the log in the paper or wrap, and twist the ends like a hard-candy wrapper.

Chill the log for several hours. Then gently roll it back and forth on a countertop, using your palms and fingers, until it forms a smooth cylinder, or hit all four sides on the countertop to create corners and shape a rectangular loaf; the recipe will tell you which shape you want. Return the log to the fridge for several hours or overnight, or freeze it for up to two weeks. When you're ready to bake, slice the log into pieces as required by the recipe and place them 1½ inches apart on a baking sheet.

Baking: Refrigerator cookies usually bake at 300° to 350°F. As a rule of thumb, thicker cookies need the lower temperature so their centers bake evenly along with the edges. The cool temperature of the dough helps them retain their shape as they bake and also contributes to their crunchiness.

Test these cookies for doneness as you would shortbread; that is, take a cookie from the oven, break it in half, and check to make sure there's no doughy strip left in the center. (If there is, return them to the oven and continue to bake the cookies until they're crunchy through and through.)

Storing: Cool refrigerator cookies on the baking sheet or on a rack, and wait at least until they reach room temperature before digging in. Store refrigerator cookies at room temperature in an airtight plastic container for a day or two. I find that this often enhances their flavor. After that, store the container in the freezer for up to two weeks. Bring the cookies to room temperature before eating.

Rolled Cookies
♥ ♥ ♥ ♥ ♥ ♥ ♥ ♥ ♥ ♥ ♥ ♥ ♥ ♥ ♥

This is the category of cookies that fill the holiday issues of women's magazines and the days of the Supermom who haunts our best intentions. It's the favored child of Christmas givers and the more-creative-than-thou baker who seems to pluck delightful cookie shapes from thin air. Fortunately, it also includes simple-to-make favorites, such as Classic Sugar Cookies and Gingerbread People.

Rolled cookies start with a stiff dough that is rolled out flat and then cut into shapes. You can use heirloom cookie cutters passed down from generation to generation, fad-of-the-month cookie cutters bought at Woolworth's or a cake decorating store, or whatever you happen to have around the house that will cut dough. I usually use a thin-rimmed glass, which cuts perfect circles, but I don't want to be a killjoy. Cookie cutters can be a lot of fun, especially for holiday baking or for baking with kids.

Mixing and Cutting: You can make the dough for rolled cookies with an electric mixer or a food processor. Form the dough into slabs, place them between layers of plastic wrap, and use a rolling pin to roll them out evenly to the designated thickness, usually ¼ to ⅛ inch.

Some doughs are so rich with egg yolks or butter that they need to be chilled after rolling so they won't be too sticky to cut easily. Just set the rolled-out dough, still sandwiched in the plastic wrap (and still on the cutting board if you like), on a refrigerator shelf for 1 to 2 hours.

When the dough is ready to be cut into shapes, dip the cookie cutter or glass in flour (to keep the dough from sticking) and cut out your cookies. Make sure you press down hard enough so that the edge of the cutter cuts totally through the dough. With your hand, gently pull the scraps away from the cookie. Then, using a spatula, carefully transfer the cookies from the cutting board to the baking sheet, placing them 1½ inches apart. Re-roll the scraps and cut out as many more cookies as possible, adding them to the rest.

Baking: Bake these cookies between 350° and 400°F until the centers are firm and the edges are just beginning to turn golden. They should be crisp through and through.

Storing: Rolled cookies are best cooled on the baking sheet, since they are too delicate to be moved when they're warm. They can be stored in cookie jars, as tradition dictates, or in your dependable airtight plastic container. If they're not gone in a day or two, refrigerate them in a plastic container to help maintain their crispness. After that, store the container in the freezer for up to two weeks. Bring the cookies to room temperature before eating.

Un-Rolling

For those who hate rolling dough, many of these doughs can also be shaped into logs and sliced like refrigerator cookies. Or you can form the dough into a mass, pinch off pieces, roll them into a ball with your hands, set them on a baking sheet, and press them flat with your hand or with the bottom of a glass. These cookies require a lower heat—325° to 350°F—because they will be thicker and need to bake more slowly.

Short-breads

Shortbread takes its name from all the butter or shortening used to give it both a rich and a pure taste. And rich it is. A very early recipe for something called Bath Shortbread required a pound of "flower," half a pound of butter, and a pound of sugar made into a paste with wine!

Shortbread has always been among my favorite cookies. I was introduced to it when my mother brought home those round tins decorated with a tartan and filled with wedges of Dundee shortbread. It was crunchy and buttery beyond belief! When I got old enough to think about what went into the food I liked, I wondered how something so simple could taste so good, and as I explored baking more, I came to appreciate how something so basic could take on so many variations. I read that Scottish business leaders feel sorely misunderstood by a world that recognizes them only for bagpipes and shortbread, and while the businesswoman in me sympathizes, every other part of me yearns to reassure them that there are few forms of immortality more noble than a really fine piece of shortbread.

Mixing: Shortbreads are dense, solid cookies. They can be eggless, like Ginger Shortbread, or can contain whole eggs or yolks or whites, like Chocolate Orange Shortbread or Little Princesses. With the exception of spritzes and piped cookies, all kinds of shortbread can be made equally well with a food processor or an electric mixer. (For spritzes and piped cookies, you need to use the paddle attachment on an electric mixer to cream the butter and sugar to the right consistency for squeezing the dough from a tube.)

If you use an electric mixer, cream room-temperature butter with the sugar until the mixture is light and fluffy. Creaming the butter and sugar this way aerates the dough nicely, making for a wonderfully crunchy shortbread. Next, beat in the eggs, and add the dry ingredients at the end, beating only enough to incorporate them into the dough.

As an alternative, you can use a food processor and incorporate the butter at any temperature. Cool or cold butter will give you the requisite crunchiness because minute particles will remain and will melt in baking, leaving tiny air pockets that create a "short," or crunchy, texture. Blend the flour and sugar, add the butter, and process the dough until it resembles coarse cornmeal. With the processor running, add the eggs through the feed tube and process until they're incorporated and the dough just comes together. Sometimes a little hand kneading is necessary.

Whatever appliance you use, take care not to overbeat the dough after you've added the flour because beating can toughen dough that contains both eggs and flour.

Baking: Shortbread doughs can be rolled out, scooped, formed, or made into a log to be refrigerated and then cut. Each variety will call for a somewhat different baking time and temperature, but shortbreads bake best between 300° and 350°F; they can even bake as low as 275°F if you have the patience. Lower temperatures ensure that they bake evenly, with the center as crunchy as the edges.

To test for doneness, remove one cookie from the oven and cut or break it in half to make sure that there is no doughy strip in the center. (If there is, continue baking.) I prefer my shortbread slightly golden for the texture that

it gives and because butter is even more flavorful when it reaches this color.

Storing: Because of their crunchy nature, shortbread cookies store beautifully. Keep them in an airtight container at room temperature for two days if you plan to snack on them during that time. After that, store the container in the freezer for up to two weeks. Bring the cookies to room temperature before eating them. If you don't have sufficient freezer space, shortbread, unlike many other cookies, can be left at room temperature for up to a week.

Bar Cookies

❤ ❤ ❤ ❤ ❤ ❤ ❤ ❤ ❤ ❤ ❤ ❤ ❤ ❤ ❤

This category is so popular at Rosie's that I've often felt like breaking into a chorus of "Belly Up to the Bar, Boys." Certainly boys, girls, women, men, and the occasional puppy line up for them regularly, making brownies and fruit bars hard to keep in stock. I don't usually think of brownies and their ilk as cookies, but they're more that than anything else, and they fill a similar role as snacks and desserts.

Brownies are an American original, something I like to offer foreign visitors as part of their authentic American experience. But bar-type cookies show up in many other cultures, and I've found them to be particularly adaptable to flavors and ingredients

from all over, which has inspired me to come up with three kinds of linzer bars, White Chocolate Brownies with Macadamia Nuts, and all kinds of fruit bars, to note just a few.

In my mind, bars fall into three categories: brownie bars, which include such variations as Sour Cherry Cheesecake Brownies and Peanut Butter Topped Brownies; shortbread bars, such as Cranberry Walnut Squares and Chunky Pecan Shortbread; and pastry bars, which subdivide further into bars with crumb crusts (Dating Bars, Cranberry Crumb Bars); bars with fine crusts (Pucker-Your-Lips Apricot Linzer Bars); and sturdy-crusted linzer bars. A couple of bars (Carrot Cake Cream Cheese Bars and Poppyseed Coffee Cake Bars) don't fit into any of these categories. Their recipes will give specific instructions.

Brownie Bars

Mixing: These batters are usually made by one of two methods. The first requires creaming the butter and sugar together and then adding the eggs,

flour, and melted chocolate. The second requires you to melt the butter and chocolate together, and then to add the eggs and flour.

Baking: I bake most of my brownies between 325° and 350°F. Since I don't want too much of the aeration that higher temperatures bring, I use a lower heat to produce a fudgier, moister bar.

Most brownies are done when the center has risen and is no longer liquidy. You want to take the bars out of the oven when their center is less crusty and set than the edges. If the center has only a thin crust, it will drop slightly as it cools to create a fudgier bar. So to test for doneness, insert a cake tester in the center of the pan; remove the pan from the oven when the tester comes out dry or with moist crumbs but no syrupy batter.

Cutting: The bars can be cut 10 minutes after they come out of the oven or when they are room temperature. Use the point of a sharp, thin knife and perhaps a spatula or cake cutter to lift them out of the pan. For frosted or glazed brownie bars, dip the knife in hot water and wipe it dry before each cut.

Storing: Although there are those who would disagree, I think a brownie, like a cheesecake or a great stew, is better the second day. The texture settles to become more what it is meant to be, and the flavor seems to intensify and become more full-bodied. I always leave the bars, cut, in the pan overnight at room temperature. (Once they have completely cooled, I cover them with plastic wrap, but it's not absolutely necessary that first night.)

The following day, if there are leftovers after you've passed the brownies around, place them in an airtight container and refrigerate them for two to three days. (If the brownies are frosted, layer them with parchment or waxed paper between.) After that, any remains can be frozen for up to two weeks.

Shortbread Bars

Mixing: These cookies are made from a shortbread dough, which may or may not be finished off with a topping. Mix the dough with an electric mixer or a food processor, as explained in the section on shortbread cookies. Then spread it over the bottom of a prepared pan with your fingertips. If the dough is too sticky, dip your fingers in flour.

Sometimes the shortbread is glazed to keep a wet topping from sinking into the base. Glazing also works as decoration when there's no topping. There are two ways to glaze: You can separate an egg white into a dish or cup, then paint it over the surface of the unbaked dough with a pastry brush. Or you can drop an egg white directly onto the unbaked dough, tilt the pan from side to side until the white covers the entire surface, and then spill the excess into the sink.

Baking: I bake plain shortbread bars at 325°F, but I raise the temperature to 350°F for bars that will get a topping. Bake both kinds until they are light golden with slightly darker edges. Once shortbread bars are topped, the baking time will vary considerably from recipe to recipe.

Cutting: Plain shortbread bars should be cut with the point of a sharp, thin knife or a cleaver. Cut them when they're hot because once they cool, they're more likely to break.

Shortbread bars with sugary toppings—Tropical Macadamia Bars or Pecan Delight Bars, for example—should be cut when they've just reached room temperature. If they get too cool, the caramelized sugar around the edges becomes hard to cut through. A cleaver or heavy knife works well here (remove any goo after each cut).

Bars topped with fruit, such as Cranberry Walnut Squares, should be cut carefully at room temperature with the point of a sharp, thin knife.

Storing: Plain shortbread bars, such as Semolina Shortbread and Cinnamon Pecan Shortbread, should be stored, when cooled, in an airtight container at room temperature for two to three days. Their buttery flavor will become even more intense as they sit. After this, store them in the freezer for up to two weeks. Bring the bars to room temperature before eating.

Shortbread bars that are topped with fruit or cream cheese or gooey toppings have individual storing needs that are too numerous to note in a general way here. As with all the recipes in this book, the storing instructions for this type of bar are included within the recipe.

Pastry Bars with Crumb Crusts

Mixing: Crumb crusts generally consist of a combination of flour, sugars, melted butter, and sometimes oats or nuts. Toss the dry ingredients in a bowl or process them gently in a food processor, then add the melted butter. Next, cover the bottom of the baking pan with a portion of this mixture to form a base, and when the recipe specifies, prebake it. Spread the filling over the base and sprinkle the remaining crumb mixture over the top.

Baking: These bars are usually baked at 350° to 375°F until their top is golden and crunchy.

Cutting: Cut crumb-crust bars when they reach room temperature.

Storing: For the ultimate crunch of the crumb mixture, these bars are particularly delicious on the first day. After that, store them in an airtight container in the refrigerator for a few days. If the bars contain fruit, you can leave them in the pan, covered, for up to two days at room temperature or layer them in an airtight container with plastic wrap, parchment, or waxed paper between the layers, and refrigerate for up to four days. Fruit bars can also be frozen; however, dried fruit bars (apricot, date) remain crisper than fresh-fruit bars (apple) when defrosted. Follow the same storage procedure with bars with cream cheese, but keep them refrigerated for easy handling. All bar cookies should be brought to room temperature before eating.

Pastry Bars with Fine Crusts

Mixing: Bars in this category are made with pastry crusts that are either pressed into the bottom of the pan by hand or rolled out like a pie crust and then fitted into the pan. These bottom crusts may be prebaked. They are then filled with a fruit mixture and covered with the remaining dough or with a lattice of dough.

Baking: These bars are usually baked at 400°F so that the bottom and top crusts both become crisp. This high heat allows the crust beneath the fruit to get crisp or crunchy, depending on the recipe, rather than becoming soggy or remaining raw tasting.

29

Cutting: Cut these bars at room temperature.

Storing: Fine pastry bars that contain fruit are best eaten the first day, when you get the full experience of the contrast between the crispness of the dough and the moisture of the fruit. After day one, store them in an airtight container in the fridge. I don't like to freeze these bars. Like the crumb crust bars, they get soggy when defrosted.

Linzer Bars

Mixing: Linzer bars use their own type of crust made of flour, sugar, butter, eggs, spices, and lots of ground nuts, all of which can be creamed together in a mixer or a food processor. A portion of this dough is then pressed into the bottom of a pan and sometimes prebaked slightly. A jam or jam-and-fruit filling is spread over this base, and the remaining crust is rolled into strips and woven into a lattice over the filling.

Baking: For recipes that require prebaking the crust, I suggest doing so at 350°F until the crust is just firm to the touch, about 20 minutes. After they're assembled, return the bars to the oven and bake them at 350° to 375°F until the top is crisp and the filling is bubbling.

Cutting: Wait until these bars have cooled completely before you cut them.

Storing: Linzer bars are very durable and are as great on day two or three as on day one. For the first few days, store them, with parchment or waxed paper between the layers, in an airtight container. After that, put the container in the refrigerator or freezer, depending on how quickly you think you'll go through them.

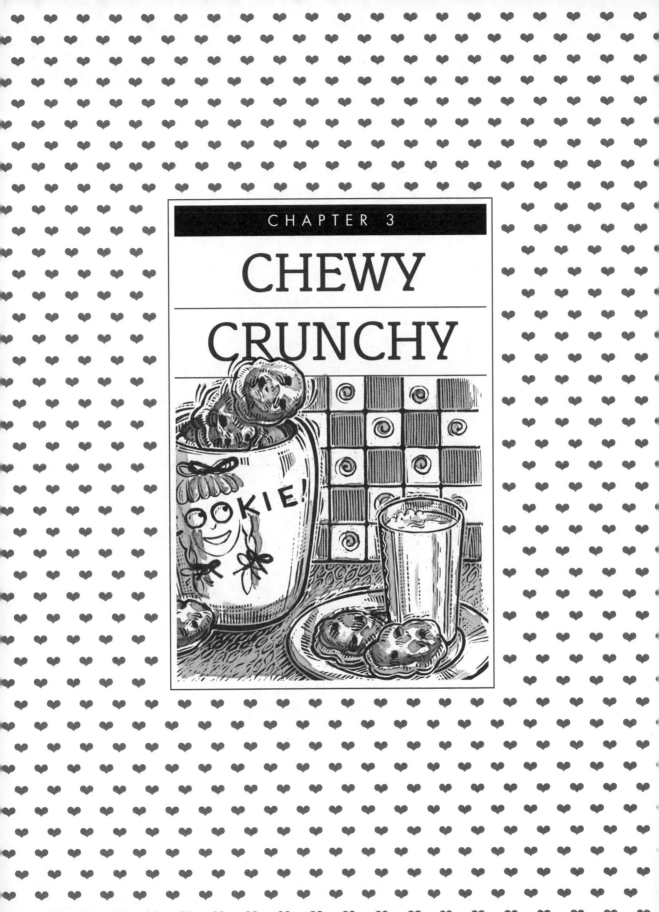

CHAPTER 3

CHEWY

CRUNCHY

usually get into trouble when I make sweeping pronouncements, but I'll go out on a limb and proclaim this category of cookie America's sweetheart. It includes such basics as chocolate chip cookies, oatmeal and peanut butter cookies, snickerdoodles and macaroons.

While I've raided other cultures and climates for some of the ingredients, most of these cookies are quintessentially American—a fistful of good taste straight out of a Norman Rockwell kitchen—and so is what goes into them. Our southern states give the world its pecans, oatmeal probably came over with the Pilgrims, great New England fortunes were founded on molasses and rum (hermit cookies were created by Cape Cod bakers to outlast the long sea voyages of American clipper ships), and what else but American ingenuity would come up with something like peanut butter?

A large part of the widespread appeal of these cookies comes, I think, from their texture. There's something so reinforcing, so comforting and rewarding, about biting through a crunchy edge and encountering a moist, chewy center and often a further prize of raisins or nuts. There's a word used in Louisiana, *lagniappe,* that means an unexpected extra something. That's how I think of my chewy cookies.

These cookies are baked large and generous and tend to keep well, so when we imagine the perfect cookie jar filler, these chewies often come to mind. Even the names are straightforward, telling us that what we see is what we get. (I know, there's "snickerdoodles," and where that name came from is anybody's guess. But it's fun to say, so who cares?)

Most of the cookies in this chapter are made from sturdy doughs, so carefully regulated mixing isn't as important as in other baking. If you're the type of baker who needs to be anxious about something, concentrate on finding the right baking time and temperature to create the texture you want. Chewier cookies are dropped in mounds on the baking sheet and removed from the oven when their centers are a little less done than their edges. Crunchier cookies can be pressed flatter on the baking sheet and baked until their centers and edges are the same doneness. Play around to get precisely the chew and crunch that your little heart desires.

Noah's Chocolate Chocolatey Chocolate Chips

drop cookie

Crunchy edges, chewy centers, dark chocolatey chocolate cookies filled to bursting with chocolate chips, and claimed for his own by my son, Noah, whom I love more than chocolate itself.

INGREDIENTS

4 ounces unsweetened chocolate
2¼ cups all-purpose flour
1 teaspoon baking soda
½ teaspoon salt
1 cup (2 sticks) unsalted butter at room temperature
1¼ cups (lightly packed) light brown sugar
½ cup plus 2 tablespoons granulated sugar
2 large whole eggs
1 large egg yolk
8 ounces (1¼ cups) semisweet chocolate chips

1. Preheat the oven to 400°F. Line several baking sheets with parchment paper, or grease them lightly with vegetable oil.

2. Melt the unsweetened chocolate in the top of a double boiler placed over simmering water. Then remove it from the heat and let it cool slightly.

3. Sift the flour, baking soda, and salt together into a small bowl and set aside.

4. Using an electric mixer on medium speed, cream the butter and both sugars together in a medium-size bowl until light and fluffy, 1½ to 2 minutes. Stop the mixer twice during the process to scrape the bowl with a rubber spatula.

5. Add the eggs and egg yolk and beat on medium speed until they are blended, about 30 seconds. Scrape the bowl. Add the melted chocolate and blend until mixed, about 10 seconds, stopping the mixer once to scrape the bowl.

6. Add the flour mixture, and mix on low speed for 15 seconds.

7. Add the chocolate chips and blend until they are mixed in, 5 to 8 seconds.

8. Drop the dough by generously rounded tablespoons onto the prepared baking sheets, spacing them 2 inches apart.

9. Bake the cookies until the centers are puffed up and lightly cracked, but still soft, 12 to 13 minutes. Remove the cookies from the oven and allow them to cool on the sheets.

10. These are best eaten the same day they are baked. Otherwise, store them in an airtight container in the freezer for up to 2 weeks. Before eating, bring them to room temperature or heat them lightly in the microwave (50 seconds on medium-high power).

Makes 24 large cookies

Fudgie Wudgies

❤ ❤ ❤ ❤ ❤ ❤ ❤ ❤ ❤ *drop cookie*

Named by my son Jake, this extra-fudgy, almost flourless, abounding-in-nuts-and-chips cookie is a dark—as dark can be—sensation. It's a chocoholic's dream, and not bad for the casual indulger too.

INGREDIENTS

6 ounces (1 cup) plus 4 ounces (¾ cup)
    semisweet chocolate chips
10 tablespoons (1¼ sticks)
    unsalted butter
6 tablespoons all-purpose flour
1 teaspoon baking powder
3 tablespoons unsweetened cocoa powder
⅛ teaspoon salt
2 large eggs
2 teaspoons pure vanilla extract
¾ cup sugar
½ cup chopped pecans or walnuts

1. Preheat the oven to 325°F. Line several baking sheets with parchment paper, or grease them lightly with vegetable oil.

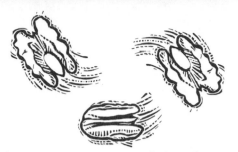

2. Melt the 6 ounces of chocolate chips and the butter in the top of a double boiler placed over simmering water. Then remove the pan from the heat and allow to cool slightly.

3. Sift the flour, baking powder, cocoa, and salt together into a small bowl and set aside.

4. Using an electric mixer on medium speed, beat the eggs and vanilla in a medium-size mixing bowl until they are blended, about 10 seconds.

5. Add the sugar to the egg mixture and blend until the mixture is thick, about 1 minute. Scrape the bowl.

6. Add the melted chocolate and blend 1 minute more. Scrape the bowl.

7. Add the flour mixture on low speed and mix until blended, 10 seconds, scraping the bowl with a rubber spatula.

8. Add the remaining 4 ounces chocolate chips and the nuts, and blend until they are mixed in, 5 to 8 seconds.

9. Drop the dough by generously rounded tablespoons about 2 inches apart onto the prepared baking sheets.

35

10. Bake the cookies until they rise slightly and form a thin crust, 14 to 16 minutes. Immediately transfer the cookies from the baking sheets to wire racks to cool.

11. If you plan to snack on them the first day, place the cookies on a plate. After that, place the cookies in an airtight container and refrigerate for a day or two or store in the freezer for up to 2 weeks. Bring the cookies to room temperature before eating.

Makes 20 large cookies

Pecan Chocolate Chips

❤ ❤ ❤ ❤ ❤ ❤ ❤ ❤ ❤ ❤   *drop cookie*

In the baking biz, the big debate is nuts versus no nuts. Nearly everyone under age twelve falls firmly in the no-nuts camp, but those of us who have made it through adolescence are less predictable and depend more on mood. I, for one, consider the nutted chocolate chip cookie to be a valuable variation on the classic, and this is one of the best of its breed. It's chewy in the center, crunchy around the edges, and enhanced by the chomp of chopped pecans.

INGREDIENTS

2¼ cups plus 2 tablespoons all-purpose flour
2 teaspoons baking soda
1 teaspoon salt
1 cup (2 sticks) unsalted butter at room temperature
1 cup (lightly packed) light brown sugar
7 tablespoons granulated sugar
1 tablespoon pure vanilla extract
2 tablespoons light corn syrup
2 teaspoons water
2 large eggs
12 ounces (2 cups) semisweet chocolate chips
1½ cups chopped pecans

1. Preheat the oven to 400°F. Line several baking sheets with parchment paper, or grease them lightly with vegetable oil.

2. Sift the flour, baking soda, and salt together into a small bowl and set aside.

3. Using an electric mixer on medium speed, cream the butter, both sugars, and the vanilla together in a medium-size bowl until light and fluffy, 1½ to 2 minutes. Stop the mixer twice during the process to scrape the bowl with a rubber spatula. Then add the corn syrup and the water, and mix for several seconds.

4. Add the eggs and beat on medium speed until they are blended, about 30 seconds. Scrape the bowl.

5. Add the flour mixture and mix on low speed for 15 seconds. Scrape the bowl.

6. Add the chocolate chips and the nuts and blend until they are mixed in, 5 to 8 seconds.

7. Drop the dough by rounded tablespoonfuls 2 inches apart onto the prepared baking sheets.

8. Bake the cookies until the edges are dark golden and the centers are light and slightly puffed up, 11 to 12 minutes. Remove from the oven and allow them to cool on the sheets.

9. These are best eaten the same day they are baked. Otherwise, store them in an airtight container in the freezer for up to 2 weeks, and bring them to room temperature before eating.

Makes 40 cookies

Chips Off the Old Block

If you were to ask any group of people anywhere in this country what their favorite cookie was, the answer, hands down, would be chocolate chip. I know this for a fact because pollsters *have* asked people everywhere just that—though I'm always a little perplexed about what we're supposed to do with the information.

The chocolate chip—or Toll House cookie, as it was first known—has topped the American hit parade almost since the fateful day sixty-five years ago when Ruth Wakefield, proprietor of the Toll House Inn in Whitman, Massachusetts, stumbled onto the perfect *ménage à trois* of butter, sugar, and chocolate. That story has been told often: How Mrs. Wakefield set out to make an old colonial recipe called the Butter Drop Do. How she didn't have the nuts the recipe

called for, so cut up a bar of semisweet chocolate, expecting it to melt evenly. How it didn't, but instead studded the cookies with luscious bits of soft chocolate. How a guest sampled the cookies and told a journalist friend in Boston about them. And how Nestle's bought out Mrs. Wakefield, created the chocolate chip, and put her recipe on the package for posterity.

Which goes to show that many an empire has been founded on a goof.

I'm grateful to Ruth Wakefield—who would want to live in a world devoid of chocolate chip cookies?—and also to Nestle's, who, I think, still make the best chocolate chips. I use no other for my cookies. You may decide otherwise, but whatever brand you use, make sure that they're real chocolate, not chocolate flavored.

Dark Brown Sugar Chocolate Chips

❤ ❤ ❤ ❤ ❤ ❤ ❤ ❤ ❤   *drop cookie*

A bit deeper in color and flavor because it uses dark brown sugar, this cookie offers up the same beloved oomph as a classic chocolate chip cookie.

INGREDIENTS

2 cups plus 5 tablespoons all-purpose flour
1 teaspoon baking soda
1 teaspoon salt
1 cup (2 sticks) unsalted butter at room temperature
1¼ cups (lightly packed) dark brown sugar
½ cup granulated sugar
1½ teaspoons pure vanilla extract
2 large eggs
6 ounces (1 cup) semisweet chocolate chips
¾ cup chopped pecans
1¼ cups shredded sweetened coconut (optional)

1. Preheat the oven to 400°F. Line several baking sheets with parchment paper, or lightly grease them with vegetable oil.

2. Sift the flour, baking soda, and salt together into a small bowl and set aside.

3. Using an electric mixer on medium speed, cream the butter, both sugars, and vanilla together in a medium-size bowl until light and fluffy, 1½ to 2 minutes. Stop the mixer twice during the process to scrape the bowl with a rubber spatula.

4. Add the eggs and beat on medium speed until they are blended, about 30 seconds. Scrape the bowl.

5. Add the flour mixture and mix on low speed for 20 seconds. Scrape the bowl.

6. Add the chocolate chips and blend until they are mixed in, 5 to 8 seconds. Then add the nuts and coconut, if using, and mix until blended, 5 to 8 seconds more.

7. Drop the dough by heaping tablespoons 2 inches apart onto the prepared baking sheets.

8. Bake the cookies until the edges are dark golden and the centers are light and slightly puffed up, 9 to 11 minutes. Remove the cookies from the oven and allow them to cool on the sheets.

9. These are best eaten the same day they are baked. Otherwise, store them in an airtight container in the freezer for up to 2 weeks. Before eating, bring them to room temperature or heat them slightly in the microwave (50 seconds on medium-high power).

Makes 24 large cookies

Chocolate Chunkers

❤ ❤ ❤ ❤ ❤ ❤ ❤ ❤ ❤   *drop cookie*

Remember Chunky, the candy?
Well, meet Chocolate Chunkers,
the cookie. They're a craggy moun-
tain stuffed full of chocolate chips,
raisins, and pecans, then coated with
a velvety chocolate ganache. For the
kid in all of us.

INGREDIENTS

THE COOKIE
3½ ounces unsweetened chocolate
8 tablespoons (1 stick) unsalted butter
1 cup plus 2 tablespoons all-purpose flour
⅛ teaspoon baking powder
1¼ cups sugar
2 whole large eggs
1 large egg yolk
1 cup raisins
¾ cup chopped pecans
4 ounces (¾ cup) semisweet chocolate chips

THE GLAZE
½ cup heavy (whipping) cream
2 tablespoons sugar
8 ounces bittersweet chocolate, chopped
    small
1 tablespoon unsalted butter

1. Preheat the oven to 325°F. Line
several baking sheets with parchment
paper, or grease them lightly with vegetable oil.

2. Make the cookies: Melt the
unsweetened chocolate and the butter

in the top of a double boiler placed
over simmering water. Remove the pan
from the heat and allow to cool slightly.

3. Sift the flour and baking powder
together into a small bowl and set
aside.

4. Place the sugar in a medium-size
mixing bowl, add the melted chocolate
mixture, and blend for 10 seconds.
Scrape the bowl with a rubber spatula.

5. Add the eggs and the yolk and mix
until blended, 10 seconds, stopping the
bowl once to scrape the sides with a
rubber spatula.

6. Add the flour mixture on low
speed and mix until blended, 10 seconds, stopping the mixer once to
scrape the bowl.

7. Add the raisins and blend 5 seconds. Then add the nuts and chocolate
chips, and blend several seconds more.
Finish the mixing by hand.

8. Scoop heaping tablespoons of
dough and form them into mounds
with your hands. Arrange them 2 inches
apart on the prepared baking sheets.

9. Bake the cookies until they form a
thin crust, 20 to 25 minutes. Allow
them to cool on the sheets.

10. Meanwhile, prepare the glaze:
Place the cream and sugar in a small
saucepan and bring to a boil, whisking
occasionally. Remove from the heat
immediately.

11. Add the chocolate and butter to the pan, cover, and let sit about 5 minutes until the chocolate melts.

12. Stir the mixture with a whisk until it is shiny and velvety.

13. Dip each cookie, upside down, in the glaze, coating the entire top. Place right side up on cooling racks or on a sheet of parchment to set for several hours.

14. Store the cookies in an airtight container, with parchment paper between the layers, for a couple of days in the refrigerator. After that, store them in the freezer for up to 2 weeks.

Makes 24 cookies

Whole-Grain Earthy Chocolate Chips

❤ ❤ ❤ ❤ ❤ ❤ ❤ ❤ ❤   *drop cookie*

Go on, sneak in a little healthiness. Your kids will never know. These cookies contain bran, wheat germ, and whole wheat flour, and they're still a hit in my house (though if my son Jake suspected that they have any nutritional value whatsoever, they'd never pass his lips again).

INGREDIENTS

2¼ cups plus 2 tablespoons whole wheat flour
1 teaspoon baking soda
1 teaspoon salt
¾ cup plus 2 tablespoons quick-cooking oats
2 tablespoons wheat bran (coarse or fine)
2 tablespoons toasted wheat germ
1 cup (2 sticks) unsalted butter at room temperature
1 cup (lightly packed) light brown sugar
½ cup granulated sugar
1½ teaspoons pure vanilla extract
2 large eggs
9 ounces (1½ cups) semisweet chocolate chips

1. Preheat the oven to 400°F. Line several baking sheets with parchment paper, or grease them lightly with vegetable oil.

2. Sift the flour, baking soda, and salt together into a small bowl and set aside.

3. Mix the oats, bran, and wheat germ together in another small bowl and set aside.

4. Using an electric mixer on medium speed, cream the butter, both sugars, and the vanilla together in a medium-size bowl until light and fluffy, 1½ to 2 minutes. Stop the mixer twice during the process to scrape the bowl with a rubber spatula.

5. Add the eggs and beat on medium speed until they are blended, about 30 seconds. Scrape the bowl.

6. Add the flour mixture and mix on low speed for 10 seconds. Scrape the bowl.

7. Add the oat mixture and mix on low speed for several seconds to blend.

8. Add the chocolate chips and blend until they are mixed in, 5 to 8 seconds.

9. Drop the dough by heaping table-spoons 2 inches apart onto the pre-pared baking sheets.

10. Bake the cookies until the edges are dark golden and the centers are light and slightly puffed up, 11 to 12 min-utes. Remove the cookies from the oven and allow them to cool on the sheets. These are best eaten the same day they are baked. Otherwise, store them in an airtight container in the freezer for up to 2 weeks, and bring them to room temperature before eating.

Makes about 26 cookies

Chocolate Chocolate Chip Meringues

❤ ❤ ❤ ❤ ❤ ❤ ❤ ❤ ❤ ❤ *drop cookie*

These are a low-fat sweet treat that both you and your kids will love. (Their only fat is in the cocoa and the chocolate chips, and that's not much.) You can determine how chewy their center is by varying the baking time.

INGREDIENTS

¼ cup unsweetened cocoa powder
¾ cup plus 2 tablespoons confectioners' sugar
3 large egg whites
¼ teaspoon cream of tartar
6 tablespoons granulated sugar
6 ounces (1 cup) semisweet chocolate chips

1. Line several baking sheets with parchment paper, or grease them lightly with vegetable oil and flour them.

2. Sift the cocoa and the confection-ers' sugar together into a small bowl.

3. Using an electric mixer on medium-low speed, beat the egg whites with the cream of tartar in a medium-size bowl until frothy, 30 to 40 seconds.

4. Gradually add the cocoa mixture and the granulated sugar to the egg whites. Then increase the mixer speed to medium-high and beat for 1 minute. Stop to scrape the bowl with a rubber spatula, increase the speed to high, and continue beating until the mixture forms stiff peaks, 60 to 75 seconds longer. Then gently fold in the choco-late chips with a rubber spatula.

5. Drop the mixture by generously rounded tablespoons onto the baking sheets, leaving 1½ inches between each of the cookies. Allow the cookies to set for 45 minutes.

6. Preheat the oven to 200°F.

7. Place the baking sheets in the oven, and bake for 1½ to 2 hours, depending on how chewy you like your meringue centers to be.

8. Cool the cookies for several minutes on the sheets; then run a spatula under each one and transfer them to cooling racks. Eat warm or at room temperature.

9. After the first day, place the cookies in an airtight plastic container with parchment paper between the layers, and store them for a couple of days at room temperature.

Makes 20 cookies

Rosie's Oatmeal Cookies

♥ ♥ ♥ ♥ ♥ ♥ ♥ ♥ ♥   *drop cookie*

This Rosie's staple—moist, chewy, and replete with golden raisins—didn't make it into my first book. Many of my customers were disappointed and pleaded with me to adapt the recipe for home use. Here it is: the perfect choice for easy baking, moist in the center and crunchy around the edges. Just guard against overbaking.

INGREDIENTS

¾ cup all-purpose flour
¾ teaspoon baking soda
¾ teaspoon ground cinnamon
½ teaspoon salt
8½ tablespoons (1 stick plus 1½ teaspoons) unsalted butter at room temperature
⅓ cup plus 2 tablespoons (lightly packed) light brown sugar
7 tablespoons granulated sugar
1 tablespoon plus 1 teaspoon molasses
2¼ teaspoons water
½ teaspoon pure vanilla extract
1 large egg
2 cups plus 1 tablespoon rolled oats
½ cup shredded sweetened coconut
½ cup plus 2 tablespoons golden raisins

1. Preheat the oven to 375°F. Line several baking sheets with parchment paper, or lightly grease them with vegetable oil.

2. Sift the flour, baking soda, cinnamon, and salt together into a small bowl and set aside.

3. Using an electric mixer on medium speed, cream the butter, both sugars, the molasses, water, and vanilla together in a medium-size bowl until light and fluffy, about 1½ minutes. Stop the mixer twice during the process to scrape the bowl with a rubber spatula.

4. Add the egg and mix on medium-low speed to incorporate it, about 20 seconds.

5. Add the flour mixture and mix on medium-low speed for 10 seconds.

Scrape the bowl, then mix until blended, about 5 seconds more. Scrape the bowl.

6. Add the oats and mix for several seconds on low speed to blend them in. Add the coconut and raisins and mix until blended.

7. Drop the dough by heaping tablespoons about 2 inches apart onto the prepared baking sheets.

8. Bake the cookies until they are golden around the edges and lighter in the center, 12 to 14 minutes. Cool them on the baking sheets.

9. If you plan to snack on them the first day, place the cookies on a plate or simply leave them on the baking sheet. After that, layer the cookies in an airtight container, using plastic wrap, parchment, or waxed paper between the layers, and store the container in the freezer for up to 2 weeks. Bring the cookies to room temperature before eating.

Makes 20 cookies

Oatmeal Chocolate Chips

❤ ❤ ❤ ❤ ❤ ❤ ❤ ❤ ❤ ❤   *drop cookie*

The perfect union of two classic cookies—more an oatmeal cookie with chocolate chips than a chocolate chip cookie with oats! Chewy in the center, crunchy around the edges, it's a hearty and delicious treat.

INGREDIENTS

1¼ cups all-purpose flour
6 tablespoons whole wheat flour
1 teaspoon baking soda
1 teaspoon salt
1¼ cups (2½ sticks) unsalted butter at
    room temperature
1¼ cups (lightly packed) light brown sugar
½ cup granulated sugar
2 teaspoons pure vanilla extract
2 large eggs
2 tablespoons milk
2¼ cups quick oats
8 ounces (1¼ cups) semisweet chocolate
    chips

1. Preheat the oven to 375°F. Line several baking sheets with parchment paper, or lightly grease them with vegetable oil.

2. Sift both flours, the baking soda, and salt together into a small bowl and set aside.

3. Using an electric mixer on medium-high speed, cream the butter, both sugars, and the vanilla together in a medium-size mixing bowl until light and fluffy, 1½ minutes. Stop the mixer twice during the process to scrape the bowl with a rubber spatula.

4. Add 1 egg and beat on medium speed for 10 seconds. Scrape the bowl and add the second egg and the milk. Beat on medium speed until blended, 10 seconds. Scrape the bowl.

5. Add the flour mixture and mix on low speed until almost blended. Once again, scrape the bowl.

6. Add the oats and blend on medium speed for 10 seconds. Scrape the bowl. Then add the chocolate chips and blend on low speed for 10 to 15 seconds, until incorporated.

7. Drop the cookies by generously rounded tablespoons 2 inches apart on the prepared baking sheets. Bake until the edges are golden and the centers are lighter in color and just set, 14 to 16 minutes. Cool them on the baking sheets.

8. Store the cookies in a plastic container at room temperature for 1 day. After that, store them in the freezer for up to 2 weeks. Bring them to room temperature before eating, or heat them in a microwave for 50 seconds on medium power.

Makes about 26 cookies

Pecan Oatmeal Chips

♥ ♥ ♥ ♥ ♥ ♥ ♥ ♥ ♥ *drop cookie*

I adapted these cookies from what was purportedly an original Neiman Marcus creation, and I must say that they're a good argument for department stores branching out into everything under the sun. The oats are ground into flour before you add them to the batter—neither chic nor expensive like the source of this recipe, they're downright earthy.

INGREDIENTS

1¼ cups rolled oats
1 cup all-purpose flour
¾ teaspoon baking soda
½ teaspoon salt
12 tablespoons (1½ sticks) unsalted butter
    at room temperature
½ cup (lightly packed) light brown sugar
½ cup granulated sugar
1½ teaspoons pure vanilla extract
1 large egg
6 ounces (1 cup) semisweet chocolate chips
½ cup chopped pecans

1. Preheat the oven to 375°F. Line several baking sheets with parchment paper, or grease them lightly with vegetable oil.

2. Process the oats in a food processor until they have the consistency of coarse flour. Set aside.

3. Sift the flour, baking soda, and salt together into a small bowl and set aside.

4. Using an electric mixer on medium speed, cream the butter, both sugars, and the vanilla together in a medium-size bowl until light and fluffy, 1 to 1½ minutes. Stop the mixer twice during the process to scrape the bowl with a rubber spatula.

5. Add the egg and beat on medium speed until blended, about 15 seconds. Scrape the bowl.

6. Add the flour mixture and mix on low speed for 15 seconds. Scrape the bowl. Add the oats and blend for 8 to 10 seconds.

7. Add the chocolate chips and pecans and blend until they are mixed in, 5 to 8 seconds.

8. Drop the dough by heaping tablespoons 2 inches apart onto the prepared cookie sheets.

9. Bake the cookies until the edges are dark golden and the centers are light and slightly puffed up, 12 to 14 minutes. Remove the cookies from the oven and allow them to cool on the sheets.

10. These are best eaten the same day they are baked. If you plan to snack on them the first day, place the cookies on a plate or simply leave them on the baking sheet. After that, layer the cookies in an airtight container, using plastic wrap, parchment, or waxed paper between the layers, and store the container in the freezer for up to 2 weeks. Bring the cookies to room temperature before eating.

Makes about 20 cookies

Chocolate Chocolate Chip Oatmeal Cookies

♥ ♥ ♥ ♥ ♥ ♥ ♥ ♥ ♥ *drop cookie*

A great combination of America's favorites, this is very much an oatmeal cookie, yet totally chocolatey at the same time.

INGREDIENTS

3½ ounces unsweetened chocolate
1 cup plus 6 tablespoons all-purpose flour
1 teaspoon baking soda
½ teaspoon salt
1 cup (2 sticks) unsalted butter at room temperature
1½ cups sugar
1 teaspoon pure vanilla extract
1 large egg
6 tablespoons milk
2½ cups quick-cooking oats
6 ounces (1 cup) semisweet chocolate chips

1. Preheat the oven to 350°F. Line several baking sheets with parchment paper, or grease them lightly with vegetable oil.

2. Melt the unsweetened chocolate in the top of a double boiler placed over simmering water. Remove the pan from the heat and allow to cool slightly.

3. Sift the flour, baking soda, and salt together into a small bowl and set aside.

4. Using an electric mixer on medium speed, cream the butter, sugar, and vanilla together in a medium-size bowl until light and fluffy, 1½ to 2 minutes. Stop the mixer twice during the process to scrape the bowl with a rubber spatula.

5. Add the egg and milk and beat on medium speed until blended, about 20 seconds. Scrape the bowl.

6. Add the flour mixture and blend on low speed for 15 seconds. Scrape the bowl. Add the oats and mix until blended, about 15 seconds. Scrape the bowl.

7. Add the melted chocolate and mix on medium speed until blended, 20 seconds. Scrape the bowl.

8. Add the chocolate chips and blend until they are mixed in, 5 to 8 seconds.

9. Drop the batter by heaping tablespoons 2 inches apart on the prepared baking sheets.

10. Bake the cookies until the centers have risen and just begun to set, about 17 minutes. Allow them to cool completely on the sheets.

11. Leave the cookies on the baking sheets or transfer them to a plate if you plan on snacking on them that day. Otherwise, store the cookies in an airtight container in the freezer for up to 2 weeks, and bring them to room temperature before eating.

Makes about 45 cookies

Cranberry Orange Oatmeal Cookies

❤ ❤ ❤ ❤ ❤ ❤ ❤ ❤ ❤ *drop cookie*

To my mind, the cranberry is most enticing when its tartness is surrounded by sweetness. So this cookie, with its chewy center and distinctive citrus-accented oatmeal taste, provides the perfect setting for the little ruby-red fruits. These cookies are best the day they're baked, especially when they've cooled just enough to put in your mouth without burning your tongue.

INGREDIENTS

¾ cup plus 2 tablespoons all-purpose flour

¾ teaspoon baking soda

¾ teaspoon salt

10 tablespoons (1¼ sticks) unsalted butter
    at room temperature

½ cup plus 1 tablespoon granulated sugar

5 tablespoons (lightly packed) light
    brown sugar

1 teaspoon fresh lemon juice

½ teaspoon pure vanilla extract

2 tablespoons grated orange zest

1 tablespoon grated lemon zest

2 large eggs

1¼ cups rolled oats

¾ cup chopped walnuts

1 cup whole cranberries

1. Preheat the oven to 375°F. Line several baking sheets with parchment paper, or lightly grease them with vegetable oil.

2. Sift the flour, baking soda, and salt together into a small bowl and set aside.

3. Using an electric mixer on medium speed, cream the butter, both sugars, lemon juice, vanilla, orange zest, and lemon zest together in a medium-size bowl until light and fluffy, about 1½ minutes. Stop the mixer twice during the process to scrape the bowl with a rubber spatula.

4. Add the eggs and mix on medium-low speed to incorporate, about 20 seconds.

5. Add the flour mixture and mix on medium-low speed for 10 seconds.

Scrape the bowl, then mix until blended, about 5 seconds more. Scrape the bowl.

6. Add the oats and mix for several seconds on low speed to blend them in. Fold in the nuts and then the cranberries by hand.

7. Drop the dough by heaping tablespoons about 2 inches apart onto the prepared baking sheets.

8. Bake the cookies until the edges are golden and the centers are still light and puffy, about 11 minutes. Allow them to cool on the sheets.

9. If you plan to snack on them the first day, place the cookies on a plate or simply leave them on the baking sheet. After that, layer the cookies in an airtight container, using plastic wrap, parchment, or waxed paper between the layers, and store the container in the freezer for up to 2 weeks. Bring the cookies to room temperature before eating.

Makes 36 cookies

47

Chocolate Peanut Butter Volcanoes

❤ ❤ ❤ ❤ ❤ ❤ ❤ ❤   *formed cookie*

With all due credit to George Washington Carver, I'm sure it was a kid who invented the peanut butter-chocolate combination. It certainly is a perfect one. The next time your kids (or you) are in the mood for a Reese's Peanut Butter Cup, bake a batch of these cookies instead. They're little peanut butter volcanoes erupting in soft chocolate lava.

INGREDIENTS

THE LAVA
3 ounces (½ cup) semisweet chocolate chips
½ ounce unsweetened chocolate
½ cup sweetened evaporated milk
1½ teaspoons pure vanilla extract

THE COOKIE
1¾ cups all-purpose flour
¼ teaspoon plus ⅛ teaspoon baking soda
¼ teaspoon salt
*11 tablespoons (1 stick plus 3 tablespoons)
    unsalted butter at room temperature*
¾ cup smooth peanut butter
*½ cup plus 1 tablespoon (lightly packed)
    light brown sugar*
6 tablespoons granulated sugar
¾ teaspoon pure vanilla extract
1 large egg

1. Preheat the oven to 350°F. Line several baking sheets with parchment paper, or lightly grease them with vegetable oil.

2. Make the lava: Melt the chocolates together in the top of a double boiler placed over simmering water.

3. Combine the evaporated milk and the vanilla in a medium-size bowl.

4. Using a whisk, stir the melted chocolate vigorously into the milk until the mixture is smooth and well blended. Set it aside.

5. Make the cookie dough: Sift the flour, baking soda, and salt together into a small bowl and set aside.

6. Using an electric mixer on medium speed, cream the butter, peanut butter, both sugars, and the vanilla together in a medium-size mixing bowl until light and fluffy, about 1½ minutes. Stop the mixer twice during the process to scrape the bowl with a rubber spatula.

7. Add the egg and beat on medium speed until blended, about 1 minute. Scrape the bowl.

8. Add the flour mixture and mix on low speed until blended, about 15 seconds. Scrape the bowl and mix several seconds more.

9. Measure out heaping tablespoons of the dough and roll them into balls with your hands. Place the balls 2 inches apart on the prepared baking sheets.

10. Using your thumb, press a deep hole into the center of each ball, and plop a heaping teaspoon of the lava mixture into the hole. Pinch the opening together just a little bit so the lava will not overflow, but so that it is still visible.

11. Bake the cookies until they are lightly golden, 16 to 18 minutes. Cool the cookies on the sheets or eat them while they're still warm for an extra-special treat.

12. Store the cookies in an airtight container in the refrigerator for 1 day. After that, store them in the freezer for up to 2 weeks. Bring them to room temperature before eating.

Makes 30 cookies

Banana-Nut Chocolate Chunks

♥ ♥ ♥ ♥ ♥ ♥ ♥ ♥ ♥ ♥   *drop cookie*

According to exhaustive surveys of monkeys in the zoo, when they get to scarf up a fallen ice cream cone, their favorite—hands and feet down—is Chunky Monkey, the dynamic flavor combo from Ben and Jerry's. So in homage to those ice cream artists and to sophisticated monkeys everywhere, I came up with this earthy oatmeal cookie, filled it with nutritious chunks of bananas and walnuts, and tossed in chocolate morsels just for the heck of it. Eat the cookies when they're warm so the chips are still squishy, then make a monkey of yourself as you squeal with delight.

INGREDIENTS

1 cup plus 3 tablespoons all-purpose flour
½ teaspoon baking soda
½ teaspoon baking powder
1 teaspoon salt
12 tablespoons (1½ sticks) unsalted butter
at room temperature
½ cup plus 3 tablespoons (lightly packed)
light brown sugar
5 tablespoons granulated sugar
1 tablespoon pure vanilla extract
2 large eggs
1 tablespoon milk
1¼ cups rolled oats
3 ounces (½ cup) plus 1 tablespoon
semisweet chocolate chips
1 cup chopped walnuts or pecans
1½ cups chopped bananas

1. Preheat the oven to 400°F. Line several baking sheets with parchment paper, or lightly grease them with vegetable oil.

2. Sift the flour, baking soda, baking powder, and salt together into a small bowl and set aside.

3. Using an electric mixer on medium speed, cream the butter, both sugars, and the vanilla together in a medium-size bowl until light and fluffy, about 1½ minutes. Stop the mixer twice during the process to scrape the bowl with a rubber spatula.

4. Add the eggs and mix on medium-low speed to incorporate, about 20 seconds. Scrape the bowl. Then add the milk and blend for several seconds.

5. Add the flour mixture and mix on medium-low speed for 10 seconds. Scrape the bowl. Then mix until blended, about 5 seconds more. Scrape the bowl again.

6. Add the oats and mix for several seconds on low speed to blend them in. Then add the chocolate chips and the nuts, and blend for several seconds.

7. Fold the banana pieces in by hand, stirring very gently with a rubber spatula.

8. Drop the dough by rounded tablespoons 2 inches apart on the prepared baking sheets.

9. Bake the cookies until the edges are golden and the centers are light and puffy and not quite set, 8 or 9 minutes.

10. Cool the cookies on the sheets and eat them soon after they cool. They are extremely fragile and cannot be stacked or stored easily.

Makes about 30 cookies

Chocolate-Dipped Almond Macaroons

❤ ❤ ❤ ❤ ❤ ❤ ❤ ❤ *formed cookie*

This cookie comes with a list of acknowledgments and thanks. First to Chagit Gluska of the Jerusalem Cafe, a kosher bakery in Flushing, New York. These macaroons are one of her to-die-for Jewish specialties. And second, to my cousins Roberta and Nathan for introducing me to the bakery and for buying me all manner of goodies from there to take back to Boston. For those of you who seldom find yourself in Flushing, all I can say is *essen* and enjoy.

INGREDIENTS

THE COOKIE
½ cup all-purpose flour
½ teaspoon plus ⅛ teaspoon baking powder
6 ounces (slightly rounded ¾ cup) almond paste (not marzipan)
½ cup plus 2 tablespoons sugar
1 teaspoon pure vanilla extract
2 large egg whites

THE GLAZE
5 ounces bittersweet chocolate

1. Sift the flour and baking powder together into a small bowl and set aside.

2. Cut the almond paste into 8 pieces and distribute them in the bowl of a food processor.

3. Add the sugar and vanilla, and process until the mixture resembles coarse meal, about 15 seconds. Distribute the flour mixture evenly over the almond mixture, and pulse 3 times to blend.

4. Pour the egg whites evenly over the almond mixture and pulse 4 or 5 times to incorporate. Scrape the bowl with a rubber spatula. Then pulse several more times, until the mixture just starts to form a sticky pastelike dough.

5. Scrape the contents of the work bowl into a small bowl, cover with plastic wrap, and refrigerate for 2 to 3 hours (or freeze for 1 to 1½ hours).

6. After that time, preheat the oven to 350°F. Line a baking sheet with parchment paper, or grease it lightly with vegetable oil.

7. Remove the dough from the refrigerator or freezer, and scoop out rounded tablespoons. Using your hands, roll them into balls and place them 2 inches apart on the prepared sheet. Press them down slightly with the palm of your hand.

8. Place the sheet on the middle rack of the oven and bake the cookies for 15 minutes. Then lower the heat to 300°F and bake until they are risen, slightly cracked, and lightly golden, 5 more minutes. Cool on the sheet for 1 hour.

9. Melt the bittersweet chocolate in the top of a double boiler placed over simmering water. Using a spatula, remove the cookies from the baking sheet. Dip half of each cookie in the chocolate.

10. Place the cookies back on the sheet and allow to set for 4 hours before eating (or place the sheet in the refrigerator for about 1 hour).

11. If you plan to snack on them the first day, place the cookies on a plate or simply leave them on the baking sheet. After that, layer the cookies in an airtight container, using plastic wrap, parchment, or waxed paper between the layers, and store the container in the refrigerator for a couple of days or in the freezer for up to 2 weeks. Bring the cookies to room temperature before eating.

Makes 12 cookies

Chocolate-Coconut Scoops

♥ ♥ ♥ ♥ ♥ ♥ ♥ ♥ ♥ ♥ *drop cookie*

Do you love Mounds Bars? Meet their cookie cousins: chewy, moist mounds of shredded coconut whose bottoms are dipped in bittersweet chocolate.

INGREDIENTS

THE COOKIE
1 cup sugar
4 large egg whites
6 tablespoons all-purpose flour
3 cups shredded sweetened
    coconut

THE GLAZE
6 ounces bittersweet chocolate
4 teaspoons vegetable oil

1. Preheat the oven to 350°F. Line one or two baking sheets with parchment paper.

2. Using a whisk, vigorously stir the sugar, egg whites, and flour together in a medium-size bowl. Then stir in the coconut.

3. Using a melon baller, or a mini cookie scoop, or a tablespoon, scoop mounds of the mixture onto the prepared baking sheets, placing them 2 inches apart. Bake until the edges and tops just begin to turn golden, about 12 minutes. Cool completely on the sheets.

4. When the cookies have cooled, prepare the glaze: Melt the chocolate in the top of a double boiler placed over simmering water. Stir in the oil.

5. Place the chocolate mixture in a small deep bowl, and dip the bottom of each coconut cookie in the glaze. Set them upside down (they will tip slightly) on a plate or rack, and refrigerate for 1 to 2 hours.

6. If you plan to snack on them the first day, place the cookies on a plate, if you haven't already done so. After that, layer the cookies in an airtight container, using plastic wrap, parchment, or waxed paper between the layers, and store the container in the refrigerator for a couple of days or in the freezer for up to 2 weeks. Bring the cookies to room temperature before eating.

Makes 14 scoops

Hazelnut Macaroons

♥ ♥ ♥ ♥ ♥ ♥ ♥ ♥ ♥   *drop cookie*

Welcome to the Hazelnut Era. Hazelnut mousse, hazelnut ganache, hazelnut coffee—you'd think the nut had never existed before ten years ago. Ever a child of my times, I offer the hazelnut macaroon as my contribution. It looks like a classic macaroon, and it's bursting forth with that ever-so-current flavor that we've come to love.

INGREDIENTS

2⅔ cups (14 ounces) hazelnuts, skins
    removed (see box)
5 large egg whites
2¼ cups sugar
7 tablespoons all-purpose flour

1. Place the nuts in a food processor and process to form a powder.

2. Combine the egg whites and the sugar in a medium-size mixing bowl and stir by hand with a wooden spoon until mixed, 10 seconds.

3. Add the flour and stir to mix. Then add the ground nuts and continue to mix by hand until blended, 10 seconds.

4. Refrigerate the dough, covered, for at least 2 hours.

5. Fifteen minutes before baking, preheat the oven to 350°F. Line several baking sheets with parchment paper. Lightly grease the paper with butter, then dust with flour.

6. Drop the dough by heaping tablespoons onto the prepared baking sheets, allowing 3 inches between cookies.

7. Bake the cookies until they are lightly golden, approximately 15 minutes.

8. While they are still warm, carefully remove the cookies from the sheets and place them on a rack to cool.

9. If you plan to snack on them the first day, place the cookies on a plate or simply leave them on the baking sheet. After that, layer the cookies in an airtight container, using plastic wrap, parchment, or waxed paper between the layers, and store the container in the refrigerator for a couple of days or in the freezer for up to 2 weeks. Bring the cookies to room temperature before eating.

Makes 20 cookies

Skinning Hazelnuts

To remove the skin from unblanched hazelnuts, toast the nuts on a baking sheet in a preheated 350°F oven for 5 minutes. Then immediately transfer the nuts (about a cupful at a time) onto a clean kitchen towel and lift all four corners to make a bundle. Using one hand to keep the bundle closed, use the other hand to squeeze and massage the nuts to loosen the skin, about 30 seconds. Then open the towel and place the nuts in a small bowl, making sure not to transfer the skins. (It will be impossible to remove all the skins from the nuts, but a good portion should come off.)

Baker's Best Snicker-doodles

♥ ♥ ♥ ♥ ♥ ♥ ♥ ♥ ♥ *drop cookie*

When my family tasted these classics at a street fair, they went wild. Those chewy centers, those crispy edges! I tracked down Michael Baker, proprietor of Baker's Best in Newton Highland, Massachusetts, and he was kind enough to share his recipe with me. You can play with the baking time to get the chewy-crisp combo just the way you want.

INGREDIENTS

3 cups all-purpose flour
1 tablespoon plus 1 teaspoon baking
*   powder*
½ teaspoon salt
2 teaspoons ground cinnamon
1½ cups plus 2 tablespoons sugar
1 cup (2 sticks) unsalted butter at room
*   temperature*
1 teaspoon pure vanilla extract
2 large eggs

1. Preheat the oven to 375°F. Line several baking sheets with parchment paper, or grease them lightly with vegetable oil.

2. Sift the flour, baking powder, and salt together into a small bowl and set aside.

3. Combine the cinnamon with the 2 tablespoons sugar in a small bowl. Stir together thoroughly, and pour into a plastic bag.

4. Using an electric mixer on medium speed, cream the butter, 1½ cups sugar, and vanilla together in a medium-size mixing bowl until light and fluffy, 1 minute. Stop the mixer once during the process to scrape the bowl with a rubber spatula, and scrape the bowl again at the end.

5. Add the eggs and beat on medium speed until they are blended, about 30 seconds. Scrape the bowl.

6. Add half of the flour mixture, and mix on low speed for 10 seconds.

Scrape the bowl. Add the remaining flour mixture and blend on low for 25 seconds, stopping the mixer twice to scrape the bowl.

7. Measure out generously rounded tablespoons of the dough, and roll them into balls with your hands.

8. Place 2 cookies at a time in the cinnamon/sugar mix and shake the bag to coat. Then place the balls 2 inches apart on the prepared baking sheets, and bake until the centers are risen and slightly cracked and the edges are crisp, 16 to 18 minutes. Cool the cookies on the baking sheets.

9. If you plan to snack on them the first day, place the cookies on a plate or simply leave them on the baking sheet. After that, layer the cookies in an airtight container, using plastic wrap, parchment, or waxed paper between the layers, and store the container in the freezer for up to 2 weeks. Bring the cookies to room temperature before eating.

Makes 30 cookies

Classic Snicker- doodles

♥ ♥ ♥ ♥ ♥ ♥ ♥ ♥ ♥ ♥   *drop cookie*

This is the classic sugar cookie baked to just the right chewiness. I think of it as a well-tailored sort of cookie: subtle, never showy, and *always* appropriate. It's perfect with a cup of tea or dunked into a glass of milk.

INGREDIENTS

THE COOKIE
3 cups all-purpose flour
1 teaspoon baking soda
½ teaspoon salt
1 teaspoon cream of tartar
Scant ½ teaspoon ground nutmeg
1 cup (2 sticks) unsalted butter at room temperature
1⅓ cups sugar
1½ teaspoons pure vanilla extract
2 large eggs

THE TOPPING
¼ cup sugar
¾ teaspoon ground cinnamon

1. Preheat the oven to 375°F. Line several baking sheets with parchment paper, or grease them lightly with vegetable oil.

2. Sift the flour, baking soda, salt, cream of tartar, and nutmeg together into a small bowl and set aside.

3. Using an electric mixer on medium speed, cream the butter, sugar, and vanilla together in a medium-size mixing bowl until light and fluffy, about 1½ minutes. Stop the mixer twice during the process to scrape the bowl with a rubber spatula.

4. Add the eggs one at a time, mixing at medium speed until each is incorpo-

rated, about 30 seconds in all. Scrape the bowl.

5. Add the flour mixture on low speed and mix until blended, 20 to 25 seconds. Scrape the bowl and blend 10 seconds more.

6. Drop the dough by rounded tablespoons about 2 inches apart onto the prepared baking sheets. Stir the topping ingredients together, and sprinkle over the cookies.

7. Bake the cookies until they are firm and have small cracks on top, about 12 or 13 minutes. Transfer the cookies to wire racks to cool. As soon as they have completely cooled, store them in an airtight plastic container at room temperature for a day. After that, store the container in the freezer for up to 2 weeks.

Makes 30 cookies

Apple 'n' Spice Drops
♥ ♥ ♥ ♥ ♥ ♥ ♥ ♥ ♥ *drop cookie*

A perfect winter cookie with the texture of a traditional Toll House: crunchy edges, soft center. With its apple pie flavor, this is a wonderful treat with a tall glass of milk on a night when you want to feel warm and cozy.

55

INGREDIENTS

*2 cups dried apples, chopped into ⅜-inch
  pieces*
½ cup apple juice or cider
2 cups plus 1 tablespoon all-purpose flour
1 teaspoon baking soda
¾ teaspoon salt
2½ teaspoons ground cinnamon
1½ teaspoons ground nutmeg
*1 cup (2 sticks) unsalted butter, at room
  temperature*
*1 cup plus 1 tablespoon (lightly packed)
  light brown sugar*
*½ cup plus 2 tablespoons
  granulated sugar*
1 teaspoon pure vanilla extract
1 teaspoon grated lemon zest
2 large eggs
½ cup raisins
½ cup chopped walnuts

1. Place the apples and juice in a small saucepan over medium heat. Bring to a simmer, and simmer for 1 minute, tossing the apples lightly once or twice with a wooden spoon.

2. Drain the apples of any juice, and place them on a double sheet of paper towels. Roll them up in the paper towels, and squeeze out any excess juice. Unroll the towels and let the apples sit, uncovered, while you prepare the dough.

3. Preheat the oven to 425°F. Line several baking sheets with parchment paper, or grease them lightly with vegetable oil.

4. Sift the flour, baking soda, salt, and spices together into a small bowl and set aside.

5. Using an electric mixer on medium speed, cream the butter, both sugars, vanilla, and lemon zest together in a medium-size bowl until light and fluffy, 1½ to 2 minutes. Stop the mixer twice during the process to scrape the bowl with a rubber spatula.

6. Add the eggs and beat on medium speed until they are blended, about 30 seconds. Scrape the bowl.

7. Add the flour mixture and mix on low speed for 15 seconds. Scrape the bowl.

8. Add the apples, raisins, and walnuts, and blend until they are mixed in, 5 to 8 seconds.

9. Drop the dough by heaping tablespoons 2 inches apart onto the prepared baking sheets.

10. Bake the cookies until the edges are dark golden and the center is light and slightly puffed, 11 to 12 minutes. Remove the cookies from the oven and allow them to cool on the sheets.

11. These are best eaten the same day; they tend to get soggy over time because of the moisture in the apples. Leave them on a plate the first day, and then freeze any leftovers in an airtight container for up to 2 weeks.

Makes 28 to 30 cookies

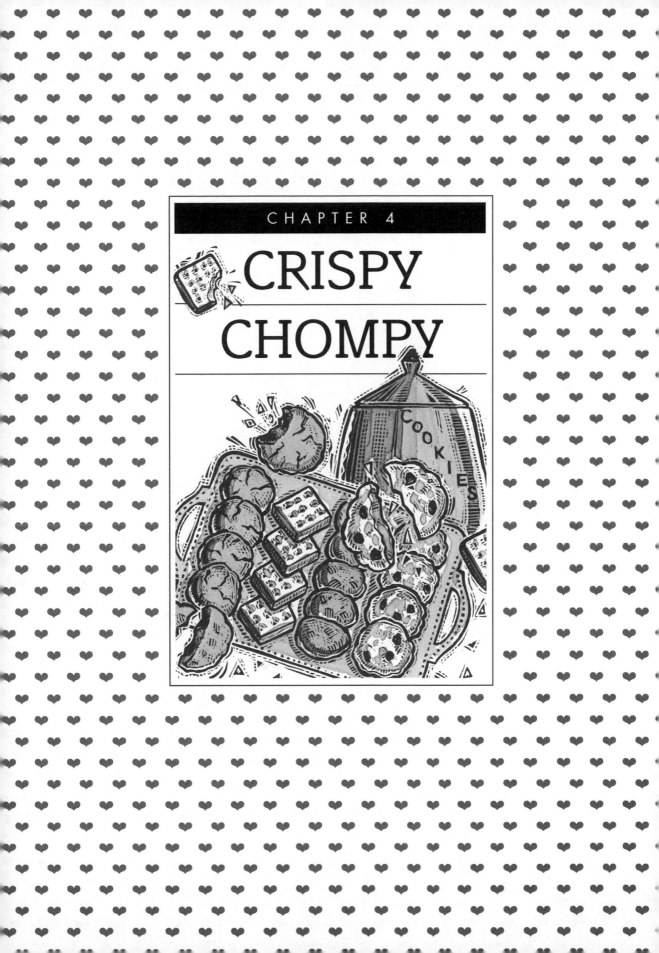

CHAPTER 4

CRISPY

CHOMPY

Crunchy Chocolate Chips

Thin Crisp Chocochips

Chocolate Chip Strips

Chocolate Chip Pecan Mounds

Hazelnut White Chocolate Chunk Cookies

Broken Brittle Crisps

Coconut Dainties

Fresh Ginger Crisps

Hazelnut Crisps

Glazed Lemon Cookies

Chinese Almond Cornmeal Wafers

Lovely Lemon Crisps

Orange Pecan Crisps

Pecan Crisps

Pecan Fingers

Très French Palmiers

Aunt Florence's Anise Biscotti

Low-Fat Almond Biscotti

Orange Walnut Mandelbrot

Chocolate Chocolate Chip Mandelbrot

Amy's Mandelbrot

Lemon Meringues

Golden Pecan Squares

Cappuccino Shortbread Sails

Chunky Chocolate Almond Shortbread

Chocolate Orange Shortbread

Chocolate-Glazed Chocolate Shortbread

Toasted Coconut Macadamia Shortbread

Chunky Pecan Shortbread

Peanut Butter Shortbread Cookies

Ginger Shortbread

Cornmeal Shortbread Cookies

This chapter encompasses the wonderful world of shortbreads, crisps, florentines, ground-nut cookies, and spritzes. Sounds a little like a cookie ride at Disneyland, doesn't it? Or better yet, something from Jane Austen: Under the watchful eye of a Shortbread, that guardian of standards, a sophisticated Florentine gossips behind her lace fan to a demure Spritz, who blushes prettily, while a gingery Crisp thumbs her nose at convention and marries well anyway.

From Disney to Austen, there's nothing like a classic shortbread cookie to win the heart of all age groups. Otherwise, crisps are pretty much the cookies of adulthood. Maybe that's because they have a certain refinement that gives them their character—and this particular character, I've found, is an acquired taste.

Though "crisp" and "chomp" are shared by all the cookies in this chapter, the texture is arrived at by different means for different cookies. Pecan cookies take their texture from their fleshy nuts, for instance, biscotti and mandelbrot are double-baked for crispness, and cookies like Cappuccino Shortbread Sails are rolled thin to achieve their crispy nature.

Shortbread, of course, depends on butter to give it its distinctive brisk texture, as do most of these cookies. That butter flavor also makes them seem to melt in your mouth—a mixed blessing, since they may disappear almost  too quickly. That's just as well because some of them may lose their crispness when left at room temperature for more than two days. Crispy cookies freeze beautifully, though, so you don't *have* to eat them all at once.

The crispier of these cookies can be fragile, so handle them carefully when removing them from the baking sheet, arranging them on a plate, and most especially, sending them through the mail.

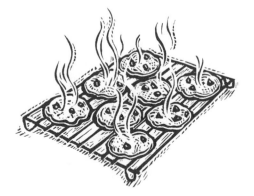

Crunchy Chocolate Chips

❤ ❤ ❤ ❤ ❤ ❤ ❤ ❤ ❤ *drop cookie*

This cookie is for those of you who share my husband's view that a good chocolate chip cookie should be crunchy. They are great alone, and a real treat broken up as a topping over ice cream.

INGREDIENTS

1¾ cups all-purpose flour
¼ teaspoon baking soda
¼ teaspoon baking powder
½ teaspoon salt
13 tablespoons (1 stick plus 5 tablespoons)
    unsalted butter at room temperature
½ cup plus 2½ tablespoons (lightly
    packed) light brown sugar
5 tablespoons granulated sugar
1½ teaspoons pure vanilla extract
1 whole large egg
½ large egg yolk
4 ounces (¾ cup) semisweet chocolate chips

1. Preheat the oven to 400°F. Line several baking sheets with parchment paper, or grease them lightly with vegetable oil.

2. Sift the flour, baking soda, baking powder, and salt together into a small bowl and set aside.

3. Using an electric mixer on medium speed, cream the butter, both sugars, and the vanilla together in a medium-size bowl until light and fluffy, 1 minute. Stop the mixer once during the process to scrape the bowl with a rubber spatula.

4. Add the egg and yolk and beat on medium speed until they are blended, about 30 seconds. Scrape the bowl.

5. Add the flour mixture and mix on low speed for 15 seconds. Scrape the bowl.

6. Add the chocolate chips and blend until they are mixed in, 5 to 8 seconds.

7. Drop the dough by heaping teaspoons 2 inches apart on the prepared baking sheets.

8. Bake the cookies until they are firm and very light golden with darker golden edges, 15 minutes. Cool on the sheets.

9. Store the cookies in an airtight container at room temperature for a day or two if you think you will be snacking on them. After that, store the container in the freezer for up to 2 weeks. Bring the cookies to room temperature before eating.

Makes 48 cookies

Thin Crisp Chocochips

drop cookie

Despite their dainty and elegant appearance, these waferlike cookies completely satisfy your chocolate chip cravings! They're lovely served as an accent with fruit, sorbet, or ice cream, or with a cup of tea in the afternoon.

INGREDIENTS

1½ cups all-purpose flour
¼ teaspoon baking powder
½ teaspoon salt
14 tablespoons (1¾ sticks) unsalted butter
    at room temperature
1 cup (lightly packed) light brown sugar
½ cup granulated sugar
1½ teaspoons pure vanilla extract
1 large egg
6 ounces (1 cup) semisweet chocolate
    chips

1. Preheat the oven to 400°F. Line several baking sheets with parchment paper, or grease them lightly with vegetable oil.

2. Sift the flour, baking powder, and salt together into a small bowl and set aside.

3. Using an electric mixer on medium speed, cream the butter, both sugars, and the vanilla together in a medium-size bowl until light and fluffy, 1 minute. Stop the mixer once during the process to scrape the bowl with a rubber spatula. Scrape the bowl again at the end.

4. Add the egg and beat on medium speed until blended, about 10 seconds. Scrape the bowl.

5. Add the flour mixture and mix on low speed for 15 seconds. Scrape the bowl.

6. Add the chocolate chips and blend until they are mixed in, 5 to 8 seconds.

7. Drop the cookies by rounded teaspoons 2 inches apart on the prepared baking sheets. Flatten each cookie to ¼ inch thickness.

8. Bake the cookies until they are firm and light golden with deep golden edges, about 12 minutes. Allow to cool on the sheets.

9. Store the cookies in an airtight container at room temperature for a day or two if you think you will be snacking on them. After that, store the container in the freezer for up to 2 weeks. Bring the cookies to room temperature before eating.

Makes 75 cookies

Chocolate Chip Strips

♥ ♥ ♥ ♥ ♥ ♥ ♥ ♥ ♥ *formed cookie*

Y ou bake these strips and then cut them to the size you want. I cut them thin and dainty for tea, wide and hearty for teen-age appetites. They're flavorful and crunchy, like the little chocolate chip cookies I used to buy at William Greenberg Bakery in New York.

I N G R E D I E N T S

1½ cups all-purpose flour
¼ teaspoon baking powder
½ teaspoon salt
14 tablespoons (1¾ sticks) unsalted butter
*   at room temperature*
½ cup plus 2 tablespoons (lightly packed)
*   light brown sugar*
6 tablespoons granulated sugar
1½ teaspoons pure vanilla extract
1 large egg
6 ounces (1 cup) semisweet chocolate chips

1. Preheat the oven to 400°F. Line two baking sheets with parchment paper, or grease them lightly with vegetable oil.

2. Sift the flour, baking powder, and salt together into a small bowl and set aside.

3. Using an electric mixer on medium speed, cream the butter, both sugars, and the vanilla together in a medium-size bowl until light and fluffy,

1 minute. Stop the mixer once during the process to scrape the bowl with a rubber spatula.

4. Add the egg and beat on medium speed until blended, about 10 seconds. Scrape the bowl.

5. Add the flour mixture and mix on low speed for 15 seconds. Scrape the bowl.

6. Add the chocolate chips and blend until they are mixed in, 5 to 8 seconds.

7. Form the dough into four equal strips 14 inches long. Place two strips of dough on each baking sheet, and using your hands, flatten each one to a width of 2½ inches. The strips should be 4 inches apart.

8. Bake until the strips are light golden with darker golden edges, about 16 minutes.

9. Remove the baking sheets from the oven, and immediately slice each strip crosswise into 14 slices for dainty cookies or 7 slices for hearty cookies. Let them cool on the sheets.

10. Store the cookies in an airtight container at room temperature for a day or two if you think you will be snacking on them. After that, store the container in the freezer for up to 2 weeks. Bring the cookies to room temperature before eating.

Makes 28 to 56 cookies, depending on how wide you slice them

Chocolate Chip Pecan Mounds

♥ ♥ ♥ ♥ ♥ ♥ ♥ ♥ ♥   *drop cookie*

This sturdy chocolate chip cookie is made with both whole wheat and white flour, which gives it a somewhat earthy texture. The recipe comes from Amy Nastasi, architect par excellence, designer of Rosie's stores, and mother of twins who are almost as cute as mine. . . . Well, all right, they're just as cute!

INGREDIENTS

1 cup whole wheat flour
2 cups all-purpose flour
1 teaspoon baking soda
1 teaspoon salt
1 cup (2 sticks) unsalted butter at room
*   temperature*
½ cup granulated sugar
1 cup (lightly packed) light brown sugar
1 teaspoon pure vanilla extract
2 extra large eggs
9 ounces (1½ cups) semisweet chocolate
*   chips*
1 cup chopped pecans (optional)

1. Preheat the oven to 375°F. Line several baking sheets with parchment paper, or grease them lightly with vegetable oil.

2. Sift both flours, the baking soda, and the salt together into a small bowl and set aside.

3. Using an electric mixer on medium speed, cream the butter, both sugars, and the vanilla together in a medium-size bowl until light and fluffy, about 1 minute.

4. Add the eggs and beat on medium speed until they are blended, about 30 seconds. Scrape the bowl.

5. Add the flour mixture and mix on low speed for 15 seconds. Scrape the bowl.

6. Add the chocolate chips and blend until they are mixed in, 5 to 8 seconds. Add the nuts, if using, and blend until smooth, 5 seconds more.

7. Drop the dough in ¼-cup mounds, spaced 2 inches apart, onto the prepared baking sheets.

8. Bake the cookies until the edges are a rich golden color and the top is lightly golden, risen, and slightly tender, 14 to 18 minutes, depending on desired chewiness. Remove the cookies from the oven and allow them to cool on the sheets.

9. If you plan to snack on them the first day (which is the best idea), place the cookies on a plate or simply leave them on the baking sheet. After that, layer the cookies in an airtight container, using plastic wrap, parchment, or waxed paper between the layers, and store the container in the freezer for up to 3 weeks. Bring the cookies to room temperature before eating.

Makes 20 cookies

Hazelnut White Chocolate Chunk Cookies

❤ ❤ ❤ ❤ ❤ ❤ ❤ ❤ ❤ *drop cookie*

Imagine peanut butter cookies with chunks of chocolate. Then imagine substituting hazelnuts for the peanuts and white chocolate for the chunks. Finally, imagine a cookie like none you've ever tasted, and now we're talking Hazelnut White Chocolate Chunks.

INGREDIENTS

1½ cups all-purpose flour
½ teaspoon baking soda
½ teaspoon salt
1¼ cups skinned toasted
     hazelnuts (see pages 53 and 89)
2 tablespoons unsalted butter, melted
7 tablespoons unsalted butter at room
     temperature
½ cup (lightly packed) light brown sugar
½ cup granulated sugar
1 teaspoon pure vanilla extract
1 large egg
6 ounces (1 cup) coarsely chopped white
     chocolate or whole white chocolate
     chips

1. Preheat the oven to 350°F. Line several baking sheets with parchment paper, or grease them lightly with vegetable oil.

2. Sift the flour, baking soda, and salt together into a small bowl and set aside.

3. Chop ½ cup of the hazelnuts coarsely and set aside.

4. Place the remaining ¾ cup hazelnuts and the 2 tablespoons melted butter in a food processor, and process until the mixture forms a crumbly paste, 30 seconds.

5. Using an electric mixer on medium speed, cream the butter, both sugars, and the vanilla together until blended, 30 seconds. Stop once during the process to scrape the bowl.

6. Add the hazelnut butter mixture and beat on medium speed for 10 seconds to blend. Scrape the bowl.

7. Add the egg and continue to beat on medium speed until blended, 10 seconds. Scrape the bowl.

8. Add the flour mixture and mix on low speed until almost blended, 20 seconds. Scrape the bowl. Then add the reserved chopped nuts and the white chocolate, and mix for 3 seconds. Finish the mixing by hand.

9. Drop the dough by generously rounded teaspoons about 2 inches apart onto the prepared baking sheets. Using the prongs of a fork, press each cookie down lightly, making a crisscross pattern.

10. Bake the cookies until they are firm and lightly golden, 16 to 18 minutes. Cool them on the baking sheets.

11. If you plan to snack on them the first day, place the cookies on a plate or simply leave them on the baking sheet. After that, layer the cookies in an airtight container, using plastic wrap, parchment, or waxed paper between the layers, and store the container in the freezer for up to 2 weeks. Bring the cookies to room temperature before eating.

Makes about 55 cookies

Broken Brittle Crisps

❤ ❤ ❤ ❤ ❤ ❤ ❤ ❤ ❤ *formed cookie*

Take a classic chocolate chip cookie, stud it with your choice of shattered Heath Bar or Skōr bar, and you've got yourself a treat. Although the chocolate coating on the candy melts into the cookie, the hard toffee remains intact once the cookie cools. A perfect candy/cookie combo.

INGREDIENTS

2 cups all-purpose flour
¼ teaspoon baking soda
1 teaspoon salt
1 cup (2 sticks) unsalted butter at room temperature
¾ cup (lightly packed) light brown sugar
¼ cup (lightly packed) dark brown sugar
½ cup granulated sugar
1½ teaspoons pure vanilla extract
1 large egg
4 ounces Heath or Skōr candy bars, chopped very coarsely and unevenly

1. Preheat the oven to 400°F. Line several baking sheets with parchment paper, or grease them lightly with vegetable oil.

2. Sift the flour, baking soda, and salt together into a small bowl and set aside.

3. Using an electric mixer on medium speed, cream the butter, three sugars, and the vanilla together in a medium-size bowl until light and fluffy, 1½ to 2 minutes. Stop the mixer twice during the process to scrape the bowl with a rubber spatula.

4. Add the egg and beat on medium speed until blended, about 10 seconds. Scrape the bowl.

5. Add the flour mixture and mix on low speed for 15 seconds. Scrape the bowl.

6. Add the candy and mix on low speed just enough to incorporate.

7. Measure out generously rounded teaspoons of the dough and roll them into balls with your hands.

8. Place the balls 2 inches apart on the prepared baking sheets, and then press each cookie down as thin as possible with your hand (dip your hand in flour for every other cookie).

9. Bake the cookies until they are golden with a deeper golden edge, 13 to 14 minutes. Cool the cookies on the sheets.

10. If you plan to snack on them the first day, place the cookies on a plate or simply leave them on the baking sheet. After that, layer the cookies in an airtight container, using plastic wrap, parchment, or waxed paper between the layers, and store the container in the freezer for up to 2 weeks. Bring the cookies to room temperature before eating.

Makes about 50 cookies

Coconut Dainties

❤ ❤ ❤ ❤ ❤ ❤ ❤ ❤ ❤   *formed cookie*

Melt-in-your-mouth coconut wafers—crisp, delicate, coated with confectioners' sugar. They came to me from Susan Allison of Healdsburg, California—they're an Allison family heirloom.

INGREDIENTS

2 cups plus 2 tablespoons cake flour
5 tablespoons granulated sugar
½ teaspoon salt
1 cup (2 sticks) unsalted butter, cold, cut into 16 pieces
½ teaspoon pure vanilla extract
1 teaspoon pure almond extract
2 cups shredded sweetened coconut
2 cups sifted confectioners' sugar for coating

1. Preheat the oven to 350°F. Line several baking sheets with parchment paper.

2. Place the flour, sugar, and salt in a food processor and process to blend, 5 seconds.

3. Scatter the butter over the flour mixture, and dribble the extracts over that. Process until the butter is blended and the dough is beginning to come together, 35 seconds. Scrape the sides and bottom of the bowl with a rubber spatula.

4. Add the coconut and pulse 7 or 8 times to blend.

5. Scoop out rounded teaspoons of the dough, and use your hands to form them into 2-inch-long logs about ¼ inch thick. Place the logs 2 inches apart on the prepared baking sheets, and flatten them with your hands so that they form an oval shape.

6. Bake the cookies until they are firm and golden around the edges,

15 to 18 minutes. Let them cool on the baking sheets.

7. Place the confectioners' sugar in a plastic bag or a bowl, and one by one drop the cookies in, tossing lightly to coat.

8. Store the cookies in an airtight container at room temperature for a day or two if you think you will be snacking on them. After that, store the container in the freezer for up to 2 weeks. Bring the cookies to room temperature before eating.

Makes about 50 cookies

Fresh Ginger Crisps

❤ ❤ ❤ ❤ ❤ ❤ ❤   *refrigerator cookie*

I'm willing to bet that these are the gingeriest cookies you'll ever taste—so gingery that you can see the strands of fresh ginger in each cookie, so gingery that the taste lingers on your tongue for a few minutes after you've eaten your last bite.

INGREDIENTS

1 cup plus 5 tablespoons all-purpose flour
¼ teaspoon baking soda
¼ teaspoon salt
10 tablespoons (1¼ sticks) unsalted butter at room temperature
½ cup (lightly packed) light brown sugar
¼ teaspoon ground cinnamon
¼ teaspoon ground allspice
2 teaspoons grated lemon zest
¼ cup grated fresh ginger (use a hand grater)
¼ cup molasses

1. Sift the flour, baking soda, and salt together into a small bowl and set aside.

2. Using an electric mixer on medium speed, cream the butter, brown sugar, cinnamon, allspice, lemon zest, and ginger together in a medium-size bowl until light and fluffy, 2½ to 3 minutes. Stop the mixer once or twice during the process to scrape the bowl with a rubber spatula.

3. Add the molasses and mix on low speed for several seconds. Scrape the bowl.

4. Add the flour mixture and mix on low speed until the mixture is fluffy again, about 45 seconds. Scrape the bowl. Divide the dough in half.

5. Place a 15-inch length of waxed paper or plastic wrap on a work surface. Shape one portion of the dough into a rough log 10 to 11 inches long and place it along one long side of the paper. Roll the dough up in the paper, and twist the ends like a hard-candy wrapper. Repeat with the second portion of dough. Refrigerate the dough for 2 hours.

6. Remove the logs from the refrigerator. Using your hands, gently roll the wrapped dough back and forth on the work surface to smooth out the cylinder. Refrigerate for 4 to 6 hours or as long as overnight.

7. Fifteen minutes before baking preheat the oven to 350°F. Line several baking sheets with parchment paper, or leave them ungreased.

8. Remove the logs from the refrigerator, unwrap them, and cut them into ¼-inch-thick slices.

9. Place the cookies 1 inch apart on the prepared baking sheets. Bake until they are crisp and firm, golden in color with brown edges, 14 to 16 minutes. Cool them on the baking sheets.

10. Store the cookies in an airtight container at room temperature for a day or two if you think you will be snacking on them. After that, store the container in the freezer for up to 2 weeks. Bring the cookies to room temperature before eating.

Makes 40 cookies

Hazelnut Crisps

❤ ❤ ❤ ❤ ❤ ❤ ❤ ❤ ❤ *drop cookie*

Lacy ladylike cookies with a strong hazelnut flavor and enough crisp to keep them interesting.

INGREDIENTS

6 tablespoons all-purpose flour
½ teaspoon baking powder
¼ teaspoon salt
⅛ teaspoon ground cinnamon
½ cup granulated sugar
¼ cup (lightly packed) light brown sugar
7 tablespoons unsalted butter at room temperature, cut into 7 pieces
1 large egg white
1¼ cups skinned toasted hazelnuts (pages 53 and 89)

1. Preheat the oven to 375°F. Line several baking sheets with parchment paper, or grease them lightly with vegetable oil.

2. Place the flour, baking powder, salt, cinnamon, and both sugars in a food processor and process for 5 seconds.

3. Distribute the butter over the flour mixture and process until blended, 10 to 15 seconds. Scrape the bowl with a rubber spatula.

4. With the machine running, add the egg white through the feed tube and process to blend, several seconds. Scrape the bowl.

5. Add the hazelnuts and process until they are ground, 90 seconds. (The grind will be somewhat irregular.) Stop the mixer once during the process to scrape the bowl.

6. Drop the dough by rounded teaspoons 2 inches apart on the prepared baking sheets. Press them down lightly with the tip of a finger.

7. Bake the cookies until they have spread and are a rich golden color with deep golden edges, 12 to 14 minutes.

8. Remove the cookies from the oven and allow them to cool completely on the sheets.

9. If you plan to snack on them the first day, place the cookies on a plate or simply leave them on the baking sheet. After that, layer the cookies in an airtight container, using plastic wrap, parchment, or waxed paper between the layers, and store the container in the freezer for up to 2 weeks. Bring the cookies to room temperature before eating.

Makes 50 cookies

Glazed Lemon Cookies

♥ ♥ ♥ ♥ ♥ ♥ ♥   *refrigerator cookie*

I love the pure citrus taste of these cookies. They're strongly flavored with lemon and topped with a tart lemon glaze. They make a lovely dessert served with fresh berries, or offer them as part of a cookie platter along with Chocolate Snowballs and Pecan Crisps.

I N G R E D I E N T S

THE COOKIE
2 cups plus 2 tablespoons cake flour
¼ teaspoon baking powder
½ teaspoon salt
1 tablespoon plus 1 teaspoon grated
     lemon zest
¾ cup confectioners' sugar
¼ cup granulated sugar
12 tablespoons (1½ sticks) unsalted butter,
     cold, cut into 12 pieces
1 teaspoon pure vanilla extract
2 tablespoons fresh lemon juice

THE GLAZE
6 tablespoons confectioners' sugar
2½ teaspoons heavy (whipping)
     cream
2 teaspoons fresh lemon juice

1. Combine the flour, baking powder, salt, lemon zest, and both sugars in a food processor and process for 10 seconds.

2. Scatter the butter over the flour mixture, and process for 45 seconds or until the dough just comes together. During this time, while the machine is running, add the vanilla and lemon juice through the feed tube.

3. Spread a 24-inch length of waxed paper on a work surface. With floured fingers, shape the dough into a rough log about 18 or 19 inches long, and place it along one long side of the paper. Roll the log up in the waxed paper and twist the ends like a hard-candy wrapper. Refrigerate the dough for 2 hours. (If necessary, cut the log in half and wrap it up in two packages in order to fit it in the refrigerator.)

4. Remove the dough from the refrigerator, and with it still in the waxed paper, gently roll it back and forth on the work surface to round the log.

5. Place the log back in the refrigerator and chill it for 2 to 3 more hours.

6. Preheat the oven to 325°F. Line two baking sheets with parchment paper, or leave them ungreased.

7. Unwrap the log and cut it into ⅜-inch-thick slices.

8. Place the cookies 2 inches apart on the prepared baking sheets, and bake until the centers are set and the edges are golden, 25 to 30 minutes.

9. Transfer the cookies to wire racks, and allow them to cool completely.

10. Meanwhile, prepare the glaze: Combine the ingredients in a small bowl, and stir vigorously with a whisk until smooth.

11. When the cookies are completely cool, drizzle the glaze randomly over the tops. If possible, place the racks in the refrigerator for the glaze to set, or leave them out for 2 to 3 hours so the glaze can harden.

12. If you plan to snack on them the first day, place the cookies on a plate. After that, layer the cookies in an air-tight container, using plastic wrap, parchment, or waxed paper between the layers, and store the container in the refrigerator for 2 days or in the freezer for up to 2 weeks. Bring the cookies to room temperature before eating.

Makes about 44 cookies

Chinese Almond Cornmeal Wafers

♥ ♥ ♥ ♥ ♥ ♥ ♥ ♥ ♥ ♥ *rolled cookie*

Beverly Jones, one of my two recipe testers, tells me that these cookies are of Chinese origin. Mimi

Santini-Ritt, my other recipe tester, insists that can't be. "Change the name immediately," she advised. "The Chinese don't eat cornmeal." My Solomonic decision was to do nothing, since I think the taste is more important than the name. In whatever culture, the addition of cornmeal to this sweet and buttery Chinese-style almond cookie was a wise move.

INGREDIENTS

THE COOKIE
1¼ cups all-purpose flour
1 cup yellow cornmeal
½ teaspoon salt
1 cup (2 sticks) unsalted butter at room temperature
½ cup (lightly packed) light brown sugar
¾ cup confectioners' sugar
½ teaspoon pure vanilla extract
1 cup finely chopped almonds

THE GLAZE
1 large egg
1 tablespoon water
1 cup sliced almonds

1. Place the flour, cornmeal, and salt in a small bowl and stir with a whisk.

2. Using an electric mixer on medium speed, cream the butter, both sugars, and the vanilla together in a medium-size mixing bowl until light and fluffy, 2 minutes. Stop the mixer three times during the process to scrape the bowl with a rubber spatula.

3. With the mixer on low, add the flour mixture and beat just until blended, 20 seconds. Scrape the bowl.

4. Add the almonds and blend on low speed for 5 seconds. Divide the dough in half. (If the dough is sticky, wrap each portion in plastic wrap and refrigerate for 1 hour before rolling.)

5. Preheat the oven to 350°F. Line several baking sheets with parchment paper, or leave them ungreased.

6. Place one portion of the dough between two pieces of plastic wrap and roll it out ⅛ inch thick.

7. Remove the top piece of plastic wrap, and using a 2¼- or 2½-inch round cookie cutter, cut out approximately 20 cookies. Place the cookies about ¾ inch apart on the prepared baking sheets. Gather up the dough scraps and reroll the dough to make as many cookies as possible. Repeat with the second portion of dough.

8. Prepare the glaze: In a small cup, stir the egg and water together with a small whisk or fork to blend. Brush glaze over each cookie with a pastry brush. Then arrange the almond slices in a circle around the edges of each cookie, and glaze gently once again to set the almonds.

9. Bake the cookies until they are a rich golden brown, about 16 minutes. Allow to cool on the sheets.

10. Store the cookies in an airtight container at room temperature for a day or two if you think you will be snacking on them. After that, store the container in the freezer for up to 2 weeks. Bring the cookies to room temperature before eating.

Makes about 48 cookies

Lovely Lemon Crisps

❤ ❤ ❤ ❤ ❤ ❤ ❤   *refrigerator cookie*

As a child I was always fond of thin crisp lemon wafers, delicate in texture yet pungent in flavor—like these. I like to dunk them in milk, but they're also lovely served with tea or as an accompaniment to sherbet.

INGREDIENTS

1½ cups all-purpose flour
½ teaspoon baking powder
¼ teaspoon baking soda
¼ teaspoon salt
10 tablespoons (1¼ sticks) unsalted butter
*   at room temperature*
½ cup plus 3 tablespoons sugar
1 teaspoon pure vanilla extract
1 tablespoon plus 1 teaspoon grated
*   lemon zest*
¼ cup fresh lemon juice

1. Sift the flour, baking powder, baking soda, and salt together into a small bowl and set aside.

2. Using an electric mixer on medium speed, cream the butter, sugar, vanilla, and lemon zest together in a medium-size mixing bowl until light and fluffy, 45 seconds. Stop the mixer once during the process to scrape the bowl with a rubber spatula.

3. Add the lemon juice and mix on medium speed for 15 seconds.

4. Add the flour mixture and mix on low speed until the mixture is fluffy again, about 30 seconds. Scrape the bowl.

5. Place a 20-inch length of waxed paper or plastic wrap on a work surface. Shape the dough into a rough log about 18 inches long, and place it along one long side of the paper. Roll the dough up in the paper, and twist the ends like a hard-candy wrapper. Refrigerate the dough for 2 hours.

6. Remove the dough from the refrigerator, and using your hands, roll the wrapped dough gently back and forth on a work surface to smooth out the log. Refrigerate it for 4 to 6 hours or as long as 2 days.

7. Fifteen minutes before baking, preheat the oven to 350°F. Line several baking sheets with parchment paper. If you don't have parchment paper, leave the baking sheets ungreased.

8. Unwrap the dough and cut it into ¼-inch-thick slices. Place the cookies 1 inch apart on the baking sheets.

9. Bake the cookies until they are golden around the edges, 10 or 11 minutes. Allow them to cool on the baking sheets.

10. Store the cookies in an airtight container at room temperature for a day or two if you think you will be snacking on them. After that, store the container in the freezer for up to 2 weeks. Bring the cookies to room temperature before eating.

Makes 72 cookies

Orange Pecan Crisps

❤ ❤ ❤ ❤ ❤ ❤ ❤   *refrigerator cookie*

A wonderful wafer-like cookie bursting with the flavor of oranges and loaded with pecans. Adjust the amount of pecans in either direction according to your taste.

INGREDIENTS

2¼ cups all-purpose flour
¼ teaspoon baking soda
½ teaspoon salt
1 cup (2 sticks) unsalted butter at room temperature
½ cup (lightly packed) light brown sugar
½ cup granulated sugar
¼ cup grated orange zest
1 large egg
2 tablespoons frozen orange juice concentrate, thawed
1 cup chopped pecans

1. Sift the flour, baking soda, and salt together into a medium-size bowl and set aside.

2. Using an electric mixer on medium speed, cream the butter, both sugars, and the orange zest together in a medium-size mixing bowl until the ingredients are light and fluffy, about 1 minute. Scrape the bowl with a rubber spatula.

3. Add the egg and orange juice concentrate, and beat on medium speed until blended, 20 seconds. Scrape the bowl.

4. Add the flour mixture and beat on medium-low speed for 20 seconds. Scrape the bowl. Then add the nuts and beat until they are completely incorporated, about 15 seconds.

5. Spread a 13-inch length of waxed paper on a work surface. With floured fingers, shape the dough into a rough log about 12 inches long, and place it along one long side of the paper. Roll the log in the waxed paper, and twist the ends like a hard-candy wrapper. Refrigerate the dough for 2 hours.

6. Remove the dough from the refrigerator, and using your hands, gently roll the dough back and forth on the work surface to round the log.

7. Refrigerate the dough for 4 hours, or up to 2 days.

8. Fifteen minutes before cooking, preheat the oven to 400°F. Line two baking sheets with parchment paper, or leave them ungreased.

9. Unwrap the dough and cut it into ⅛-inch-thick slices. Place the slices 2 inches apart on the baking sheets.

10. Bake the cookies until they are firm to the touch and golden around the edges, 7 to 8 minutes. (They should be crisp through and through when cooled.) Let them cool on the baking sheets.

11. Store the cookies in an airtight container at room temperature for a day or two if you think you will be snacking on them. After that, store the container in the freezer for up to 2 weeks. Bring the cookies to room temperature before eating.

Makes about 90 cookies

Pecan Crisps

❤ ❤ ❤ ❤ ❤ ❤ ❤ ❤ ❤ *drop cookie*

For the pecan purist. The wonderful nutty flavor of this crispy delight is enhanced only by butter and vanilla.

INGREDIENTS

2 cups plus 2 tablespoons all-purpose flour
1 teaspoon baking soda
1½ teaspoons salt
1¼ cups (2½ sticks) unsalted butter at
    room temperature
¾ cup plus 2 tablespoons granulated sugar
¾ cup plus 2 tablespoons (lightly packed)
    light brown sugar
2½ teaspoons pure vanilla extract
2 large eggs
2 cups coarsely chopped pecans

1. Preheat the oven to 400°F. Line several baking sheets with parchment paper, or grease them lightly with vegetable oil.

2. Sift the flour, baking soda, and salt together into a small bowl and set aside.

3. Using an electric mixer on medium speed, cream the butter, both sugars, and the vanilla together in a medium-size bowl until light and fluffy, 1 minute. Stop the mixer once during the process to scrape the bowl with a rubber spatula.

4. Add the eggs and beat on medium speed until they are blended, about 20 seconds. Scrape the bowl.

5. Add the flour mixture and mix on low speed for 15 seconds, stopping the mixer once to scrape the bowl.

6. Add the pecans and blend them in by hand with the rubber spatula.

7. Drop the dough by generously rounded teaspoons 2 inches apart onto the prepared baking sheets.

8. Bake the cookies until they are firm and light golden with darker golden edges, 10 to 12 minutes. Let them cool on the baking sheets; then remove them carefully with a spatula.

9. Store the cookies in an airtight container at room temperature for a day or two if you think you will be snacking on them. After that, store the container in the freezer for up to 2 weeks. Bring the cookies to room temperature before eating.

Makes about 30 cookies

Pecan Fingers

❤ ❤ ❤ ❤ ❤ ❤ ❤ ❤ ❤   *formed cookie*

This is a taste memory that's bred in the bone: Biting into these thin crispy cookies and being greeted with a browned-butter-pecan flavor brings back my childhood in the form of a Danish butter cookie that my mother used to buy at a sensational gourmet store called the Danish Bowl. I was always thrilled when she went there because it meant a dinner of lobster salad finished off with Pecan Fingers.

INGREDIENTS

THE COOKIE
1¼ cups all-purpose flour
¼ teaspoon baking powder
¼ teaspoon salt
12 tablespoons (1½ sticks) unsalted butter
     at room temperature
5 tablespoons (lightly packed) light brown
     sugar
5 tablespoons granulated sugar
2½ teaspoons pure vanilla extract
1 large egg (optional)

THE GLAZE
2 teaspoons milk
2 tablespoons granulated sugar
6 pecans, finely chopped

1. Sift the flour, baking powder, and salt together into a small bowl and set aside.

2. Using an electric mixer on medium speed, cream the butter, both sugars, and the vanilla in a medium-size mixing bowl until light and fluffy, 1 minute. Stop the mixer twice during the process to scrape the bowl with a rubber spatula.

3. Add the egg, if using, and mix at medium-high speed until blended, 15 seconds. Scrape the bowl.

4. Add the flour mixture and beat on medium-low speed until blended,

20 seconds, stopping the mixer once to scrape the bowl. Then scrape the bowl again at the end.

5. Divide the dough in half, wrap each half in plastic wrap, and refrigerate for 4 hours or as long as 2 days.

6. Fifteen minutes before cooking, preheat the oven to 300°F. Line two baking sheets with parchment paper, or grease them lightly with vegetable oil.

7. Using a frosting spatula or your fingertips repeatedly dipped in flour, spread each portion of the dough out on one of the baking sheets to form a rough rectangle ⅛ inch thick (the shape is not important).

8. To glaze, using a pastry brush, lightly brush each portion of dough with the milk. Then sprinkle each with the sugar and the chopped pecans.

9. Bake for 30 minutes. Then remove the baking sheets from the oven and cut the shortbreads into approximately 20 pieces each. Move the pieces ½ inch apart, and return the sheets to the oven. Bake until the cookies are a deep golden color, 15 to 20 minutes.

10. Allow the cookies to cool completely on the baking sheets before eating. These store beautifully in an airtight container for several days. After that, place the container in the freezer for up to 2 weeks.

Makes about 40 small fingers

Très French Palmiers

❤ ❤ ❤ ❤ ❤ ❤ ❤ ❤ ❤ ❤   *rolled cookie*

I confess that these elegant cookies look more like elephant ears than palm leaves to me, but I know better than to argue with French chefs. After all, who would want to eat an elephant's ear? These palmiers are made of a very buttery puff pastry that's swirled into concentric circles and baked to crunchy perfection. *Magnifique!* And just the right thing to accompany a *tisane*.

INGREDIENTS

THE DOUGH
1 cup (2 sticks) unsalted butter, cold
2 cups all-purpose flour
¼ teaspoon salt
½ cup heavy (whipping) cream, cold,
*   plus 2 tablespoons if needed*

THE FILLING
⅓ cup plus ¾ cup sugar
1½ teaspoons ground cinnamon

1. Melt ¼ cup (½ stick) of the butter in a microwave oven or in a small saucepan over low heat. Remove from the heat.

2. Cut the remaining butter into 12 pieces, and cut the 12 pieces in half. Place these chunks in the freezer for 5 minutes.

3. Place the flour and salt in a food processor and process for 5 seconds.

4. Distribute the butter over the flour mixture and pulse 5 or 6 times, just to break up the pieces.

5. Pour the ½ cup cream evenly over the flour-butter mixture. Pulse several times, until the crumbs appear to be evenly moist (the size of the butter chunks will stay fairly large and inconsistent, ranging from a grain of rice to a pea). Test for moistness: pinch some crumbs together. If the mixture holds together like pie dough, there is enough cream. If it doesn't, add 1 tablespoon of cream and pulse twice. Retest. If the dough is still not moist enough, add 1 more tablespoon of cream and pulse twice.

6. Place the (crumbly) dough on a work surface and gently mold it into a 4 × 12-inch rectangle.

7. Place the dough between two pieces of plastic wrap, and roll it out to form a 10 × 20-inch rectangle. Remove the top piece of plastic wrap.

8. Using a pastry brush, brush the yellow part of the melted butter (the milky solids will have sunk to the bottom) over the surface of the dough.

9. With the point of a sharp knife, lightly score the dough lengthwise in thirds. Take the right-hand third of the dough and fold it over the middle third. Then take the left-hand third and fold it over the double thickness. You will have a rectangle measuring about 3½ by 20 inches.

10. Beginning at one end of the length, using the plastic wrap to lift it, roll the dough up like a jelly roll, to form one big fat roll.

11. Place a piece of plastic wrap over this roll and using a rolling pin, roll out a 5-inch square. Cut the square in half, forming two rectangles, each 2½ x 5 inches. Wrap each rectangle in plastic wrap, and refrigerate for several hours or as long as overnight (no more than 48 hours).

12. Prepare the filling: Mix the ⅓ cup sugar and the cinnamon together in a small bowl and set aside. Remove one rectangle of dough from the refrigerator and unwrap it.

13. Sprinkle 1½ tablespoons of the remaining sugar on a large piece of plastic wrap, and place the dough on the plastic. Sprinkle another 1½ tablespoons sugar on top of the dough, cover it with a second piece of plastic, and roll it out, flipping the dough several times, to form a 6 × 12-inch rectangle.

14. Remove the top piece of plastic, sprinkle half of the cinnamon-sugar mixture over the dough, replace the plastic, and roll it out to form a 9 × 12-inch rectangle.

15. Remove the top plastic. Take the long sides of the rectangle and fold them toward the center so that the edges just meet. Then fold in half the long way, as if closing a book. You should have a 9 × 3-inch rectangle.

16. Sprinkle 1½ tablespoons sugar over the long rectangle, then flip it over and sprinkle 1½ tablespoons sugar over the other side.

17. Roll a rolling pin very gently over the length of the rectangle—just to seal it, not to flatten it. Wrap it in plastic wrap and chill for 1 hour.

18. Repeat steps 13 through 17 with the second rectangle.

19. When you are ready to bake the palmiers, preheat the oven to 350°F. Line several baking sheets with parchment paper.

20. Remove the dough from the refrigerator, and cut the rectangles into ⅓-inch-thick slices. Place them, cut side down, 1½ inches apart on the prepared baking sheets.

21. Bake until crisp in texture and deep golden in color, 18 to 21 minutes. Cool on the baking sheets.

22. Because of their incredibly flaky nature, these are best if eaten the first day. However, if storing is a must, place them in an airtight plastic container in the freezer for up to 2 weeks.

Makes 54 palmiers

Aunt Florence's Anise Biscotti

♥ ♥ ♥ ♥ ♥ ♥ ♥ ♥   *formed cookie*

Aunt Florence is ninety years old. She is the eldest of three sisters, all of whom are stellar cooks. For the sake of efficiency or maybe family feeling, each carved out her domain. Florence's is biscotti. For many years the recipe existed only in her mind, so her niece, Mary Susan DeLaura, petitioned her aunt to teach her the secret of the biscotti, which she wrote down and brought back to us. I can't believe a crunchier, more delicious biscotti exists. If you store biscotti correctly, in an airtight container at room temperature, they'll return the favor and last forever.

I N G R E D I E N T S

2¾ cups plus 2 tablespoons all-purpose flour
3 teaspoons baking powder
¼ teaspoon salt
3 large eggs
¾ cup plus 2 teaspoons sugar
1 teaspoon anise flavoring
8 tablespoons (1 stick) unsalted butter, melted

1. Preheat the oven to 325°F. Line two baking sheets with parchment paper, or grease them lightly with vegetable oil.

Biscottibrot?

You say biscotti, I say mandel-brot. Time was when biscotti were one thing and mandelbrot another, and never the twain did meet. Nowadays they're acknowledged as essentially the same crunchy cookie, separated only by different names and pedigrees. I've long harbored the belief that Jews and Italians view the world in similar ways, and this congruence is just one more manifestation. Dip your mandelbrot in cappuccino or your biscotti in hot milk. The beauty of multiculturalism is that you don't have to choose.

2. Sift the flour, baking powder, and salt together into a small bowl and set aside.

3. Using an electric mixer on medium speed, beat the eggs in a medium-size bowl until foamy, 30 seconds. Add the sugar gradually, continuing to beat on medium speed until mixed, 30 seconds. Add the anise flavoring and the melted butter and beat until blended, 10 seconds.

4. With the mixer on low speed, add the flour mixture and mix only until blended, 20 seconds, stopping the mixer once to scrape the bowl with a rubber spatula.

5. Turn the dough out onto a work surface and divide it in half. Form a

strip about 2½ inches wide and 12 inches long with one of the portions, and place it on one of the prepared baking sheets.

6. Form a second strip and place it on the second sheet.

7. Bake the dough strips until firm to the touch, 30 minutes. Remove the baking sheets from the oven and lower the oven temperature to 275°F. Allow the strips to cool for 10 minutes.

8. Using a serrated knife, cut each strip into ½-inch-thick slices. Arrange the slices, standing up, about ½ inch apart on the baking sheets. Bake until thoroughly crisp and lightly golden, about 30 minutes. Let the biscotti cool on the baking sheets.

9. Store in an airtight container at room temperature for up to 2 weeks.

Makes 48 cookies

Low-Fat Almond Biscotti

♥ ♥ ♥ ♥ ♥ ♥ ♥ ♥ *formed cookie*

If you like your biscotti hard and crunchy, this is the one for you. Just dunk them in some coffee or skim milk, and you've got yourself one scrumptious low-fat dessert.

INGREDIENTS

2 cups plus 2 tablespoons all-purpose flour
1 teaspoon baking powder
⅛ teaspoon baking soda
¼ teaspoon salt
2 large eggs at room temperature
2 large egg whites at room temperature
1 cup sugar
4 teaspoons pure almond extract
1 cup coarsely chopped almonds

1. Preheat the oven to 325°F. Line two baking sheets with parchment paper, or grease them lightly with vegetable oil.

2. Sift the flour, baking powder, baking soda, and salt together into a medium-size bowl and set aside.

3. Using an electric mixer on medium speed, beat the eggs, egg whites, sugar, and almond extract together until well blended, 20 seconds. Scrape the bowl with a rubber spatula.

4. Using the rubber spatula, mix in half the flour mixture by hand. Then blend with the electric mixer on low speed for several seconds. Add the remaining flour mixture and mix on low speed until the dough is smooth, about 5 seconds. Add the nuts with a few more turns of the mixer.

5. Turn the dough out onto a work surface and divide it in half. Form a strip about 2½ inches wide and 12 inches long with one of the portions, and place it on one of the prepared baking sheets.

6. Form a second strip and place it on the second sheet.

7. Bake the dough strips until firm to the touch and lightly golden, 20 to 25 minutes.

8. Remove the sheets from the oven and lower the oven temperature to 300°F. Let the strips cool for 10 minutes. Then, using a serrated knife, cut each strip into ½-inch-thick slices. Arrange the slices, standing up, about ½ inch apart on the baking sheets. Bake until crisp and very lightly golden, about 35 minutes.

9. Store in an airtight container at room temperature for up to 2 weeks.

Makes about 48 cookies

Orange Walnut Mandelbrot

❤ ❤ ❤ ❤ ❤ ❤ ❤ ❤   *formed cookie*

Although we usually think of mandelbrot as flavored with cinnamon and vanilla, it's actually a very versatile base for a variety of flavors—and there's no reason to ignore a great flavor like orange. Feel free to substitute chocolate chips for the nuts if you're in the mood for something sweeter. For a fruitier experience, substitute dried cranberries.

INGREDIENTS

2 cups all-purpose flour
1 teaspoon baking powder
Pinch of baking soda
1 teaspoon salt
4 tablespoons (½ stick) unsalted butter at room temperature
¼ cup vegetable oil
¾ cup sugar
1 tablespoon pure vanilla extract
¼ cup grated orange zest
2 large eggs
½ cup plus 2 tablespoons chopped walnuts

1. Preheat the oven to 350°F. Line two baking sheets with parchment paper, or lightly grease them with vegetable oil.

2. Sift the flour, baking powder, baking soda, and salt together into a medium-size bowl.

3. Using an electric mixer on medium-high speed, cream the butter, oil, sugar, vanilla, and orange zest together in a medium-size mixing bowl until light and fluffy, 1 to 1½ minutes. Stop the machine twice during the process to scrape the bowl with a rubber spatula.

4. Add the eggs one at a time on medium speed, mixing until each egg is partially incorporated, about 5 seconds. Scrape the bowl after each addition.

5. Using the rubber spatula, mix in half the flour mixture by hand. Then blend with the electric mixer on low speed for several seconds. Add the remaining flour mixture and mix on low speed until the dough is smooth, about 5 seconds. Add the nuts with a few more turns of the mixer.

6. Turn the dough out onto a work surface and divide it in half (it will be somewhat sticky). Form a strip about 3 inches wide and 11 inches long with one of the portions, and place it on one of the prepared baking sheets.

7. Form a second strip and place it on the second sheet.

8. Bake the dough strips until firm to the touch and lightly golden, 20 to 25 minutes.

9. Remove the baking sheets from the oven and lower the oven temperature to 275°F. Let the strips cool for 10 minutes. Then, using a serrated knife, cut each strip into ½-inch-thick slices. Arrange the slices, standing up, about ½ inch apart on the sheets. Bake until crisp and golden, about 20 minutes.

10. Turn the oven off and leave the cookies in for 15 minutes more. Then remove them from the oven and let them cool on the baking sheets.

11. Store the cookies in an airtight container at room temperature or in the freezer for up to 2 weeks. Bring them to room temperature before eating.

Makes about 44 cookies

Chocolate Chocolate Chip Mandelbrot

♥ ♥ ♥ ♥ ♥ ♥ ♥ ♥ *formed cookie*

This is a brownie-like version of a traditional mandelbrot, note-worthy for its richness, density, and ever-so-chocolately chocolateness. Bake it for the designated length of time if you like your mandelbrot crunchy. For a fudgier texture, take it out of the oven a little sooner.

INGREDIENTS

4 ounces bittersweet chocolate
1 ounce unsweetened chocolate
1¼ cups all-purpose flour
1 teaspoon baking powder
¼ teaspoon salt
2 tablespoons grated orange zest, or
*   1 teaspoon instant espresso or*
*   coffee powder*
1 teaspoon pure vanilla extract
7 tablespoons unsalted butter at room
*   temperature*
5 tablespoons granulated sugar
¼ cup (lightly packed) light brown sugar
1 whole large egg
1 large egg yolk
3 ounces (½ cup) semisweet chocolate chips

THE GLAZE
2 ounces bittersweet or semisweet
*   chocolate*
2 teaspoons pure vegetable oil

1. Preheat the oven to 350°F. Line a baking sheet with parchment paper, or lightly grease it with vegetable oil.

2. Melt the bittersweet and unsweet-ened chocolate in the top of a double boiler placed over simmering water. Then let it cool to room temperature.

3. Sift the flour, baking powder, and salt together into a medium-size bowl. If you are using instant coffee, dissolve it in the vanilla.

4. Using an electric mixer on medium-high speed, cream the butter, both sugars, the vanilla, and the orange zest, if using, together in a medium-size mixing bowl until light and fluffy, 1 to 1½ minutes. Stop the machine twice during the process to scrape the bowl with a rubber spatula.

5. Add the egg and the egg yolk and mix on medium speed until blended, 10 seconds.

6. Add the melted chocolate with the mixer on medium-low speed and mix to blend, 10 seconds, stopping the mixer once to scrape the bowl.

7. Add the flour mixture with the mixer on low, and blend until almost incorporated, 10 seconds. Then add the chocolate chips and blend to mix, 5 more seconds.

8. Lay the dough on the prepared baking sheet, and mold it to form a cylindrical strip about 10 inches long and 3 inches wide.

9. Bake until firm to the touch, about 50 minutes.

10. Remove the sheet from the oven, and lower the oven temperature to 275°F.

11. Let the strip cool for 10 minutes. Then, using a serrated knife, cut the strip into ½-inch-thick slices. Arrange the slices, standing up, about ½ inch apart on the baking sheet. Bake until crunchy through and through, 20 minutes. Then turn off the oven and allow the cookies to sit in the oven for an additional 15 minutes. Remove the sheets from the oven and allow the cookies to cool on the sheets.

12. Meanwhile, prepare the glaze: Melt the chocolate in the top of a double boiler placed over simmering water. Using a whisk, stir in the oil and mix until smooth.

13. When the cookies have cooled, use a pastry brush to paint one side, or the top of the cookies with the chocolate glaze.

14. When the glaze has completely set, 3 hours, place the cookies in an airtight container, with parchment or waxed paper between the layers, and store it in a cool place or in the refrigerator for 2 to 3 days. (At room temperature, the glaze may discolor after several days.) After that, store the container in the freezer for up to 2 weeks. Bring to room temperature before eating.

Makes about 20 cookies

Amy's Mandelbrot

❤ ❤ ❤ ❤ ❤ ❤ ❤ ❤ *formed cookie*

After all the recipes for this book had been completed and the manuscript was actually in my editor's hands, I received this recipe in the mail from my old friend, Amy Etra, who lives in Los Angeles. Although I needed a brief respite from baking, the recipe was just too tempting—I tried it and loved it! The cookies are not too rich and so are great any time of the day. Thanks, Amy.

INGREDIENTS

1 cup water
½ cup raisins
3 cups all-purpose flour
2½ teaspoons baking powder
1 teaspoon salt
¾ cup vegetable oil
1 cup plus 1½ tablespoons sugar
2 teaspoons pure vanilla extract
1½ teaspoons lemon zest
1½ teaspoons orange zest
3 large eggs
½ cup chopped walnuts
1½ teaspoons ground cinnamon

1. Preheat the oven to 375°F. Line two baking sheets with parchment paper, or lightly grease them with vegetable oil.

83

2. Bring the water to a boil in a small saucepan. Turn off the heat, place the raisins in the pan, and cover while you prepare the dough.

3. Sift the flour, baking powder, and salt together in a medium-size bowl, and set aside.

4. Using an electric mixer on medium-high speed, cream the oil, 1 cup of the sugar, the vanilla, and both zests together in a medium-size bowl until light and fluffy, 30 to 45 seconds. Stop the machine once during the process to scrape the bowl with a rubber spatula.

5. Add the eggs one at a time on medium speed, mixing until each egg is partially incorporated, about 5 seconds. Scrape the bowl after each addition.

6. Add half the flour mixture to the egg mixture and blend with the mixer on medium speed for 10 to 15 seconds. Scrape the bowl with a rubber spatula. Then, add the remaining flour mixture and mix on medium speed until the dough is smooth, about 5 seconds.

7. Drain the raisins and pat dry with paper towels. Add the nuts and the raisins to the dough with a few more turns of the mixer.

8. Remove the dough from the bowl and divide it into quarters. Using floured hands, lay one-quarter of the dough lengthwise on a prepared baking sheet, molding it into a strip 2½ inches wide and 7 inches long. Make sure it sits about 2 inches from the edge of the pan. Form the remaining dough quarters into strips and place them on the pans, 2 inches from the edge and 3 inches from each other (there should be 2 strips on each pan).

9. Mix the remaining 1½ tablespoons sugar with the cinnamon. Sprinkle the cinnamon sugar generously over each strip.

10. Bake the dough strips until firm to the touch and lightly golden, 25 to 30 minutes.

11. Remove the sheets from the oven and lower the oven temperature to 350°F. Let the strips cool for 10 minutes. Then, using a serrated knife, cut each strip into ½-inch-thick slices. Arrange the slices, standing up, about ½ inch apart on the sheets. Bake until crisp and lightly golden, about 15 minutes. Remove the cookies from the oven and let them cool on the baking sheets.

12. Store the cookies in an airtight container at room temperature for up to 2 weeks. Otherwise, store the container in the freezer for up to 2 weeks. Bring them to room temperature before eating.

Makes 56 cookies

Lemon Meringues

❤ ❤ ❤ ❤ ❤ ❤ *refrigerator cookie*

Built of three parts—a crunchy shortbread cookie, a dollop of tart lemon curd, and a cap of airy meringue—this confection offers a contrast of flavors and textures with each bite. If you don't eat them all on the first day, you'll need to freeze them, since they wilt at room temperature.

INGREDIENTS

THE COOKIE
1½ cups sifted all-purpose flour
5 tablespoons confectioners' sugar
3 tablespoons granulated sugar
10 tablespoons (1¼ sticks)
     unsalted butter, cold,
     cut into 10 pieces
1 large egg yolk

THE CURD
¼ teaspoon unflavored gelatin powder
⅓ cup plus 1 tablespoon fresh lemon juice
4 large egg yolks
½ cup plus 1 tablespoon sugar
1 tablespoon unsalted butter

THE MERINGUE
4 large egg whites at room temperature
Pinch of salt
2 cups confectioners' sugar, sifted
¼ teaspoon pure vanilla extract

1. Prepare the cookie dough: Place the flour and both sugars in a food processor and process for 5 seconds.

2. Distribute the butter over the flour mixture and process until the mixture resembles coarse meal, about 20 seconds.

3. With the machine running, add the egg yolk through the feed tube and process for 5 seconds. Stop the machine, scrape the bowl, and process until the yolk has been absorbed and the dough is just coming together, 30 seconds.

4. Form the dough into two logs, each about 4½ inches long and 1½ inches in diameter. Wrap each log in plastic wrap and refrigerate.

5. Next, prepare the curd: In a small cup, stir the gelatin into the lemon juice until dissolved. Place the yolks and sugar in a small saucepan, and mix to blend.

6. Add the gelatin mixture to the yolk mixture and stir. Then cook this mixture over low heat, stirring constantly, until it just comes to a boil and starts to thicken, about 5 minutes.

7. Remove the pot from the heat, pour the mixture through a strainer into a small bowl, and stir in the butter. Place plastic wrap directly on the surface, and refrigerate both the curd and the cookie dough for 4 to 6 hours.

8. When you are ready to bake, preheat the oven to 375°F. Fit a pastry bag with a ¼-inch round tip, and place the bag, tip side down, in a tall glass. Line several baking sheets with parchment paper, or grease them lightly with vegetable oil.

9. Unwrap the logs of dough, and cut them into slices that are a generous ⅛ inch thick. Place them 1 inch apart on the prepared baking sheets. Bake until the edges are golden, 10 to 11 minutes.

10. While the cookies are baking, prepare the meringue: Place the egg whites in the top of a double boiler set over tepid water. Add the salt, and stir with a whisk until foamy but not stiff. Whisk in the confectioners' sugar, a teaspoon at a time. Then whisk in the vanilla.

11. Place the double boiler over low heat and continue to stir the meringue with the whisk until it thickens, about 8 minutes. (When it is ready, it will leave a thick trail when the whisk is lifted out of the mixture.) Fill the pastry bag with the meringue.

12. When the cookies have finished baking, remove them from the oven. Place a generous ½ teaspoon of the curd in the center of each cookie, and then pipe a mound of meringue over the curd. Return the cookies to the oven and bake until the meringue starts to turn golden, 8 or 9 minutes. Remove the cookies from the oven and allow them to cool on the baking sheets, or on wire racks for 4 hours. These cookies should be eaten on the same day they are baked.

Makes about 55 cookies

Golden Pecan Squares

❤ ❤ ❤ ❤ ❤ ❤ *refrigerator cookie*

The little bit of maple syrup in this primarily brown sugar shortbread enhances and enriches the flavor and combines perfectly with the pecans. It is a beautiful glazed square cookie, which on a dessert platter is a wonderful complement to all its round cookie cousins.

INGREDIENTS

THE COOKIE
1½ cups all-purpose flour
½ teaspoon salt
¼ teaspoon ground nutmeg
¼ teaspoon ground cinnamon
6 tablespoons (lightly packed) light brown sugar
2 tablespoons granulated sugar
11 tablespoons (1 stick plus 3 tablespoons) unsalted butter, cut in pieces
2 tablespoons maple syrup
½ cup chopped pecans

THE GLAZE
1 large egg yolk
1 teaspoon water
½ teaspoon ground cinnamon
2 tablespoons granulated sugar

1. Preheat the oven to 325°F. Line several baking sheets with parchment paper, or grease them lightly with vegetable oil.

2. Place the flour, salt, nutmeg, cinnamon, and both sugars in a food processor and process for 10 seconds.

3. Scatter the butter over the flour mixture and process until the mixture resembles coarse meal, 10 to 15 seconds.

4. Add the maple syrup and process just until the dough comes together, 45 seconds.

5. Break the dough apart with your hands. Then add the nuts and pulse 30 times to distribute.

6. Place a 16-inch length of waxed paper or plastic wrap on a work surface. Shape the dough into a rough log 12 inches long, and place it along one long side of the paper. Roll the dough up in the paper and twist the ends like a hard-candy wrapper. Refrigerate the dough for 1½ hours.

7. Remove the dough from the refrigerator. Slap each side of the log against a work surface to flatten it so the cookies will be square.

8. Refrigerate it again for 4 to 6 hours or as long as overnight.

9. Fifteen minutes before baking, preheat the oven to 350°F. Line several baking sheets with parchment paper, or leave them ungreased.

10. Prepare the glaze: Stir the egg yolk and the water together in a cup. Mix the cinnamon and sugar in another cup.

11. Remove the dough from the refrigerator, unwrap it, and cut it into ¼-inch-thick slices.

12. Place the cookies 1 inch apart on the baking sheets. Using a pastry brush, glaze each cookie with the yolk mixture and sprinkle with the cinnamon-sugar mix.

13. Bake the cookies on the center rack of the oven until they are a rich golden color and completely firm, 25 minutes. (To test for doneness, remove a cookie from the oven and cut it in half. There should be no doughy strip in the center.) Allow the cookies to cool on the sheets.

14. If you plan to snack on them the first day, place the cookies on a plate or simply leave them on the baking sheet. After that, layer the cookies in an airtight container, using plastic wrap, parchment, or waxed paper between the layers, and store the container in the freezer for up to 2 weeks. Bring the cookies to room temperature before eating.

Makes 48 cookies

Cappuccino Shortbread Sails

❤ ❤ ❤ ❤ ❤ ❤ ❤ ❤ ❤ *rolled cookie*

This is the way I trim my sails: I take triangular wedges of coffee-flavored shortbread and dip them in chocolate before coating them with nuts. They'd probably sink the boat, but what a way to go!

INGREDIENTS

THE COOKIE
2 tablespoons instant coffee powder
1¾ cups plus 2 tablespoons all-purpose
    flour
⅛ teaspoon baking powder
¾ teaspoon salt
6 tablespoons granulated sugar
3 tablespoons light brown sugar
1 teaspoon ground cinnamon
1 cup (2 sticks) unsalted butter, cold,
    cut into 1-inch chunks
1 tablespoon strong brewed coffee
¼ teaspoon pure vanilla extract

THE GLAZE
7 ounces bittersweet chocolate
1½ cups finely chopped toasted almonds
    (see box, facing page)

1. Place the instant coffee, flour, baking powder, salt, both sugars, and the cinnamon in a food processor and process for 5 seconds.

2. Distribute the butter over the flour mixture, and process until the mixture resembles coarse meal, 10 seconds.

3. With the processor running, pour the brewed coffee and vanilla through the feed tube and process just until the mixture comes together, 45 seconds. Stop the machine once during the mixing to scrape the bowl with a rubber spatula.

4. Place the dough between two pieces of plastic wrap, and roll it out to form a 10-inch square that is ⅜ inch thick. Slide this square onto a baking sheet and refrigerate it for 45 minutes.

5. Preheat the oven to 300°F. Line several baking sheets with parchment paper, or grease them lightly with vegetable oil.

6. Cut the dough into 25 squares, and then cut each square in half diagonally to make triangles.

7. Using a spatula, carefully transfer the triangles to the prepared baking sheets, leaving 1½ inches between each cookie. Bake the cookies until they are lightly golden and firm to the touch, 25 to 30 minutes. Transfer the cookies to a rack to cool.

8. Meanwhile, prepare the glaze: Melt the chocolate in the top of a double boiler placed over simmering water. Place the almonds in a small bowl. When the cookies have cooled, dip the base of each triangle about ¾ inch deep into the chocolate and then into the almonds. Set the cookies aside on parch-

Toasting Nuts

It's best to chop nuts before toasting them to ensure a more even result. Place the chopped nuts on an ungreased baking sheet and place them in a preheated 350°F oven for 5 minutes. Open the oven door and toss the nuts by shaking the pan gently back and forth. Close the door and continue until the nuts give off a toasted aroma and are lightly golden, 3 to 5 minutes more.

ment paper, waxed paper, or aluminum foil, and allow them to set for several hours (slide the paper onto baking sheets and refrigerate them to speed up the process).

9. If you plan to snack on them the first day, place the cookies on a plate or simply leave them on the baking sheet. After that, layer the cookies in an airtight container, using plastic wrap, parchment, or waxed paper between the layers, and store the container in the freezer for up to 2 weeks. Bring the cookies to room temperature before eating.

Makes 50 cookies

Chunky Chocolate Almond Shortbread

❤ ❤ ❤ ❤ ❤ ❤ ❤ ❤ *formed cookie*

Wandering the streets of SoHo, NYC, one day, I spotted a big log of almond shortbread studded with chopped chocolate sitting in a bakery window. It called out to me. Here is a mini version of that memory.

INGREDIENTS

1 cup plus 3 tablespoons all-purpose
    flour
¼ teaspoon baking powder
½ teaspoon salt
8 tablespoons (1 stick) unsalted butter
    at room temperature
½ cup (lightly packed) light brown sugar
¾ teaspoon pure vanilla extract
1 large egg white
½ cup ground almonds (from 1 scant cup
    whole almonds)
4 ounces coarsely chopped bittersweet
    chocolate
⅓ cup coarsely chopped almonds
¼ cup granulated sugar in a plastic bag

1. Preheat the oven to 325°F. Line several baking sheets with parchment paper, or leave them ungreased.

2. Sift the flour, baking powder, and salt together into a small bowl and set aside.

3. Using an electric mixer on medium speed, cream the butter, brown sugar, and vanilla in a medium-size mixing bowl until the ingredients are light and fluffy, about 1 minute. Scrape the sides of the bowl with a rubber spatula.

4. Add the egg white and mix until blended, 10 seconds.

5. Add the flour mixture and the ground almonds, and beat on medium-low speed for 20 seconds. Scrape the bowl.

6. Add the chocolate chunks and coarsely chopped almonds, and beat on low speed until incorporated, 10 seconds.

7. Measure out rounded teaspoons of the dough and roll them into balls with your hands.

8. Place each ball in the bag of sugar and toss to coat.

9. Place the balls 2 inches apart on the baking sheets. Using your hands or the bottom of a glass that has been dipped in sugar, flatten each cookie to form a round approximately 1¾ inches in diameter. Bake until the cookies are firm and crunchy through and through, 20 to 22 minutes. (To test for doneness, remove a cookie from the oven and cut it in half. There should be no doughy strip in the center.) Cool on the baking sheets.

10. Store the cookies in an airtight container at room temperature for a day or two if you think you will be snacking on them. After that, store the container in the freezer for up to 2 weeks. Bring the cookies to room temperature before eating.

Makes 40 cookies

Chocolate Orange Shortbread

♥ ♥ ♥ ♥ ♥ ♥ *refrigerator cookie*

I'm convinced that feasts of the gods on Olympus included chocolate and oranges since it's such a divine pairing. It's embodied here in a crunchy orange-flavored wafer, festooned with chunks of bittersweet chocolate.

INGREDIENTS

1 large egg
1 teaspoon pure vanilla extract
2¼ cups all-purpose flour
¼ teaspoon baking soda
½ teaspoon salt
6 tablespoons confectioners' sugar
2 tablespoons granulated sugar
1 tablespoon grated orange zest
1 cup (2 sticks) unsalted butter, cold, cut into 8 pieces
5 ounces bittersweet chocolate, chopped

1. Mix the egg and vanilla together in a cup and set aside.

2. Combine the flour, baking soda, salt, both sugars, and the orange zest in a food processor and process for 10 seconds.

3. Distribute the butter over the flour mixture, and process to form coarse crumbs, 5 seconds.

4. With the machine running, pour the egg mixture through the feed tube and process until the dough comes together, about 10 seconds. Stop the processor once during the blending to scrape the sides of the bowl with a rubber spatula.

5. Remove the dough from the processor and place it on a work surface. Knead the chocolate in by hand.

6. Place a 20-inch length of waxed paper or plastic wrap on a work surface. Shape the dough into a rough log 16 inches long and place it along one long side of the paper. Roll the dough up in the paper and twist the ends like a hard-candy wrapper. Refrigerate the dough for 2 hours.

7. Remove the log from the refrigerator. Using your hands, roll the wrapped dough gently back and forth on a work surface to smooth out the log. Refrigerate it again for 4 to 6 hours or as long as overnight.

8. Fifteen minutes before baking, preheat the oven to 325°F. Line several baking sheets with parchment paper, or leave them ungreased.

9. Remove the dough from the refrigerator, unwrap it, and cut the log into slices that are a slight ½ inch thick. Place the cookies 1 inch apart on the baking sheets.

10. Bake the cookies until they are firm and crisp, about 16 minutes. (To test for doneness, remove a cookie from the oven and cut it in half. There should be no doughy strip in the center.) Cool the cookies on the baking sheets.

11. Store the cookies in an airtight container at room temperature for a day or two if you think you will be snacking on them. After that, store the container in the freezer for up to 2 weeks. Bring the cookies to room temperature before eating.

Makes about 42 cookies

Chocolate-Glazed Chocolate Shortbread

❤ ❤ ❤ ❤ ❤ ❤ ❤ ❤ ❤ *formed cookie*

G ood chocolate shortbread is hard to come by. This one is very chocolatey, delicious, and really easy to throw together. Cut it into rectangles, diamonds, strips, or squares to complement any cookie platter.

INGREDIENTS

THE COOKIE
1 cup all-purpose flour
⅔ cup sugar
⅓ cup unsweetened cocoa powder
8 tablespoons (1 stick) unsalted butter,
   cold, cut into 8 pieces

THE GLAZE
3 ounces bittersweet chocolate, chopped
1 teaspoon vegetable oil

1. Preheat the oven to 300°F. Lightly grease a 9 × 12-inch baking dish with vegetable oil, or line it with parchment paper.

2. Place the flour, sugar, and cocoa in a food processor and process for 10 seconds.

3. Scatter the butter over the flour mixture, and pulse 60 times to blend. (The mixture will still be crumbly.)

4. Press the mixture evenly into the baking dish. Place the dish on the center rack of the oven, and bake until the shortbread is firm to the touch, 40 to 45 minutes.

5. Remove the dish from the oven and place it on a cooling rack. Using a sharp knife, immediately cut the shortbread into 24 pieces (3 long slices by 8 crosswise). Then allow it to cool completely in the pan.

6. When the shortbread is cool, prepare the glaze: Melt the chocolate in the top of a double boiler placed over simmering water.

7. Whisk in the oil, stirring until the mixture is smooth, several seconds. Then pour the mixture into a small deep bowl.

8. Working quickly, dip the prongs of a fork into the glaze, and moving your wrist rapidly from side to side, drizzle lines of chocolate over the shortbread. Use the tip of a knife to go over the cut lines. Allow the shortbread to set for 4 to 6 hours, or place it in the refrigerator or freezer for 1 hour.

9. Any cookies not eaten on the first day should be layered in an airtight container, using plastic wrap, parchment, or waxed paper between the layers, and stored in the refrigerator for up to 2 days or in the freezer for up to 2 weeks.

Makes 24 cookies

Toasted Coconut Macadamia Shortbread

❤ ❤ ❤ ❤ ❤ ❤ ❤ ❤ *formed cookie*

Delicate, crunchy, and chock-full of two of my favorite ingredients, these tropical cookies are good during any season.

INGREDIENTS

THE COATING
1 large egg white
2 cups flaked sweetened coconut

THE COOKIE
2 cups all-purpose flour
¼ teaspoon baking powder
½ teaspoon salt
1 cup (2 sticks) unsalted butter at room
*   temperature*
7 tablespoons confectioners' sugar
4 tablespoons granulated sugar
2 teaspoons pure vanilla extract
½ cup flaked sweetened coconut
¾ cup coarsely chopped macadamia
*   nuts*

1. Preheat the oven to 325°F. Line several baking sheets with parchment paper.

2. Place the egg white for the coating in a small bowl, and set it aside. Place the 2 cups coconut in another small bowl, and set aside.

3. Sift the flour, baking powder, and salt together into a small bowl, and set aside.

4. Using an electric mixer on medium-high speed, cream the butter, both sugars, and vanilla together in a medium-size mixing bowl until light and fluffy, 1½ minutes. Stop the mixer once during the process to scrape the bowl with a rubber spatula.

5. Add the flour mixture, and mix on low speed for 5 seconds. Scrape the bowl. Then increase the speed to medium-high and mix until fluffy, 1 minute. Scrape the bowl again.

6. Add the ½ cup coconut and mix for 10 seconds; scrape the bowl. Then add the nuts and mix until blended, 5 seconds.

7. Measure out generously rounded teaspoons of the dough, and roll them between your hands to form cylinders about 2 inches long by ½ inch thick. Press each cylinder between your palms to form an oval shape about 1½ by 2½ inches.

8. Dip each cookie into the egg white so that it is completely covered; then lift it up, allowing any excess white to slide off. Place the cookie in the bowl of coconut, and shake the bowl gently so that the cookie is completely coated with coconut.

9. Place the cookies 1 inch apart on the prepared baking sheets. Bake until the cookies are a deep golden color,

about 20 minutes. Then reduce the heat to 300°F, and continue to bake for 10 to 15 minutes (to ensure crispness). Allow the cookies to cool on the baking sheets.

10. Store the cookies in an airtight container at room temperature for a day or two if you think you will be snacking on them. After that, store the container in the freezer for up to 2 weeks. Bring the cookies to room temperature before eating.

Makes 58 cookies

Chunky Pecan Shortbread

♥ ♥ ♥ ♥ ♥ ♥ ♥ ♥ ♥ *formed cookie*

There are moments in baking when I feel like a matchmaker for the most obvious of unions. Here it's the natural trio of brown sugar, butter, and pecans. Together they create a solid, chunky cookie with incredible depth of flavor and a texture that's enhanced by the oats I threw in to keep them company.

INGREDIENTS

THE COOKIE
1¼ cups (2½ sticks) unsalted butter
    at room temperature
1 cup plus 2 tablespoons (lightly packed)
    light brown sugar
2 teaspoons pure vanilla extract
2½ cups all-purpose flour
¾ teaspoon salt
7 tablespoons rolled oats
6 tablespoons chopped pecans

THE GLAZE
1 large egg white
24 pecan halves

1. Preheat the oven to 325°F. Line two baking sheets with parchment paper, or leave them ungreased.

2. Using an electric mixer on medium speed, cream the butter, brown sugar, and vanilla together in a medium-size mixing bowl until light and fluffy, about 1½ minutes. Stop the mixer once or twice during the process to scrape the bowl with a rubber spatula.

3. Add the flour and salt, and blend on medium speed for about 1 minute. Scrape the bowl.

4. Add the oats and blend until incorporated, 30 seconds. Then scrape the bowl and add the nuts. Mix until blended, 5 seconds.

5. Measure out rounded tablespoons of dough, and form them into balls with your hands. Place the balls at least

1½ inches apart on the baking sheets. Flatten them with the palm of your hand to form cookies 2¼ inches in diameter and ½ inch thick.

6. Using a pastry brush, glaze each cookie with egg white. Place a pecan half in the center of each cookie. Bake until the cookies are firm and deep golden with darker edges, 35 minutes. Allow them to cool on the baking sheets.

7. Store the cookies in an airtight container at room temperature for a day or two if you think you will be snacking on them. After that, store the container in the freezer for up to 2 weeks. Bring the cookies to room temperature before eating.

Makes 24 cookies

Peanut Butter Shortbread Cookies

♥ ♥ ♥ ♥ ♥ ♥ *refrigerator cookie*

A sophisticated version of the peanut butter cookie, these small, crunchy refrigerator cookies are a cinch to make and a favorite for people of all ages.

INGREDIENTS

1¾ cups plus 2 tablespoons all-purpose flour
⅛ teaspoon baking powder
½ teaspoon salt
12 tablespoons (1½ sticks) unsalted butter at room temperature
7½ tablespoons smooth peanut butter
5 tablespoons granulated sugar
6 tablespoons (lightly packed) light brown sugar
¾ teaspoon pure vanilla extract
1 large egg

1. Sift the flour, baking powder, and salt together into a small bowl and set aside.

2. Using an electric mixer on medium speed, cream the butter, peanut butter, both sugars, and the vanilla together in a medium-size mixing bowl until light and fluffy, 1 or 2 minutes. Stop the mixer once or twice during the process to scrape the bowl with a rubber spatula.

3. Add the egg and mix on medium speed until incorporated, 15 to 20 seconds. Scrape the bowl.

4. Add the flour mixture and mix on low speed until the mixture is smooth, about 45 seconds. Divide the dough in half.

5. Place two 16-inch lengths of waxed paper or plastic wrap on a work surface. Shape each half of the dough into a rough log 10 inches long and place it along one long side of the paper. Roll the logs up in the waxed paper, and twist the ends like a hard-candy wrapper. Refrigerate the dough for 1½ to 2 hours.

6. Remove the dough from the refrigerator. Using your hands, roll the wrapped dough gently back and forth on a work surface to smooth out the logs. Refrigerate again for 1 to 2 hours.

7. Fifteen minutes before baking, preheat the oven to 300°F. Line several baking sheets with parchment paper, or leave them ungreased.

8. Remove the dough from the refrigerator, unwrap it, and cut the logs into slices that are ⅓ inch thick. Place the cookies 1 inch apart on the prepared baking sheets.

9. Bake the cookies until they are lightly golden and crisp to the touch, about 20 minutes. (To test for doneness, remove a cookie from the oven and cut it in half. There should be no doughy strip in the center.) Cool the cookies on the sheets.

10. Store the cookies in an airtight container at room temperature for a day or two if you think you will be snacking on them. After that, store the container in the freezer for up to 2 weeks. Bring the cookies to room temperature before eating.

Makes about 60 cookies

Ginger Shortbread

♥ ♥ ♥ ♥ ♥ ♥   *refrigerator cookie*

Instead of a tea cake, I like to offer this as a tea cookie. I save it for the true ginger lover because it's loaded both with ground and candied ginger. Like tea, it's an acquired taste—unless, of course, you hang out with very sophisticated children. Whatever the age of the palate, it's a shortbread that packs a punch.

INGREDIENTS

2 cups plus 2 tablespoons all-purpose flour
¼ teaspoon baking powder
¾ teaspoon salt
1 cup (2 sticks) unsalted butter at room temperature
⅔ cup plus 1 tablespoon (lightly packed) light brown sugar
¾ teaspoon pure vanilla extract
3 tablespoons ground ginger
1 cup coarsely chopped candied ginger (chopped by hand)

1. Sift the flour, baking powder, and salt together into a small bowl and set aside.

2. Using an electric mixer on medium speed, cream the butter, brown sugar, vanilla, and ground ginger together in a medium-size mixing bowl until light and fluffy, about 2 minutes. Stop the mixer once or twice during the process to scrape the bowl with a rubber spatula.

3. Add the flour mixture and mix on low speed until the mixture is fluffy again, about 45 seconds. Scrape the bowl.

4. Remove the dough from the bowl and place it on a work surface. Work the candied ginger into the dough with your hands.

5. Divide the dough in half. Place two 16-inch lengths of waxed paper or plastic wrap on a work surface. Shape each half of the dough into a rough log, about 10 inches long and 1½ inches in diameter, and place it along one long side of the paper. Roll the dough up in the paper, and twist the ends like a hard-candy wrapper. Refrigerate the dough for 1 to 2 hours.

6. Remove the dough from the refrigerator. Using your hands, roll the wrapped dough gently back and forth on the work surface to smooth out the logs. Refrigerate again for 4 to 6 hours.

7. Fifteen minutes before baking, preheat the oven to 350°F. Line several baking sheets with parchment paper, or leave them ungreased.

8. Remove the dough from the refrigerator, unwrap the logs, and cut them into slices that are a generous ⅓ inch thick.

9. Place the cookies 1 inch apart on the prepared baking sheets, and bake until they are golden and firm to the touch, 28 to 30 minutes. (To test for doneness, remove a cookie from the oven and cut it in half. There should be no doughy strip in the center.) Cool the cookies on the sheets.

10. Store the cookies in an airtight container at room temperature for a day or two if you think you will be snacking on them. After that, store the container in the freezer for up to 2 weeks. Bring the cookies to room temperature before eating.

Makes about 60 cookies

Cornmeal Shortbread Cookies

❤ ❤ ❤ ❤ ❤ ❤ *refrigerator cookie*

There's a lot to be said for cornmeal. The richness of its history, rooted in Native American culture, and the flavor reminiscent of one of our favorite holiday meals make this a very special ingredient. I put cornmeal in my kids' pancakes and cook them cornmeal mush for breakfast. With all that, why not cornmeal cookies, too? These have the crunchy butteryness of shortbread plus the texture of the cornmeal—light, delicious, and grainy.

INGREDIENTS

1 large egg
1 teaspoon pure vanilla extract
1¾ cups plus 2 tablespoons all-purpose
  flour
1 cup yellow cornmeal
⅛ teaspoon baking powder
½ teaspoon salt
¾ cup sugar
1 cup (2 sticks) unsalted butter, cold,
  cut into 16 pieces

1. Using a fork, stir the egg and vanilla together in a small cup and set aside.

2. Place the flour, cornmeal, baking powder, salt and sugar in a food processor and process to blend, 5 seconds.

3. Distribute the butter over the flour mixture and process until the mixture resembles coarse cornmeal, 20 to 30 seconds.

4. With the machine running, add the egg mixture through the feed tube; process for 30 seconds. Scrape the bowl, then process for 3 seconds more. Remove the dough and knead it for several seconds on a work surface.

5. Place a 16-inch length of plastic wrap on a work surface. Shape the dough into a rough log 11 inches long and 2 inches in diameter, and place it along one long side of the plastic wrap. Roll the dough up in the plastic wrap, and twist the ends like a hard-candy wrapper. Refrigerate the dough for 1 hour.

6. Remove the dough from the refrigerator. Using your hands, roll the wrapped dough gently back and forth on a work surface to smooth out the cylinder. Refrigerate it again for 4 to 6 hours or as long as overnight.

7. Fifteen minutes before baking, preheat the oven to 350°F. Line several baking sheets with parchment paper, or leave them ungreased.

8. Remove the dough from the refrigerator, unwrap it, and cut it into slices that are a generous ¼ inch thick. Place them 1 inch apart on the baking sheets.

9. Bake the shortbread cookies until they are firm and lightly golden around the edges, 20 minutes. Let them cool on the baking sheets.

10. Store the cookies in an airtight container at room temperature for a day or two if you think you will be snacking on them. After that, store the container in the freezer for up to 2 weeks. Bring the cookies to room temperature before eating.

Makes 44 cookies

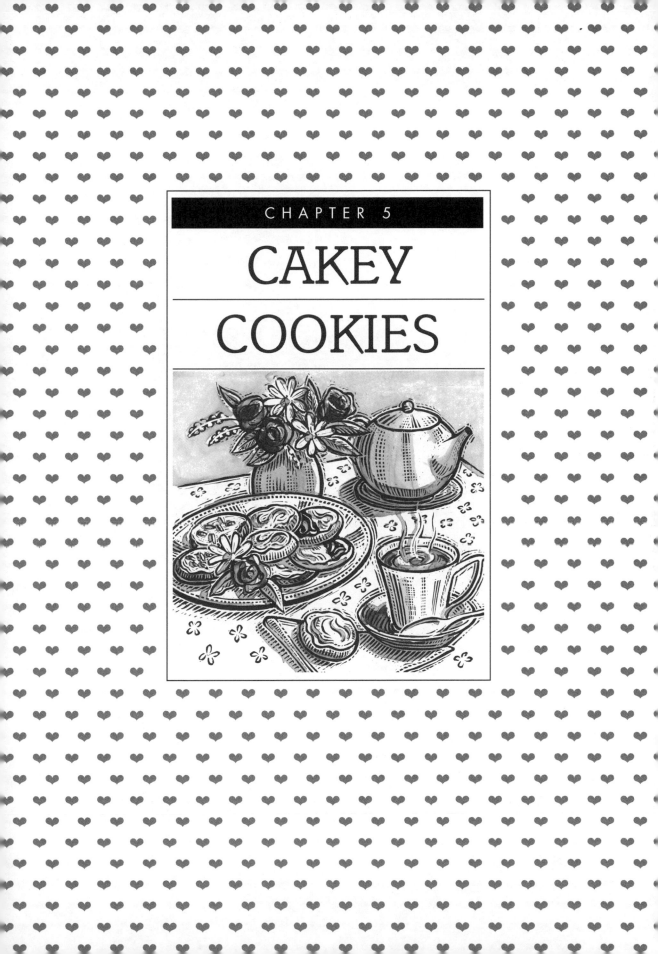

CHAPTER 5

CAKEY

COOKIES

Sacher Tortes

Banana Cream Cheese Mounds

Lemon Orange Sour Cream Cookies

Carrot Cake Cookies

Lemon-Glazed Hermits

Maple Softies

Glazed Molasses Cake Cookies

Half Moons

Chippy Jaker Cakers

Glazed Molasses Cookies, Banana Cream Cheese Mounds, Half Moons. These luscious little heaps of cake, glazed or frosted and passed off as cookies, have a special place in my heart because they allow me to have my cake and eat my cookie too. It seems I'm not alone in this. When I told a friend I was writing a book of cookie recipes, the first thing he said was, "I certainly hope you plan to include Half Moons"—which reaffirmed for me why we're friends.

As my children have gone off to school, cakey cookies have risen even higher in my esteem, because they make wonderful child-size treats for school birthday parties. They're easier for the teacher to hand out and less messy than cake, but they taste just as good and are just as filling. They look great too, especially with a piece of candy or a birthday doodad perched atop the frosting. Best of all, they're separate but equal—and as anyone who has spent any time around kids knows, the child who has her own is a happy child.

Because these cookies are essentially miniature cakes, their batters require more delicate mixing than the other types of cookies. They're also

Cover-ups

Many of these cookies are topped with a glaze or frosting. I use a liquidy confectioners' sugar glaze, and if the glaze is loose enough, I dip the top of the cookie directly in it. If it's too dense for dipping, I spread the glaze with a small spatula or a butter knife. Frostings are always too thick for dipping, so you have to spread them, using the same utensils.

Frostings and glazes are most attractive when they're spread evenly over the cookie with a narrow border left around the edge. When toppings are left to dribble over the sides, they look more like a mistake than an adornment.

fussier about baking time and temperature, and they don't hang around well, so you need to eat them the day of or the day after baking, or you can freeze them for later on. Don't let their demands put you off, though. Once you've made any of these cookies, you'll know their quirks, and you'll agree that the effort is certainly worth it.

Sacher Tortes

♥ ♥ ♥ ♥ ♥ ♥ ♥ ♥ ♥ *drop cookie*

The Sacher torte is a Viennese specialty, a chocolate cake layered with apricot preserves and glazed with more chocolate. I've transformed it into a cookie, keeping all the original ingredients but making it more compact. If you're not a fan of apricots, you can still enjoy the essence of the torte; just leave the preserves out to create a great devil's food cookie with a fudge glaze.

INGREDIENTS

THE COOKIE

2 ounces unsweetened chocolate
1 cup all-purpose flour
1 cup cake flour
6 tablespoons unsweetened cocoa powder
½ teaspoon salt
1 teaspoon baking powder
¼ teaspoon baking soda
4 tablespoons (½ stick) unsalted butter at
*   room temperature*
¼ cup vegetable oil
1 cup (lightly packed) light brown sugar
3 tablespoons granulated sugar
1½ teaspoons pure vanilla extract
3 large eggs
1 cup sour cream

THE TOPPING

⅓ cup apricot preserves

THE GLAZE

8 ounces bittersweet chocolate
2 tablespoons light corn syrup
2 tablespoons unsalted butter
2 tablespoons hot water

1. Preheat the oven to 400°F. Line two baking sheets with parchment paper, or grease them lightly with vegetable oil.

2. Melt the chocolate in the top of a double boiler placed over simmering water. Remove it from the heat and set it aside.

3. Sift both flours, the cocoa powder, salt, baking powder, and baking soda together into a small bowl and set aside.

4. Using an electric mixer on medium-high speed, cream the butter, oil, both sugars, and the vanilla together in a medium-size bowl until light and fluffy, 1½ to 2 minutes. Stop the mixer once or twice during the process to scrape the bowl with a rubber spatula.

5. Add the eggs one at a time, blending on medium speed for 5 seconds after each addition and scraping the bowl with the rubber spatula each time.

6. Add the sour cream and beat on medium speed until blended, about 5 seconds, then on high speed for 3 seconds.

7. Using the spatula, fold in the melted chocolate, mixing until the batter is uniform in color.

8. Fold in the flour mixture with six or seven broad strokes of the spatula. Then mix with the electric mixer on low speed until the batter is velvety, about 10 seconds, stopping once to scrape the bowl with the rubber spatula.

9. Drop the batter by slightly rounded tablespoons about 2 inches apart on the prepared baking sheets.

10. Bake the cookies until they are puffed and just set, about 11 minutes.

11. As soon as the cookies come out of the oven, heat the apricot preserves in a saucepan over low heat just until liquid.

12. Drop a generous ½ teaspoon of the preserves on top of each cookie, and spread it over the surface with a pastry brush. Let the cookies sit for 5 minutes. Then slide the sheet of parchment onto the counter (or, using a spatula, carefully transfer each cookie to a sheet of aluminum foil or waxed paper on the counter) and let them cool further.

13. While the cookies are cooling, prepare the glaze: Melt the chocolate in the top of a double boiler placed over simmering water. Remove the pan from the heat.

14. Add the corn syrup, butter, and hot water to the chocolate, and whisk vigorously until smooth and shiny.

15. Loosen the cookies from the paper with a spatula, and dip their tops into the warm glaze; or use a spatula or a butter knife to spread the glaze over the top. Then return the cookies to the paper, and allow the glaze to set for 2 hours (or refrigerate for 1 hour to set quickly). If you plan to eat them the first day,

store them at room temperature on a plate. After that, place them in an airtight plastic container with plastic wrap, parchment, or waxed paper between the layers, and store them in the refrigerator for up to 3 days or in the freezer for up to 2 weeks. Bring the cookies to room temperature before eating.

Makes about 30 cookies

Banana Cream Cheese Mounds

♥ ♥ ♥ ♥ ♥ ♥ ♥ ♥ ♥   *drop cookie*

Soft and moist, these cookies are among my favorites in this book. It has to do with a cherished memory from my childhood: a banana layer cake my mother sometimes brought home as a treat. When I bite into these cookies, I'm transported back to our dining room table, with my feet not quite reaching the floor and my fork poised to let the glory begin.

INGREDIENTS

THE COOKIE

1½ cups plus 1 tablespoon sifted cake flour
1 teaspoon baking powder
⅛ teaspoon baking soda
¼ teaspoon salt
6 tablespoons (¾ stick) unsalted butter at
*   room temperature*
5 tablespoons granulated sugar
¼ cup (lightly packed) light brown sugar
1 teaspoon pure vanilla extract
1 large egg
½ cup plus 2 tablespoons mashed very ripe
*   bananas*

THE FROSTING

¾ cup cream cheese at room temperature
6 tablespoons confectioners' sugar
3 tablespoons unsalted butter at room
*   temperature*

1. Preheat the oven to 400°F. Line several baking sheets with parchment paper, or lightly grease them with vegetable oil.

2. Sift the flour, baking powder, baking soda, and salt together into a small bowl and set aside.

3. Using an electric mixer on medium speed, cream the butter, both sugars, and the vanilla in a medium-size bowl until light and fluffy, 1 to 1½ minutes. Scrape the bowl.

4. Add the egg and mix on medium speed until blended, about 15 seconds. Scrape the bowl.

5. Add the banana and mix on medium-low speed until blended, about 10 seconds. Scrape the bowl.

6. Fold in the flour mixture by hand. Then blend with the mixer on low speed for 5 seconds. Scrape the bowl with the rubber spatula, and mix on low speed until the batter is smooth and velvety, about 10 seconds. Give the batter a stir or two with the spatula.

7. Drop the batter by heaping tablespoons 2 inches apart onto the prepared baking sheets.

8. Bake the cookies until they are puffed and just firm to the touch (but not golden), about 10 minutes. Let the cookies sit for 2 to 3 minutes. Then slide the sheet of parchment onto the counter (or, using a spatula, carefully transfer each cookie to a sheet of aluminum foil or waxed paper on the counter), and let them cool further.

9. Meanwhile prepare the frosting: Place all the frosting ingredients in a food processor and process until smooth, 40 seconds.

10. Using a small spatula or a butter knife, spread a generous tablespoon of the frosting over the top of each cookie.

11. If you plan to eat the cookies that day, leave them sitting out. To store them, place them in an airtight plastic container with plastic wrap, parchment, or waxed paper between the layers. Store them in the refrigerator if you plan to eat them the next day. Otherwise, place the container in the freezer for up to 2 weeks. Bring the cookies to room temperature before eating.

Makes about 13 large cookies

Lemon Orange Sour Cream Cookies

♥ ♥ ♥ ♥ ♥ ♥ ♥ ♥ ♥   *drop cookie*

Does everyone have some food that makes them close their eyes and moan blissfully, or is it just me? That's certainly what happens when I bite into this cookie. It's so moist, tender, and flavorful—I feel as if I'm indulging in a sumptuous orange layer cake with lots of lemon frosting.

I N G R E D I E N T S

THE COOKIE
1 cup plus 1 tablespoon cake flour
½ cup plus 2 tablespoons all-purpose flour
½ teaspoon baking powder
½ teaspoon baking soda
½ teaspoon salt
8 tablespoons (1 stick) unsalted butter at room temperature
1 cup minus 2 tablespoons sugar
1½ tablespoons grated orange zest
1½ teaspoons pure vanilla extract
1 large egg
½ cup plus 3 tablespoons sour cream

THE GLAZE
1 cup confectioners' sugar
2 tablespoons unsalted butter, melted
1 tablespoon plus 2 teaspoons fresh lemon juice

1. Preheat the oven to 400°F. Line several baking sheets with parchment paper, or lightly grease them with vegetable oil.

2. Sift both flours, the baking powder, baking soda, and salt together into a small bowl and set aside.

3. Using an electric mixer on medium speed, cream the butter, sugar, orange zest, and vanilla in a medium-size bowl until light and fluffy, about 1 minute. Scrape the bowl.

4. Add the egg and mix on medium speed until blended, about 10 seconds. Scrape the bowl.

5. Add the sour cream and mix on medium-low speed until blended, about 8 seconds.

6. Fold in the flour mixture by hand. Then blend with the mixer on low speed for 5 seconds. Scrape the bowl with the rubber spatula, and mix on low speed until the batter is smooth and velvety, 10 seconds. Give the batter a stir or two with the spatula.

7. Drop the batter by large rounded tablespoons about 2 inches apart onto the prepared baking sheets.

8. Bake until the cookies have puffed up, are firm to the touch, and are just beginning to turn golden around the edges, 10 minutes. Let the cookies sit for 2 to 3 minutes. Then slide the sheet of parchment onto the counter (or, using a spatula, carefully transfer each cookie to a sheet of aluminum foil or waxed paper on the counter), and let them cool further.

9. Meanwhile, prepare the glaze: Place the confectioners' sugar in a medium-size bowl. Add the butter and lemon juice, and beat vigorously with a whisk until the mixture is smooth and creamy.

10. Once the cookies have cooled, drop generously rounded ½ teaspoons of the glaze onto each cookie and spread with small butter knife. Allow them to sit until the glaze hardens, about 2 hours (or pop them into the refrigerator for 1 hour).

11. If you plan to eat the cookies that day, leave them sitting out. To store them, place them in an airtight plastic container with plastic wrap, parchment, or waxed paper between the layers. Store them in the refrigerator if you plan to eat them the next day. Otherwise, place the container in the freezer for up to 2 weeks. Bring the cookies to room temperature before eating.

Makes about 24 cookies

Carrot Cake Cookies

❤ ❤ ❤ ❤ ❤ ❤ ❤ ❤   *drop cookie*

Although carrot cake is not quite the hot ticket that it was in the 1970s, it still ranks as a favorite in the repertoire of American desserts. This moist, cakey cookie is topped appropriately with a cream cheese frosting—just like in the old days!

INGREDIENTS

THE COOKIE
2 cups all-purpose flour
1 teaspoon baking powder
¾ teaspoon baking soda
1 teaspoon salt
1 teaspoon ground cinnamon
½ teaspoon ground allspice
¾ teaspoon ground mace
½ teaspoon ground ginger
2 cups grated carrots (2 or 3 good-size
   carrots)
12 tablespoons (1½ sticks) unsalted butter
   at room temperature
7 tablespoons (lightly packed) light brown
   sugar
7 tablespoons granulated sugar
2 teaspoons pure vanilla extract
2 large eggs
1 cup drained crushed pineapple
   (one 16-ounce can)

THE FROSTING
1 cup cream cheese at room temperature
½ cup confectioners' sugar
4 tablespoons (½ stick) unsalted butter
   at room temperature

1. Preheat the oven to 425°F. Line several baking sheets with parchment paper or grease them lightly with vegetable oil.

2. Sift the flour, baking powder, baking soda, salt, and all the spices together into a medium-size bowl and set aside.

3. Place the grated carrots in a food processor and pulse 8 times to chop the shreds. Set aside.

4. Using an electric mixer on medium-high speed, cream the butter, both sugars, and vanilla in a medium-size bowl until light and fluffy, 1 minute. Stop the mixer once during the process to scrape the bowl with a rubber spatula.

5. Add the eggs one at a time, blending on medium speed for 10 seconds after each addition and scraping the bowl with the rubber spatula each time.

6. Add the carrots and the pineapple, and mix on medium speed until blended, 10 seconds, stopping the mixer once to scrape the bowl and then scraping it once again at the end.

7. Add the flour mixture with the mixer on low speed, and blend for 8 seconds. Scrape the bowl thoroughly, then turn the mixer to medium-high and blend for 5 more seconds. Scrape the bowl and finish mixing the batter by hand with a few additional turns of the spatula.

8. Drop the batter by heaping tablespoons onto the prepared baking sheets, and bake on the center rack of the oven until the centers are puffed, set, and lightly golden, about 13 minutes. Allow the cookies to cool 2 to 3 minutes on the baking sheets. Then slide the sheet of parchment onto the counter (or, using a spatula, carefully transfer each cookie onto a sheet of aluminum foil or waxed paper on the counter) and let them cool further.

9. Meanwhile, prepare the frosting: Place all the ingredients in a food processor and process until smooth, 40 seconds.

10. Using a small spatula or a butter knife, spread a generous tablespoon of the frosting over the top of each cookie.

11. If you plan to eat the cookies that day, leave them sitting out. To store them, place them in a single layer in large airtight plastic containers. Store them in the fridge if you plan to eat them the next day. Otherwise, store the container in the freezer for up to 2 weeks. Bring the cookies to room temperature before eating.

Makes about 20 cookies

Lemon-Glazed Hermits

♥ ♥ ♥ ♥ ♥ ♥ ♥ ♥ ♥ ♥   *drop cookie*

Hermits always seem misnamed to me because they're so popular, though it's true that they keep to themselves very well. This version is a moist cakey mound of molasses-and-spice-flavored cookie topped with a white glaze.

INGREDIENTS

THE COOKIE

2¼ cups all-purpose flour

1 teaspoon baking soda

½ teaspoon salt

*14 tablespoons (1¾ sticks) unsalted butter
    at room temperature*

*1 cup plus 2 tablespoons (firmly packed)
    light brown sugar*

*1 tablespoon plus 1 teaspoon ground
    cinnamon*

2 tablespoons ground ginger

2 teaspoons ground cloves

*1 tablespoon plus 1 teaspoon instant
    coffee powder*

1 whole large egg

2 large egg yolks

2 tablespoons dark molasses

THE GLAZE

1¼ cups confectioners' sugar

3 tablespoons fresh lemon juice

1. Preheat the oven to 400°F. Line several baking sheets with parchment paper, or lightly grease them with vegetable oil.

2. Sift the flour, baking soda, and salt together into a small bowl and set aside.

3. Using an electric mixer on medium-high speed, cream the butter, brown sugar, all the spices, and coffee powder together in a medium-size bowl until light and fluffy, about 2 minutes. Stop the mixer twice during the process to scrape the bowl with a rubber spatula. Scrape the bowl a third time before going on to the next step.

4. Add the whole egg and blend on medium speed for about 10 seconds. Scrape the bowl, and then add the yolks. Blend on medium speed for 20 seconds. Scrape the bowl again.

5. Add the molasses and mix on medium-low speed for about 5 seconds. Scrape the bowl.

6. Fold in the flour mixture by hand. Then turn the mixer on low speed and mix for about 5 seconds. Scrape the bowl with the rubber spatula, and mix on low speed until the batter is smooth and velvety, 10 seconds. Give the batter a stir or two with the spatula.

7. Drop the batter by generously rounded tablespoons about 2 inches apart onto the prepared baking sheets.

8. Bake the cookies until they are puffed but the tops are not set (they should leave an indentation when touched), about 12 minutes depending on how chewy you like your hermits. Using a metal spatula, carefully transfer the cookies to wire racks to cool completely.

9. Meanwhile, prepare the glaze: Place the confectioners' sugar and the lemon juice in a small bowl and beat vigorously with a whisk until the mixture is smooth and creamy.

10. Drizzle the glaze over the cooled cookies, or spread it over the surface with a butter knife. Allow the cookies to sit until the glaze hardens, 2 to 3 hours.

11. Then place the cookies, with plastic wrap, parchment, or waxed paper between the layers, in an airtight container and keep them at room temperature if you plan to eat them the first day. Otherwise, store them in the freezer for up to 2 weeks. Bring the cookies to room temperature before eating.

Makes about 22 hermits

Maple Softies

❤ ❤ ❤ ❤ ❤ ❤ ❤ ❤ ❤ ❤   *drop cookie*

One of my most vivid memories from my college years is my mornings at King Pin Donuts on Telegraph Avenue in Berkeley. I'd go there before classes and inhale a maple bar—a fresh-from-the-oven rectangular doughnut swathed in a maple glaze. This is a tribute to that memory: a tender, cakey drop cookie, finished off with a confectioners' sugar–maple glaze.

INGREDIENTS

THE COOKIE
2 cups plus 6 tablespoons cake flour
½ teaspoon plus ⅛ teaspoon baking powder
½ teaspoon plus ⅛ teaspoon baking soda
½ teaspoon salt
9 tablespoons (1 stick plus 1 tablespoon)
    unsalted butter at room temperature
¾ cup granulated sugar
6 tablespoons (lightly packed) light brown
    sugar
½ teaspoon pure vanilla extract
¾ teaspoon pure maple extract
2 large eggs
¾ cup sour cream

THE GLAZE
3 cups confectioners' sugar
¼ cup water
3 tablespoons pure maple syrup
1½ tablespoons light corn syrup
1½ tablespoons (lightly packed) light
    brown sugar
2 teaspoons pure maple extract

THE TOPPING
About 24 pecan halves

1. Preheat the oven to 400°F. Line several baking sheets with parchment paper, or lightly grease them with vegetable oil.

2. Sift the flour, baking powder, baking soda, and salt together into a small bowl and set aside.

3. Using an electric mixer on medium-high speed, cream the butter, both sugars, vanilla, and maple extract together until light and fluffy, 1 minute. Stop the mixer twice during the process to scrape the bowl with a rubber spatula. Scrape the bowl a third time before going on to the next step.

4. Add the eggs one at a time, blending for about 10 seconds on medium speed after each addition. Scrape the bowl.

5. Add one third of the flour mixture with the mixer on low speed, and blend for 5 seconds. Scrape the bowl.

6. Add half of the sour cream, and blend on low speed for 5 seconds. Scrape the bowl.

7. Repeat steps 5 and 6. Then add the remaining flour mixture and mix on low speed for 5 seconds.

8. Give the batter a few broad strokes with a rubber spatula.

9. Drop the batter by heaping tablespoons 2 inches apart on the prepared baking sheets.

10. Bake the cookies until they are just golden and firm to the touch but not crusty, 11 to 12 minutes.

11. Let the cookies sit for 2 to 3 minutes. Then slide the sheet of parchment onto the counter (or, using a spatula, carefully transfer each cookie to a sheet of aluminum foil or waxed paper on the counter), and let them cool further.

12. When the cookies have cooled, prepare the glaze: Place the confectioners' sugar in a medium-size bowl and set aside.

13. Place the water, maple syrup, corn syrup, and brown sugar in a small saucepan and bring to a boil over medium heat. Remove from the heat and add the maple extract.

14. Immediately add this hot mixture to the confectioners' sugar and beat it vigorously with a whisk until velvety smooth, 20 to 30 seconds.

15. Dip the rounded top of each cooled cookie into the glaze, and place a pecan half on top of the cookie. Return the cookies to the paper or foil, and allow them to sit until the glaze hardens, 2 to 3 hours (or pop them into the fridge for 1 hour to set quickly).

16. If you plan to eat the cookies that day, leave them sitting out. To store them, place them in an airtight plastic container with plastic wrap, parchment, or waxed paper between the layers. Store them in the refrigerator if you plan to eat them the next day. Otherwise, place the container in the freezer for up to 2 weeks. Bring the cookies to room temperature before eating.

Makes about 24 cookies

Glazed Molasses Cake Cookies

♥ ♥ ♥ ♥ ♥ ♥ ♥ ♥ ♥ ♥   *drop cookie*

This moist and flavorful molasses cookie is like a tasty piece of gingerbread in cookic form. Glaze a single cookie or sandwich two cookies together with Marshmallow Filling (see page 140). Either way, they're best on the day they are baked.

INGREDIENTS

THE COOKIE
1½ cups all-purpose flour
1 cup plus 2 tablespoons cake flour
1 teaspoon salt
¾ teaspoon baking soda
1 teaspoon ground ginger
1 teaspoon ground cinnamon
¼ teaspoon ground cloves
13 tablespoons (1½ sticks plus 1 table-
  spoon) unsalted butter at room
  temperature
2 teaspoons grated lemon zest
2 whole large eggs
2 large egg yolks
1 cup dark molasses

THE GLAZE
1½ cups confectioners' sugar
2 tablespoons plus 2 teaspoons heavy
  (whipping) cream
1 tablespoon plus 1 teaspoon fresh
  lemon juice

1. Preheat the oven to 400°F. Line several baking sheets with parchment paper, or grease them lightly with vegetable oil.

2. Sift both flours, the salt, baking soda, ginger, cinnamon, and cloves together into a small bowl and set aside.

3. With an electric mixer on medium-high speed, cream the butter and lemon zest together in a medium-size bowl until light and fluffy, 1 minute.

4. Add the whole eggs and the yolks, and mix on medium speed until blended, 20 seconds. Stop the mixer once to scrape the bowl.

5. Add the molasses and mix to blend, 10 seconds. Scrape the bowl.

6. Add half the flour mixture with the mixer on low speed, and blend for 10 seconds. Scrape the bowl with the rubber spatula, add the rest of the flour mixture, and blend on low speed for 10 seconds. Finish the mixing by hand until the batter is smooth.

7. Drop the batter by large rounded tablespoons about 2 inches apart on the prepared baking sheets.

8. Bake until the cookies have puffed up and are firm to the touch, about 13 minutes. Let the cookies sit for 2 to 3 minutes. Then slide the sheet of parchment onto the counter (or, using a spatula, carefully transfer each cookie

111

to a sheet of aluminum foil or waxed paper on the counter), and let them cool further.

9. Meanwhile, prepare the glaze: Place the confectioners' sugar, cream, and the lemon juice in a small bowl and whisk vigorously until smooth.

10. Using a small spatula or a butter knife, frost the top of each cookie with a generously rounded teaspoon of glaze. Let the cookies set for 2 to 3 hours (or pop them into the fridge for 1 hour to set quickly).

11. If you plan to eat the cookies that day, leave them sitting out. To store them, place them in a large airtight plastic container in no more than two layers, with plastic wrap, parchment, or waxed paper between the layers. Store them in the refrigerator if you plan to eat them the next day. Otherwise, place the container in the freezer for up to 2 weeks. Bring the cookies to room temperature before eating.

Makes 20 to 24 cookies

Half Moons

❤ ❤ ❤ ❤ ❤ ❤ ❤ ❤ ❤ ❤   *drop cookie*

However many days there were in the academic years of 1961 to 1964 probably exactly equals the number of Half Moons I consumed. It was only a short jaunt from school to the little neighborhood bakery that supplied me with these oversized yellow cake cookies, one half frosted in chocolate and one half in vanilla. Half Moons are close to perfection.

INGREDIENTS

THE COOKIE
1¼ cups cake flour
½ cup plus 1 tablespoon all-purpose flour
1¼ teaspoons baking powder
½ teaspoon salt
10 tablespoons (1¼ sticks) unsalted butter at room temperature
¾ cup plus 2 tablespoons sugar
1½ teaspoons pure vanilla extract
1 teaspoon grated lemon zest
2 large egg yolks
2 whole large eggs
1 tablespoon milk

THE VANILLA GLAZE
¾ cup confectioners' sugar
2 tablespoons plus 1 teaspoon heavy (whipping) cream
1½ teaspoons unsalted butter, melted

THE CHOCOLATE GLAZE
¼ cup heavy (whipping) cream, heated just to boiling
1 ounce unsweetened chocolate, melted
2 teaspoons unsalted butter
¼ cup confectioners' sugar

1. Preheat the oven to 400°F. Line several baking sheets with parchment paper, or lightly grease them with vegetable oil.

2. Sift both flours, the baking powder, and the salt together into a small bowl and set aside.

3. Using an electric mixer on medium-high speed, cream the butter, sugar, vanilla, and lemon zest together in a medium-size bowl until light and fluffy, about 2 minutes. Stop the mixer once during the process to scrape the bowl with a rubber spatula. Scrape the bowl a third time before going on to the next step.

4. Add the egg yolks and blend on medium speed until incorporated, 15 seconds, stopping the mixer once to scrape the bowl with a rubber spatula.

5. Add the whole eggs one at a time, blending on medium speed for 10 seconds after each addition. Stop the mixer once to scrape the bowl. Then blend on high speed for 5 seconds.

6. Fold in half of the flour mixture by hand. Then turn the mixer on low speed and mix for about 10 seconds. Add the milk. Scrape the bowl with the spatula. Then turn the mixer to medium speed and blend for 5 seconds. Scrape the bowl. With the mixer on low speed, add the remaining flour mixture and blend for 5 seconds. Scrape the bowl. Then turn the mixer to high speed and blend until velvety, 5 seconds.

7. Drop the batter by quarter-cupfuls about 3 inches apart on the prepared baking sheets.

8. Bake the cookies until they are just set and firm to the touch but not crusty, about 12 minutes. Let the cookies sit for 2 to 3 minutes. Then slide the sheet of parchment onto the counter (or, using a spatula, carefully transfer each cookie to a sheet of aluminum foil or waxed paper on the counter), and let them cool further.

9. While the cookies are cooling, prepare the glazes: Place all the ingredients for the vanilla glaze in a small bowl and stir vigorously with a whisk until smooth and velvety.

10. To make the chocolate glaze, place the hot cream in a small bowl and stir in the melted chocolate and the butter until blended. Add the confectioners' sugar and stir with a whisk until smooth and shiny. Allow both glazes to set for 10 minutes.

11. When the cookies are completely cool, turn them upside down, brush off any excess crumbs, and using a small spatula or a butter knife, spread half of the flat side with the vanilla glaze, half with the chocolate. Allow to set for 2 to 3 hours (or pop them into the fridge for 1 hour to set quickly).

12. If you plan to eat the cookies that day, leave them sitting out. To store them, place them in an airtight plastic container with plastic wrap, parchment, or waxed paper between the layers. Store them in the refrigerator if you plan to eat them the next day. Otherwise, place the container in the freezer for up to 2 weeks. Bring to room temperature before eating.

Makes about 10 very large cookies

Chippy Jaker Cakers

drop cookies

Favorites of my son Jake, these cookies are a nice change from the classic chocolate chip. Their texture is like a soft, light cake, so they're best eaten the day they're baked—which hardly presents a problem in my household.

INGREDIENTS

1½ cups plus 2 tablespoons
    all-purpose flour
½ teaspoon baking soda
½ teaspoon salt
8 tablespoons (1 stick) unsalted butter
    at room temperature
1 cup (lightly packed) light brown sugar
2 teaspoons pure vanilla extract
1 large egg
¼ cup buttermilk
6 ounces (1 cup) semisweet chocolate
    chips

1. Preheat the oven to 400°F. Line several baking sheets with parchment paper, or grease them lightly with vegetable oil.

2. Sift the flour, baking soda, and salt together into a small bowl and set aside.

3. Using an electric mixer on medium speed, cream the butter, brown sugar, and vanilla together in a medium-size bowl until light and fluffy, 1½ to 2 minutes. Stop the mixer during the process twice to scrape the bowl with a rubber spatula.

4. Add the egg and beat on medium speed until blended, about 30 seconds. Scrape the bowl.

5. Add one third of the flour mixture, and mix on low speed for 5 seconds. Scrape the bowl.

6. Add the buttermilk and mix for 5 seconds. Then add the rest of the flour mixture and mix until blended, 5 seconds. Scrape the bowl.

7. Add the chocolate chips and blend until they are mixed in, 5 to 8 seconds.

8. Drop the dough by generously rounded tablespoons 2 inches apart on the prepared baking sheets.

9. Bake the cookies until the edges are light golden and the centers are slightly puffed, 11 to 12 minutes.

10. Allow any cookies that don't get eaten right away to cool completely on the sheets; then store them in an airtight plastic container. Leave them at room temperature for the first day if you plan to eat them. Otherwise, place the container in the freezer for up to 2 weeks. Bring the cookies to room temperature before eating.

Makes about 30 cookies

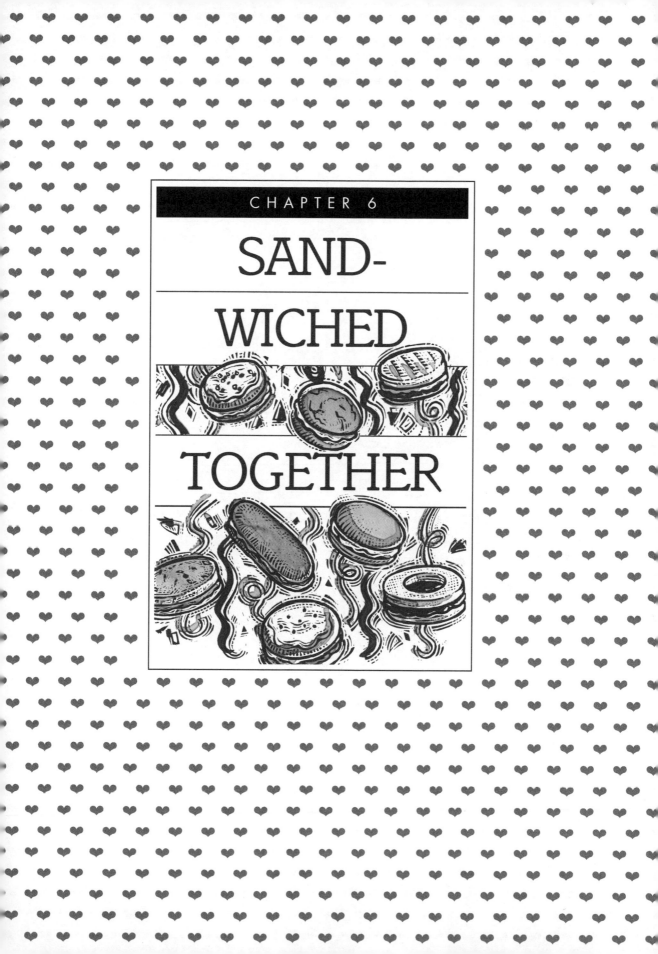

CHAPTER 6

SAND-WICHED TOGETHER

Were there Nobel Prizes in his day, the Earl of Sandwich would surely have been nominated for his culinary contribution to lunch boxes everywhere. The same goes for the unknown genius who translated the Earl's invention into a cookie. I imagine her slaving over a hot Bunsen burner all those long nights in the laboratory, until one red-eyed dawn, just when it seems all has been in vain, she looks up from her calculations, whips off her glasses, and shouts, "Victory is mine! I've got it!"

There before her lies the perfect solution to the age-old problem of how to keep the filling inside the cookie—and on top of that, she's come up with the added prize of two cookies in one. Nothing stands between her and a bright future full of Nutter Butters, Oreos, and vanilla creams. Though history cruelly has denied our inventor immortality, it has given us the sandwich cookie to smoosh apart, lick the frosting off, and eat in pieces, or, being a democratic people, to eat in one piece if we're so inclined. And for that I am grateful.

Sandwich cookies can be made from many types of cookies: cakey, shortbread, and drops, both chewy and crispy. What are they, anyway, but tiny layer cakes in cookie form? Construction of the sandwich isn't hard, but following certain steps helps. Before proceeding, be sure to read the tips in the box on this page.

Frosting the Sandwich

For all kinds of sandwiches, let the cookies cool before you fill them. Pair the cookies up, and turn half of them upside down to receive the filling; the other half will be tops.

For cookies that use buttercream, such as Peanut Butter Sandwiches, dab the right amount of filling in the center of an upside-down cookie and gently press the bottom of its partner down onto it. Let the filling ruffle slightly out the sides to give it a sumptuous look.

Cookies with jam, like Almond Apricot Sandwiches, look better and are easier to eat when they're neater. Spread the jam sparingly here, so that it doesn't ooze out.

For cookies with melted chocolate fillings, such as Shortbread Sandwiches, let the chocolate firm up just a bit after it has melted. Spoon the appropriate amount onto the center of the bottom cookie, and using a butter knife, spread the filling very gently toward the outer edge, stopping just short of it. Then carefully place the top cookie over the chocolate and press ever so lightly until the chocolate comes just to the edge. Allow cookies to set for several hours before eating, though refrigeration will speed up the process.

Boston Cream Pies

❤ ❤ ❤ ❤ ❤ ❤   *cakey drop cookie*

Boston cream pie isn't actually a
pie—it's a cake. Variations have
been floating around for at least a couple of centuries, and Fanny Farmer
codified it as a "Favorite Cake" in her
1896 cookbook. For all that history, I
remain loyal to my version: two buttery vanilla cake cookies sandwiched
together with vanilla custard and
topped with a glossy chocolate glaze.

INGREDIENTS

THE CUSTARD
1 cup milk
6 tablespoons heavy (whipping) cream
6 tablespoons sugar
3 tablespoons cornstarch
¼ teaspoon salt
1 large egg yolk
2 teaspoons pure vanilla extract

THE COOKIE
1 cup all-purpose flour
1 cup plus 2 tablespoons cake flour
¾ teaspoon baking soda
½ teaspoon salt
*9 tablespoons (1 stick plus 1 tablespoon)
    unsalted butter at room temperature*
1 cup plus 1 tablespoon sugar
2 teaspoons pure vanilla extract
½ teaspoon grated lemon zest
2 large egg yolks at room temperature
1 whole large egg at room temperature
*½ cup plus 2 tablespoons buttermilk at
    room temperature*

THE GLAZE
½ cup heavy (whipping) cream
*2 ounces unsweetened chocolate, chopped
    fine or melted*
*1 tablespoon plus 1 teaspoon unsalted
    butter at room temperature*
6 tablespoons confectioners' sugar

1. Prepare the custard: Place ½ cup
plus 2 tablespoons of the milk, all the
cream, and the sugar in a medium-size
saucepan over medium-low heat and
bring just to a boil. Remove from the
heat.

2. Dissolve the cornstarch and salt in
the remaining milk.

3. Add the egg yolk to the cornstarch
mixture, and stir it rapidly with a fork
or whisk. Add this to the scalded cream
mixture and whisk over medium-low
heat constantly until it thickens, 2 to 3
minutes. Then cook, stirring, for 30
seconds more.

4. Remove the custard from the heat,
stir in the vanilla, and pour it into a ce-
ramic or plastic bowl. Allow it to cool
for 10 minutes, stirring it gently several
times.

5. Puncture a piece of plastic wrap in
several places, and place it directly over
the surface of the custard. Refrigerate
until completely chilled, 2 to 3 hours.

6. Meanwhile, make the cookies:
Preheat the oven to 400°F. Line several
baking sheets with parchment paper,
or lightly grease them with vegetable
oil.

7. Sift both flours, the baking soda, and the salt together in a small bowl and set aside.

8. With an electric mixer on medium-high speed, cream the butter, sugar, vanilla, and lemon zest together in a medium-size bowl until light and fluffy, about 2 minutes. Stop the mixer twice during the process to scrape the bowl with a rubber spatula. Scrape the bowl a third time before going on to the next step.

9. Add the egg yolks and blend on medium speed for about 10 seconds. Scrape the bowl. Then add the whole egg and mix until blended, about 10 seconds. Scrape the bowl again.

10. Add the buttermilk and mix on medium-low speed for about 10 seconds. The mixture will appear curdled. Scrape the bowl.

11. Fold in the flour mixture by hand. Then turn the mixer to low speed and mix for about 5 seconds. Scrape the bowl with the spatula, and mix on low speed until the batter is smooth and velvety, 10 seconds. Give the batter a stir or two with the spatula.

12. Drop the batter by generous tablespoons about 2 inches apart onto the prepared baking sheets.

13. Bake the cookies until they are just firm, yet spongy to the touch (not crusty), 10 to 11 minutes. Using a metal spatula, carefully transfer the cookies to wire racks to cool.

14. When the custard and the cookies have cooled, turn half the cookies upside down and spread each bottom half with a generously rounded tablespoon of custard. Top them with the remaining cookies.

15. Then prepare the glaze: Heat the cream in a small saucepan over medium-low heat just to the boiling point. Place the hot cream in a small bowl and add the chocolate and butter. Cover the bowl with a pot lid or a small plate and leave it for several minutes. Then uncover and stir with a small whisk until smooth. Add the confectioners' sugar and stir vigorously until smooth and velvety.

16. Frost each cookie by spreading a scant tablespoon of the chocolate glaze evenly across the top. If you plan to eat the cookies that day, leave them sitting out. To store them, first allow the glaze to set for several hours, then place the cookies in a large airtight plastic container, with parchment, plastic wrap, or waxed paper between the layers (no more than two layers). Store them in the refrigerator if you plan to eat them the next day. Otherwise, place the container in the freezer for up to 2 weeks. Bring the cookies to room temperature before eating.

Makes about 13 cookie sandwiches

Birthday Cakes On The Go

❤ ❤ ❤ ❤ ❤ ❤ *cakey drop cookie*

If your idea of the perfect birthday cake is the same as mine—a yellow cake with raspberry preserves and white frosting—then you'll love these sumptuous cookies. I find them ideal for school birthday treats. For an additional thrill, you can sprinkle colored jimmies or sugar confetti over the glaze immediately after spreading it.

INGREDIENTS

THE COOKIE
1 recipe Boston Cream Pies cookie batter (page 118)

THE GLAZE
1½ cups confectioners' sugar
6 tablespoons (¾ stick) unsalted butter at room temperature
3 tablespoons fresh lemon juice

THE FILLING
Approximately ¾ cup raspberry preserves

1. Preheat the oven to 400°F. Line several baking sheets with parchment paper, or lightly grease them with vegetable oil.

2. Prepare the cookie batter (steps 6 through 11), and drop it by generous tablespoons onto the prepared baking sheets. Bake until just firm, 10 or 11

minutes. Using a metal spatula, carefully lift the cookies from the sheet and place them on wire racks to cool.

3. Prepare the glaze: Place all the glaze ingredients in a food processor and process until smooth, about 10 seconds.

4. When the cookies are completely cool, turn half of them upside down, and spread each bottom half with a slightly rounded teaspoon of preserves. Top them with the remaining cookies.

5. Using a small spatula or a butter knife, frost the top of each cookie with a generously rounded teaspoon of the glaze. Allow the cookies to sit until the glaze has set, 2 hours.

6. You can store the cookies in an airtight container and eat them the next day. They will continue to soften overnight. Otherwise, store the cookies in an airtight plastic container in the freezer for up to 2 weeks. Bring them to room temperature before eating.

Makes about 13 cookie sandwiches

Chocolate Minteos

❤ ❤ ❤ ❤ ❤ ❤ *crispy drop cookie*

It is my firm belief that no matter how sophisticated our palates become and no matter how we hone our culinary skills, we will never lose the taste memory of Oreos. So here's a tribute to that cookie of our youth. It's thick and crunchy and filled with mint-flavored buttercream, and as my oldest son, Jake, does, you may eat the inside first. They are especially good when chilled in the fridge—I eat them cold all the time!

I N G R E D I E N T S

THE COOKIE
2½ cups all-purpose flour
1 teaspoon baking soda
12 tablespoons (1½ sticks) unsalted butter
*   at room temperature*
1 cup plus 2 tablespoons sugar
2 teaspoons peppermint extract
2 large eggs
2 tablespoons water
12 ounces (2 cups) semisweet chocolate
*   chips, melted*

THE FILLING
8 tablespoons (1 stick) unsalted butter
*   at room temperature*
2 cups confectioners' sugar
2 tablespoons plus 2 teaspoons
*   half-and-half or light cream*
½ teaspoon peppermint extract

1. Preheat the oven to 375°F. Line several baking sheets with parchment paper, or grease them lightly with vegetable oil.

2. Sift the flour and baking soda together into a small bowl and set aside.

3. Using an electric mixer on medium speed, cream the butter, sugar, and peppermint extract together in a medium bowl until light and fluffy, 1 minute. Scrape the bowl with a rubber spatula.

4. Add the eggs and water and beat on medium speed until they are blended, about 20 seconds. Scrape the bowl.

5. Add the melted chocolate chips and mix until blended, 5 seconds. Scrape the bowl.

6. Add the flour mixture and mix on low speed for 15 seconds. Scrape the bowl.

7. Scoop rounded teaspoons of the batter 2 inches apart onto the prepared baking sheets. Using the bottom of a glass that has been dipped in water, press each cookie down so that it forms a round 1½ inches in diameter.

8. Bake the cookies until they are firm to the touch, 17 minutes. Cool them completely on wire racks.

9. Meanwhile, prepare the filling: Place all the filling ingredients in a small bowl and whisk until smooth.

10. When the cookies are completely cool, turn half of them upside down, and spread a rounded teaspoon of filling on each bottom half. Top them with the remaining cookies. Allow them to set for 2 to 3 hours or pop them into the refrigerator for 1 hour to set quickly. If you plan to eat the cookies that day, leave them sitting out. If not, store them in an airtight plastic container in the freezer for up to 2 weeks, and bring to room temperature before eating. Or try eating them cold for a refreshing treat.

Makes about 40 cookie sandwiches

Chocolate Raspberry Sandwiches

♥ ♥ ♥ ♥ ♥   *rolled shortbread cookie*

Two delicate, crisp deeply chocolate wafers sandwiched with raspberry preserves: an elegant addition to a dessert of ice cream or fresh fruit. These cookies are also lovely as the chocolate component on a dessert platter, accompanying Lemon Curd Tartlets and Coconut Dainties.

INGREDIENTS

THE COOKIE
2 cups plus 2 tablespoons all-purpose flour
½ cup unsweetened cocoa powder
⅛ teaspoon baking soda
1 cup (2 sticks) unsalted butter at room temperature
¾ cup confectioners' sugar
½ cup granulated sugar
1 teaspoon pure vanilla extract

THE FILLING
1 cup raspberry preserves

THE GLAZE
12 ounces bittersweet chocolate

1. Sift the flour, cocoa powder, and baking soda together into a small bowl and set aside.

2. Using an electric mixer on medium speed, cream the butter, both sugars, and the vanilla together in a medium-size bowl until light and fluffy, 2½ to 3 minutes. Stop the mixer once or twice during the process to scrape the bowl with a rubber spatula.

3. Add the flour mixture and blend on low speed until the mixture is fluffy again, about 45 seconds. Scrape the bowl.

4. Divide the dough in half and shape it into two thick disks. Wrap each disk in plastic wrap and refrigerate for at least 2 hours or as long as overnight.

5. When you're ready to bake the cookies, preheat the oven to 325°F. Lightly grease several baking sheets with vegetable oil. Remove the dough from the refrigerator, unwrap it, and allow it to soften slightly, about 10 minutes.

6. Place each piece of dough between two new pieces of plastic wrap or waxed paper, and roll it out ⅛ inch thick.

7. Remove the top piece of plastic wrap, and using a 2-inch round cookie cutter, cut out approximately 20 rounds from each half. Place the rounds about ¾ inch apart on the prepared baking sheets. Gather up the scraps and reroll the dough to make as many cookies as possible.

8. Bake the cookies just until they are firm to the touch, 10 to 12 minutes. Cool the cookies on the sheets.

9. When the cookies are completely cool, turn half of them upside down, and spread each bottom half with a scant teaspoon of preserves. Top them with the remaining cookies.

10. Meanwhile, melt the chocolate in the top of a double boiler placed over simmering water.

11. Pour the melted chocolate into a small deep bowl, and dip half of each sandwich into the chocolate, using the rim of the bowl to scrape any excess chocolate off the bottom of the cookie. Or rotate just the outer edge of the cookie in the chocolate for an alternative design.

12. As they are dipped, place the cookies on a large sheet of waxed or parchment paper and allow them to sit until the chocolate hardens, 2 to 3 hours (or pop them into the fridge for 1 hour to set quickly, especially if it is a humid day).

13. If you plan to eat the cookies the first day, leave them sitting out. If not, store them in an airtight plastic container in the freezer for up to 2 weeks, and bring to room temperature before eating.

Makes 25 to 30 cookie sandwiches

Double Crispy Sandwiches

♥ ♥ ♥ ♥ ♥ ♥ *crispy drop cookie*

When my friend Allen Helschein told me that he had a great cookie recipe using cornflakes, I had my doubts. Well, Allen was right. Nothing besides cornflakes provides the satisfying crunch that contrasts so perfectly with the chocolate filling.

INGREDIENTS

THE COOKIE
1½ cups all-purpose flour
1 teaspoon baking soda
1 teaspoon salt
1½ cups quick-cooking oats
1¼ cups (2½ sticks) unsalted butter
*   at room temperature*
½ cup plus 2 tablespoons granulated sugar
1 cup minus 2 tablespoons (lightly packed)
*   light brown sugar*
2 teaspoons pure vanilla extract
2 large eggs
2 cups cornflakes

THE FILLING
9 ounces (1½ cups) semisweet chocolate
*   chips*

1. Preheat the oven to 375°F. Line several baking sheets with parchment paper, or lightly grease them with vegetable oil.

2. Sift the flour, baking soda, and salt together into a medium-size bowl. Stir in the oats and set aside.

3. Using an electric mixer on medium speed, cream the butter, both sugars, and the vanilla together in a medium-size bowl until light and fluffy, about 1½ minutes. Stop the mixer during the process to scrape the bowl with a rubber spatula.

4. Add the eggs one at a time, mixing on medium-low speed for 10 seconds each time, scraping the bowl after each addition and at the end.

5. Add the flour mixture and mix on medium-low speed for 10 seconds. Scrape the bowl, then mix until blended, about 5 seconds more. Scrape the bowl.

6. Add the cornflakes and mix until they're crushed and blended in, 10 seconds. Stop the mixer once during this process to scrape the bowl with a rubber spatula.

7. Drop the dough by rounded teaspoons about 2 inches apart onto the prepared baking sheets.

8. Bake until the cookies are crisp and lightly golden with darker golden edges, 12 to 14 minutes. Allow the cookies to cool completely on the sheets.

9. Prepare the filling: Melt the chocolate chips in the top of a double boiler placed over simmering water. Remove from the heat and allow to cool for 10 minutes.

10. Turn half the cookies upside down, and spread 1 rounded teaspoon of the chocolate on each bottom half. Place the other cookies over the filling, but don't press down. Allow the cookies to sit for 2 to 3 hours until the chocolate hardens (or refrigerate them for 1 hour to speed up the process).

11. If you plan to eat the cookies the first day, leave them sitting out. If not, store them in an airtight plastic container in the freezer for up to 2 weeks, and bring them to room temperature before eating.

Makes about 46 cookie sandwiches

Glazed Almond Raspberry Sandwiches

❤ ❤ ❤ ❤ ❤ ❤ ❤ ❤ *rolled cookie*

To me, almonds and raspberries are an inspired combination whose taste, texture, and color speak of luxury and abundance. They unite here in delicate almond butter cookies, held together with raspberry preserves and accented with a light lemon glaze.

INGREDIENTS

THE COOKIE
2 large egg yolks
1 teaspoon pure vanilla extract
½ cup sugar
1 package (7 ounces) almond paste (not
marzipan)
1 cup (2 sticks) unsalted butter, cold, cut
into 16 pieces
1 cup plus 3 tablespoons all-purpose flour
1 teaspoon salt
1 teaspoon grated lemon zest

THE FILLING
½ cup raspberry preserves

THE GLAZE
1 cup confectioners' sugar
1½ teaspoons almond extract
2 tablespoons hot water

1. Using a fork, stir the egg yolks and vanilla together in a cup. Set aside.

2. Process the sugar and almond paste in a food processor until the mixture looks like coarse sand, 25 seconds. Scatter the butter over the mixture and process for 15 seconds.

3. Add the flour, salt, and lemon zest, and pulse for 40 to 50 seconds to blend.

4. With the machine running, add the yolk mixture through the feed tube, and process for 5 seconds. Scrape the bowl. Then process just until the liquid is evenly absorbed, 5 to 8 seconds.

5. Remove the dough, place it on a work surface, and form it into two rectangular slabs. Wrap each in plastic wrap and refrigerate for an hour or two.

6. Place each slab of dough between two new pieces of plastic wrap, and roll it out ⅛ inch thick. Place the dough, still covered with the plastic wrap, in the freezer or refrigerator and allow it to chill again for 1 to 2 hours.

7. When you are ready to bake the cookies, preheat the oven to 375°F. Line several baking sheets with parchment paper, or grease them lightly with vegetable oil.

8. Remove the top piece of plastic wrap, and using a 2-inch round cookie cutter, cut out approximately 35 rounds from each half. Place the rounds about ¾ inch apart on the prepared baking sheets. Gather up the dough scraps and reroll the dough to make as many more cookies as possible.

9. Bake the cookies until the edges are just beginning to turn golden, about 8 or 9 minutes. Remove them from the oven and cool on the sheets.

10. When the cookies are completely cool, turn half of them upside down, and spread each bottom cookie with a scant ½ teaspoon of preserves. Top them with the remaining cookies.

11. Prepare the glaze: Place ingredients in a small bowl, and whisk until smooth.

12. Using a spoon, drizzle the glaze over the tops of the cookies. Allow to set for 2 to 3 hours (or place in the refrigerator for 1 hour to speed up the process).

13. If you plan to eat the cookies the first day, leave them sitting out. If not, store them in an airtight plastic container in the freezer for up to 2 weeks, and bring to room temperature before eating.

Makes about 40 cookie sandwiches

Katz Tongues
❤ ❤ ❤ ❤ ❤ ❤   *crispy piped cookie*

Within walking distance of my house is a great place called the Bentonwood Bakery and Cafe. Katz Tongues are owner and pastry chef, Rick Katz's rendition of the classic French *langues du chat*, so named because they resembled a cat's tongue. This version, made of two thin, crispy butter wafers sandwiched together with chocolate, is one of my favorites—particularly because their daintiness belies the ease with which they're made.

INGREDIENTS

THE COOKIE
¾ cup all-purpose flour
¾ teaspoon salt
8 tablespoons (1 stick) unsalted butter
    at room temperature
1 cup sugar
½ teaspoon pure vanilla extract
½ cup egg whites (from 3 or 4 large eggs),
    lightly beaten

THE FILLING
4 ounces bittersweet chocolate

1. Preheat the oven to 375°F. Line several baking sheets with parchment paper (do not grease them). If possible, have ready a pastry bag with a No. 9 tip; flatten the tip to form a thin oval so the batter comes out thin.

2. Sift the flour and salt together into a small bowl, and set aside.

3. Using an electric mixer on medium speed, beat the butter just until fluffy, 15 seconds. Scrape the bowl with a rubber spatula.

4. Turn the mixer to medium-low speed and gradually add the sugar, then the vanilla. Scrape the bowl.

5. Turn the mixer to low speed and gradually add the egg whites. Mix until blended, 30 seconds, stopping the mixer once to scrape the bowl.

6. Add the flour mixture, stirring it in by hand. Then blend thoroughly with the mixer on low speed for 10 seconds. Stop the mixer once during the process to scrape the bowl.

7. Place some of the batter in the pastry bag, and pipe out strips approximately 2½ inches long onto the parchment leaving 2 inches between cookies. Alternatively, use a spoon to drop the batter onto the baking sheet, and then flatten it to ⅛ inch thickness with a butter knife or spatula.

8. Bake the cookies until they are crisp to the touch in the center and rich golden around the edges, 14 to 16 minutes. Watch them carefully as they can overbake within seconds. Cool completely on the baking sheets. Then carefully loosen them with a thin spatula.

9. Prepare the filling: Melt the chocolate in the top of a double boiler placed over simmering water. Remove from the heat and let cool to spreading consistency.

10. Turn half the cookies upside down. Spread each bottom half with a teaspoon of chocolate, and top with the remaining cookies. Allow to set completely before eating, about 2 hours (or refrigerate to speed up the process).

11. If you plan to eat the cookies the first day, leave them sitting out. If not, store them in an airtight plastic container in the freezer for up to 2 weeks, and bring to room temperature before eating.

Makes about 24 cookie sandwiches

Shortbread Sandwiches

♥ ♥ ♥ *shortbread refrigerator cookie*

This perfect union of shortbread and chocolate offers two thick, not-too-sweet, crunchy cookies with bittersweet chocolate sandwiched between. Eat them as is or do as my son Jake does—pull them apart and devour the filling first.

INGREDIENTS

THE COOKIE
1 cup (2 sticks) unsalted butter, cold, cut
    into 16 pieces
1 cup confectioners' sugar
2 teaspoons pure vanilla extract
2½ cups cake flour
½ teaspoon baking powder
½ teaspoon salt

THE FILLING
8 ounces bittersweet chocolate
2 tablespoons plus 2 teaspoons vegetable oil

1. Place the flour, confectioners' sugar, baking powder, and salt in a food processor and process for 10 seconds.

2. Scatter the butter over the flour mixture, add the vanilla, and process until the dough just comes together, 30 to 40 seconds.

3. Place a 2-foot length of waxed paper on a work surface. Shape the dough into a rough log 13 or 14 inches long (or into two logs each 6 to 7 inches long) along the length of one side of the paper. Roll the dough up in the waxed paper, and twist the ends like a hard-candy wrapper. Refrigerate the dough for 2 hours.

4. Remove the log from the refrigerator. Using your hands, roll the wrapped dough gently back and forth on the work surface to smooth out and round the cylinder. Refrigerate for another 3 hours or overnight.

5. Fifteen minutes before baking, preheat the oven to 350°F. Line several baking sheets with parchment paper or leave them ungreased.

6. Remove the log from the refrigerator, unwrap it, and cut it into slices that are a scant ¼ inch thick.

7. Place the cookies 1 inch apart on the prepared baking sheets, and bake until the edges are golden and the centers are firm, 15 to 17 minutes. (To test for doneness, remove a cookie from the sheet and cut it in half. There should be no doughy strip down the center.) Cool on the baking sheets.

8. While the cookies are cooling, prepare the filling: Melt the chocolate in the top of a double boiler placed over simmering water. Remove from the heat and whisk in the oil until smooth. Let sit 15 to 20 minutes to reach spreading consistency.

9. When the cookies are completely cool, turn half of them upside down, making them the bottom half. Spread each bottom half with 1 teaspoon of the chocolate and top them with the remaining cookies. Do not press down. Allow to set for 2 to 3 hours. (They can be chilled in the refrigerator for 1 hour to speed up the process.)

10. If you plan to eat the cookies the first day, leave them sitting out. If not, store them in an airtight plastic con-

tainer in the freezer for up to 2 weeks, and bring to room temperature before eating.

Makes about 28 cookie sandwiches

Little Princesses

❤ ❤ ❤ *formed shortbread cookie*

These rich, buttery vanilla cookies, paired with raspberry preserves and then dusted with powdered sugar, truly live up to their name. Crisp the first day, they tend to soften a bit by the second day no matter how you store them—but either way, they are royally divine.

INGREDIENTS

THE COOKIE
6 large egg yolks
¾ teaspoon pure vanilla extract
2 cups all-purpose flour
⅔ cup sugar
½ teaspoon salt
1 tablespoon plus 1 teaspoon grated lemon zest
1 cup (2 sticks) unsalted butter, cold, cut into 16 pieces

THE FILLING
5 to 6 tablespoons raspberry preserves

THE COATING
¼ cup confectioners' sugar

128

1. Preheat the oven to 375°F. Line several baking sheets with parchment paper, or grease them lightly with vegetable oil.

2. Using a fork, stir the egg yolks and vanilla together in a small cup.

3. Place the flour, sugar, salt, and lemon zest in a food processor, and process for 5 seconds.

4. Scatter the butter over the flour and process until the mixture resembles coarse meal, 20 to 30 seconds.

5. With the machine running, add the yolk mixture through the feed tube and process for 5 seconds. Scrape the bowl. Then process until the dough comes together, 10 to 15 seconds.

6. Scoop out rounded teaspoons of the dough and roll them into balls with your hands. Place them 2 inches apart on the prepared baking sheets.

7. Using the bottom of a glass that has been lightly dipped in flour, flatten each ball to a generous ⅛-inch thickness, about 2¼ inches in diameter.

8. Bake the cookies until the edges are deep golden, 14 to 16 minutes. Allow them to cool on the baking sheets.

9. When the cookies are completely cool, turn half of them upside down. Spread each bottom half with a generous ½ teaspoon of the preserves, and top with the remaining cookies. Sift confectioners' sugar over the tops.

10. If you plan to eat the cookies the first day, leave them sitting out. If not, store them in an airtight plastic container in the freezer for up to 2 weeks, and bring to room temperature before eating.

Makes about 16 cookie sandwiches

Linzer Sandwiches

❤ ❤ ❤ ❤ ❤ ❤ ❤ ❤   *rolled cookie*

One of my most vivid food memories comes from the William Greenberg bakery in New York City, where I recall savoring the nutty crunch of a giant linzer cookie, then enjoying a second taste as I licked at the confectioners' sugar mustache it left on my upper lip. I tried to get the recipe from Greenberg's, but without success, so I worked and worked to come as close as I could on my own. I've made my version smaller than the original (a function of age), but other than that, it matches my memory cookie right down to the mustache.

INGREDIENTS

THE COOKIE
1 whole large egg
1 large egg yolk
1 teaspoon pure vanilla extract
1½ cups all-purpose flour
1½ cups sugar
2 cups coarsely ground almonds
1 teaspoon ground cinnamon
¼ teaspoon ground cloves
½ teaspoon baking powder
1 tablespoon unsweetened cocoa powder
¾ teaspoon salt
2½ tablespoons grated lemon zest
12 tablespoons (1½ sticks) unsalted butter,
    cold, cut into 10 pieces

THE FILLING
½ cup raspberry preserves

THE COATING
2 to 3 tablespoons confectioners' sugar

1. Preheat the oven to 350°F. Line several baking sheets with parchment paper or grease them lightly with vegetable oil.

2. Using a fork, stir the egg, egg yolk, and vanilla together in a small cup. Set aside.

3. Place the flour, sugar, almonds, cinnamon, cloves, baking powder, cocoa powder, salt, and lemon zest in a food processor and process to blend, 5 seconds.

4. Distribute the butter over the surface of the flour mixture, and process until the mixture resembles coarse meal, 20 to 30 seconds.

5. With the machine running, add the egg mixture through the feed tube and process for 3 seconds. Scrape the bowl, then process for 3 more seconds.

6. Remove the dough from the machine and shape it into two disks. Place each piece of dough between two pieces of plastic wrap or waxed paper, and roll it out to a generous ⅛-inch thickness.

7. Remove the top piece of plastic wrap, and, using a 2-inch round cookie cutter, cut out approximately 20 rounds from each half. Using a smooth bottle cap, a sharp knife, or a tiny cookie cutter, make small holes in the center of half the rounds. Place all the rounds about ¾ inch apart on the prepared baking sheets. Gather up the dough scraps and reroll the dough to make as many more cookies as possible, again making small holes in the center of half of them.

8. Bake the cookies until they are firm, 14 minutes. Remove them from the oven and let them cool on the sheets.

9. When the cookies are completely cool, turn the cookies with no holes upside down. Spread each one with a level ½ teaspoon of raspberry preserves, then place another ½ teaspoon of the preserves in a mound in the center of each cookie. Sprinkle confectioners' sugar over the cookies with holes, and place them on top of the cookie bottoms so that the jam forms a perfect little mound in the middle.

10. If you plan to eat the cookies the first day, leave them out. If not, store them in an airtight plastic container in the freezer for up to 2 weeks, and bring to room temperature before eating.

Makes 20 to 25 cookie sandwiches

Almond Apricot Sandwiches

❤ ❤ ❤ *shortbread refrigerator cookie*

Apricot jam holds these rich, nutty cookies together, while a bittersweet chocolate drizzle over the top does double duty as decoration and decadent finishing touch.

INGREDIENTS

THE COOKIE
1 large egg
1 teaspoon pure almond extract
2 cups all-purpose flour
¾ cup confectioners' sugar
6 tablespoons granulated sugar
1½ cups finely ground almonds
¾ teaspoon salt
*1 cup (2 sticks) unsalted butter,
    cold, cut into 16 pieces*

THE FILLING
¾ cup apricot preserves

THE GLAZE
3 ounces bittersweet chocolate
1 tablespoon vegetable oil

1. Using a fork, stir the egg and almond extract together in a cup and set aside.

2. Place the flour, all but 2 tablespoons of the confectioners' sugar, the granulated sugar, almonds, and salt in a food processor, and process for 5 seconds.

3. Scatter the butter over the flour mixture, and process until the mixture resembles coarse crumbs, 30 seconds.

4. With the machine running, add the egg mixture through the feed tube and process just until the dough comes together, 45 seconds.

5. Spread a 2-foot length of waxed paper on a work surface. With floured fingers, shape the dough into a rough log about 20 inches long along the length of one side of the paper. Roll the log in the waxed paper and twist the ends like a hard-candy wrapper. Refrigerate the dough for 2 hours. (You can cut the log in half in order to fit it in the refrigerator.)

6. Remove the log from the refrigerator, and with the dough still in the waxed paper, gently roll it back and forth on the work surface to smooth out and round the cylinder.

7. Place the log back in the refrigerator and chill it at least 3 hours more.

8. Fifteen minutes before baking, preheat the oven to 350°F. Line two baking sheets with parchment paper or leave them ungreased.

131

9. Place the log on the counter, unwrap it, and cut it into scant ¼-inch-thick slices.

10. Place the cookies 1 inch apart on the baking sheets and bake until they are firm and lightly golden around the edges, 20 minutes. Cool them completely on the sheets.

11. Turn half the cookies upside down, and spread 1 scant tablespoon of the preserves over each bottom half. Top them with the remaining cookies. Sift the remaining 2 tablespoons confectioners' sugar over the cookies.

12. Prepare the glaze: Melt the chocolate in the top of a double boiler placed over simmering water. Remove from the heat and whisk in the oil until smooth.

13. Using a spoon or fork, drizzle the chocolate over the tops of the cookies in a zigzag or crisscross fashion. Allow the glaze to set for 2 to 3 hours (or refrigerate for 1 hour to speed up the process).

14. If you plan to eat the cookies the first day, leave them sitting out. If not, store them in an airtight plastic container in the freezer for up to 2 weeks, and bring to room temperature before eating.

Makes about 42 cookie sandwiches

Chocolate Jam Sandwiches

❤ ❤ ❤ ❤ ❤ *rolled shortbread cookie*

Two crunchy, buttery shortbread cookies sandwiched together with a double dose of delectableness: chocolate and raspberry or orange. As an alternative, sandwich the cookies with the preserves or marmalade and use the chocolate as a glaze. You can either dip half the cookie in the glaze or drizzle the glaze over the top.

INGREDIENTS

THE COOKIE
1 large egg yolk
½ teaspoon pure vanilla extract
1¼ cups all-purpose flour
5 tablespoons confectioners' sugar
3 tablespoons granulated sugar
2 tablespoons grated orange zest
½ teaspoon salt
*8 tablespoons (1 stick) unsalted butter,
    cold, cut into 8 pieces*

THE FILLING
3 tablespoons heavy (whipping) cream
4 ounces bittersweet chocolate
*Approximately 6 tablespoons raspberry
    preserves or orange marmalade*

1. Using a fork, stir the egg yolk and vanilla together in a small cup. Set aside.

2. Place the flour, both sugars, the

orange zest, and salt in a food processor, and process for about 10 seconds.

3. Add the butter and process until the mixture resembles coarse meal, 20 to 30 seconds.

4. With the machine running, add the yolk mixture though the feed tube and process for 5 seconds. Scrape the bowl, then process until the liquid is evenly absorbed, about 10 seconds.

5. Place the dough on a work surface, and work it with your hands just until you can form it into a mass. Divide the dough in half and shape it into two thick disks. Wrap each disk in plastic wrap. Refrigerate the dough for at least 1½ hours or overnight.

6. When you're ready to bake the cookies, preheat the oven to 350°F. Line several baking sheets with parchment paper, or lightly grease them with vegetable oil. Remove the dough from the refrigerator and allow it to soften slightly, about 10 minutes.

7. Place each piece of dough between two new pieces of plastic wrap or waxed paper, and roll it out ⅛ inch thick. Slide the dough, still sandwiched in the plastic wrap, onto a plate or tray and refrigerate it for 15 minutes for easier handling.

8. Remove the top piece of plastic wrap, and using a 2-inch round cookie cutter, cut out approximately 16 rounds from each half. Place the cookies about ¾ inch apart on the prepared baking

sheets. Gather up the scraps and reroll the dough to make as many more cookies as possible.

9. Bake the cookies just until the edges begin to turn golden, 14 to 15 minutes. Remove them from the oven and let them cool on the sheets.

10. Meanwhile, prepare the filling: Heat the cream in a small saucepan over medium heat just to the boiling point, about 40 seconds.

11. Remove the pan from the heat and stir in the chocolate. Cover and set aside until the chocolate is melted, about 3 minutes. Then stir until smooth, 10 seconds.

12. Turn half the cookies over, and spread ¾ teaspoon of the chocolate filling over each bottom half. Turn the remaining cookies over, and spread ½ teaspoon of the preserves over each one.

13. Sandwich the two filled halves together, and allow to set for 3 to 4 hours (or refrigerate for 1 hour to speed up the process).

14. If you plan to eat the cookies the first day, leave them sitting out. If not, store them in an airtight plastic container in the freezer for up to 2 weeks, and bring to room temperature before eating.

Makes about 26 cookie sandwiches

Crispy Fingers

♥ ♥ ♥ ♥ ♥ ♥ ♥ ♥ ♥ *piped cookie*

For fans of Pepperidge Farm's Brussels cookie, here's a home-made version. These thin, crispy almond oatmeal wafers sandwiched with bittersweet chocolate make a wonderful teatime cookie or a delicate, elegant garnish for a dish of ice cream at the end of a meal.

INGREDIENTS

THE COOKIE

¾ cup all-purpose flour
¼ teaspoon baking soda
¼ teaspoon cream of tartar
8 tablespoons (1 stick) unsalted butter
    at room temperature
¾ cup sugar
½ teaspoon orange extract
½ teaspoon pure vanilla extract
¼ teaspoon grated orange zest
2 large egg whites, lightly beaten
½ cup finely chopped almonds
¼ cup quick-cooking oats

THE FILLING

1 ounce unsweetened chocolate
4 ounces semisweet chocolate

1. Preheat the oven to 350°F. Line several baking sheets with parchment paper, or lightly grease them with vegetable oil. Have ready a pastry bag fitted with a ½-inch tip.

2. Sift the flour, baking soda, and cream of tartar together into a small bowl and set aside.

3. Using an electric mixer on medium speed, cream the butter, sugar, both extracts, and the orange zest together in a medium-size bowl until light and fluffy, 2 minutes. Stop the mixer twice during the process to scrape the bowl with a rubber spatula.

4. Add the egg whites and beat on medium-high speed until blended, about 1 minute.

5. Add the flour mixture to the batter, and mix by hand with a rubber spatula until blended.

6. Add the almonds and oats, and mix by hand until blended.

7. Fill the pastry bag with batter, and pipe 2-inch-long fingers 3 inches apart on the prepared baking sheets. Bake until lightly golden with darker golden edges, about 12 minutes. Using a spatula, immediately transfer the cookies to wire racks to cool.

8. When the cookies have cooled, prepare the filling: Melt the chocolates together in a double boiler placed over simmering water.

9. Turn half the cookies upside down, and using a small frosting spatula or a butter knife, spread a thin layer of chocolate over each bottom half. Immediately place the remaining cookies on top, pressing down gently.

10. Allow the cookies to set for 2 hours, or place them in the refrigerator for 1 hour to speed up the process.

11. If you plan to eat the cookies the first day, leave them sitting out. If not, store them in an airtight plastic container in the freezer for up to 2 weeks, and bring to room temperature before eating.

Makes about 24 cookie sandwiches

Summer's Day Sandwiches

♥ ♥ ♥ ♥ ♥   *piped shortbread cookie*

Little lemon wafers sandwiched together with white chocolate—perfect with a glass of iced mint tea on a summer's day.

I N G R E D I E N T S

THE COOKIE
1 cup all-purpose flour
Generous ¼ teaspoon salt
Pinch of baking powder
7 tablespoons confectioners' sugar
1½ tablespoons granulated sugar
1 tablespoon grated lemon zest
8 tablespoons (1 stick) plus 1 teaspoon
  unsalted butter at room temperature
¼ cup milk

THE FILLING
3½ ounces good-quality white chocolate,
  grated or chopped fine (do not use
  white chocolate chips)
1½ tablespoons vegetable oil

1. Preheat the oven to 375°F. Line several baking sheets with parchment paper, or grease them lightly with vegetable oil. Prepare a pastry bag fitted with a ½-inch round tip.

2. Place the flour, salt, baking powder, both sugars, and the lemon zest in a food processor and process for 10 seconds.

3. Add the butter and process until partially incorporated, 30 seconds. Scrape the bowl with a rubber spatula.

4. Add the milk and process until the batter comes together, 20 seconds. It will be quite wet.

5. Fill the pastry bag with batter, and pipe 1-inch-diameter cookies, approximately ⅜ inch thick, 2 inches apart on the prepared baking sheets.

6. Using the bottom of a glass that has been dipped in flour, press each cookie into a diameter of 1½ inches.

7. Bake the cookies until the edges are golden and the centers are firm, 14 minutes.

8. Cool the cookies on wire racks.

9. Meanwhile, prepare the filling: Bring a pot of water to a boil, and remove it from the heat. Set a small metal bowl inside a larger bowl, and pour the hot water around it. The water should come about halfway up the sides of the smaller bowl. Make sure the inside of the smaller bowl stays dry. Place the white chocolate in the small bowl, cover the small bowl, and allow the chocolate to sit until it is melted. (You may need to change the water a couple of times to keep it hot.)

10. Stir the oil into the melted chocolate, whisking until the mixture is smooth. Let this set for 30 minutes. It will be fairly loose in texture.

11. Turn half the cookies upside down and place a generous ½ teaspoon of the chocolate mixture on each bottom half. Place the remaining cookies on top, pressing just enough for the filling to come to the edge of the sandwich.

12. Refrigerate the cookies for 1 hour to harden the filling, or let them set at room temperature for 2 to 3 hours.

13. If you plan to eat the cookies the first day, leave them sitting out. If not, store them in an airtight plastic container in the freezer for up to 2 weeks, and bring to room temperature before eating.

Makes about 22 cookie sandwiches

Orange Almond Spritzes

❤ ❤ ❤ ❤ ❤ *piped shortbread cookie*

Spritzes are squeezed from a cookie press, so you find them in all different shapes and sizes. As I worked on this recipe, I discovered that spritzes made with vegetable shortening hold their shape and thickness best, but that spritzes made with butter taste better, even if they spread and flatten out a little more. For the best results, be sure to cream the butter and sugar well, so the batter is soft enough to squeeze through the cookie press. If you don't have a press, scoop the batter out by the teaspoonful and flatten the cookies slightly before baking them. Either way, these cookies are delicious.

INGREDIENTS

THE COOKIE
2¼ cups all-purpose flour
¾ teaspoon baking powder
¼ teaspoon salt
4 ounces (7 tablespoons) almond paste (not
    marzipan), cut into 8 pieces
½ cup confectioners' sugar
5 tablespoons granulated sugar
1 cup (2 sticks) unsalted butter at room
    temperature, cut into 16 pieces
2 tablespoons grated orange zest
½ teaspoon orange extract
2 large egg yolks

THE FILLING
About ½ cup orange marmalade

THE GLAZE
Approximately 6 ounces bittersweet chocolate

1. Preheat the oven to 325°F. Line several baking sheets with parchment paper, or grease them lightly with vegetable oil. Have ready a cookie press. Choose your favorite tips.

2. Sift the flour, baking powder, and salt together into a medium-size bowl and set aside.

3. Place the almond paste, both sugars, butter, orange zest, and orange extract in a food processor and process until smooth, 25 to 30 seconds.

4. Transfer this mixture to a medium-size mixing bowl.

5. Add the flour mixture, and mix on medium speed until thoroughly blended, 1½ minutes. Stop the mixer once to scrape the bowl.

6. Add the egg yolks with the mixer on medium-low speed, and mix until blended, 30 seconds. Stop the mixer once to scrape the bowl.

7. Feed the dough into the cookie press, and pipe the cookies onto the prepared baking sheets, leaving 1 inch between cookies.

8. Bake the cookies until they are firm and lightly golden around the edge. The baking time will vary depending on shape, but the range will probably be 16 to 20 minutes. Cool the cookies on the sheets.

9. When the cookies have cooled completely, prepare the glaze: Melt the chocolate in the top of a double boiler placed over simmering water.

10. Turn half the cookies upside down on a piece of parchment paper. Spread each bottom half with a teaspoon (this may vary depending on the size and shape of cookie you have chosen) of marmalade, and top them with the remaining cookies.

11. Place the melted chocolate in a small deep bowl, and dip a portion of each sandwich into the glaze (or paint the chocolate on with a pastry brush).

12. Return the cookies to the parchment and allow them to set for 2 to 3 hours, or place them in the refrigerator for 1 hour to set quickly.

13. If you plan to eat the cookies the first day, leave them sitting out. If not, store them in an airtight plastic container in the freezer for up to 2 weeks, and bring to room temperature before eating.

Makes about 25 cookie sandwiches

Triple-Ginger Lemon Sandwiches

❤ ❤ ❤ ❤ ❤ ❤ ❤ *refrigerator cookie*

Here's a triple threat of ground, candied, and fresh ginger, combined to pack a genuine wallop. The lemon buttercream filling adds a wonderful accent. These small, stylish, and sophisticated refrigerator cookies may single-handedly change the perceived wisdom about the appropriateness of cookies as dinner party fare.

INGREDIENTS

THE COOKIE
⅓ cup grated fresh ginger
½ cup granulated sugar
1½ cups all-purpose flour
1½ teaspoons baking soda
½ teaspoon salt
1¼ teaspoons ground ginger
¼ teaspoon ground cloves
1 teaspoon ground cinnamon
13 tablespoons (1½ sticks plus 1 table-
　　spoon) unsalted butter at room
　　temperature
½ cup (lightly packed) light brown sugar
¼ cup molasses
1 large egg
1½ cups quick-cooking oats
⅓ cup minced candied ginger or stem ginger

THE FILLING
2 cups confectioners' sugar
3 tablespoons light corn syrup
3 tablespoons unsalted butter, melted
1½ teaspoons grated lemon zest
2 tablespoons fresh lemon juice

1. Place the fresh ginger and 2 tablespoons of the granulated sugar in a food processor and process for several seconds to break up the ginger strands.

2. Sift the flour, baking soda, salt, ground ginger, cloves, and cinnamon into a small bowl and set aside.

3. Using an electric mixer on medium speed, cream the butter, brown sugar, the remaining 6 tablespoons granulated sugar, and the fresh ginger mixture in a medium-size mixing bowl until light and fluffy, 1 minute. Stop the mixer once during the process to scrape the bowl with a rubber spatula.

4. Add the molasses and beat for 10 to 15 seconds on medium speed. Scrape the bowl. Then add the egg and beat to incorporate it, 10 seconds.

5. Add the flour mixture and beat on medium-low speed for 10 seconds. Scrape the bowl, then mix until blended, about 5 seconds more. Then scrape the bowl again.

6. Add the oats and candied ginger. Blend for several seconds on low speed.

7. Spread a 13-inch length of waxed paper or plastic wrap on a work surface.

Shape one fourth of the dough into a rough log 9 inches long and 1 inch in diameter along the length of one side of the paper. Roll the log up in the waxed paper and twist the ends like a hard-candy wrapper. Make three more logs with the remaining batter, wrap them, and refrigerate for at least 2 hours.

8. Remove the logs from the refrigerator, and with the dough still in the paper, gently roll them back and forth on the work surface to round them.

9. Chill the logs in the refrigerator for 2 to 3 more hours.

10. Fifteen minutes before baking, preheat the oven to 350°F. Line two baking sheets with parchment paper, or grease them lightly with vegetable oil.

11. Unwrap the logs and cut them into scant ¼-inch-thick slices.

12. Place the cookies 1 inch apart on the prepared baking sheets, and bake until they are a deep golden color and set but still soft to the touch, 8 to 10 minutes.

13. Allow the cookies to cool on the sheets for 3 or 4 minutes. Then remove the cookies carefully with a spatula, and place them on wire racks to cool completely.

14. Meanwhile, prepare the filling: Place the confectioners' sugar, corn syrup, melted butter, and lemon zest in a small saucepan over low heat, and stir constantly with a whisk until the mix-

ture is of pouring consistency, 4 minutes. Add the lemon juice and stir to mix. Cool for 5 minutes.

15. Turn half the cookies upside down. Drop a scant teaspoon of the filling onto the center of each bottom half. Then top them with the remaining cookies, pressing down just enough to bring the filling to the edge of the cookie. Allow to set for about 3 hours. If it's a very hot day, refrigerate them.

16. If you plan to eat the cookies the first day, leave them sitting out. If not, store them in an airtight plastic container in the freezer for up to 2 weeks, and bring to room temperature before eating.

Makes about 70 cookie sandwiches

Pumpkin Whoopee Pies

♥ ♥ ♥ ♥ ♥ ♥   *cakey drop cookie*

Yes, the day came when I got down from my high horse and used Marshmallow Fluff in a recipe. And you know what? The world didn't end. In fact, it's now all the richer for this yummy filling, which I use here to hold two pumpkin-flavored cakey cookies together. The result is a classic whoopie pie and then some.

INGREDIENTS

THE COOKIE

½ cup plus 1 tablespoon all-purpose
    flour
¾ cup plus 1 tablespoon cake flour
½ teaspoon baking soda
1 teaspoon baking powder
½ teaspoon salt
9 tablespoons (1 stick plus 1 tablespoon)
    unsalted butter at room temperature
½ cup plus 2 tablespoons (lightly packed)
    light brown sugar
7 tablespoons granulated sugar
2½ teaspoons ground cinnamon
2 teaspoons ground nutmeg
¾ teaspoon ground allspice
½ teaspoon ground cloves
½ teaspoon ground ginger
1 teaspoon pure vanilla
    extract
2 large eggs
1½ tablespoons molasses
½ cup plus 2 tablespoons
    canned puréed pumpkin
¼ cup buttermilk

MARSHMALLOW FILLING

8 tablespoons (1 stick) unsalted butter at
    room temperature
5 heaping tablespoons Marshmallow Fluff
1 cup confectioners' sugar, sifted
½ teaspoon pure vanilla extract

1. Preheat the oven to 400°F. Line several baking sheets with parchment paper, or lightly grease them with vegetable oil.

2. Sift both flours, the baking soda, the baking powder, and the salt together into a small bowl and set aside.

3. Using an electric mixer on medium-high speed, cream the butter, both sugars, the spices, and the vanilla together in a medium-size bowl until light and fluffy, about 1½ minutes. Stop the mixer twice during the process to scrape the bowl with a rubber spatula. Scrape the bowl a third time before going on to the next step.

4. Add the eggs, one at a time, blending on medium speed for about 10 seconds after each addition.

5. Add the molasses and pumpkin, and mix on medium-low speed until well blended, about 10 seconds. Scrape the bowl. Add the buttermilk and blend for 5 seconds.

6. Fold in the flour mixture by hand. Then turn the mixer to low speed and mix for about 5 seconds. Scrape the bowl with the spatula, and mix on low speed until the batter is smooth and velvety, 10 seconds. Give the batter a stir or two with the spatula.

7. Drop the batter by generously rounded tablespoons about 2 inches apart onto the prepared baking sheets.

8. Bake the cookies until they are risen and firm to the touch, but not crusty, about 12 minutes. Using a metal spatula, carefully transfer the cookies to wire racks to cool.

9. While the cookies are cooling, prepare the filling: Place all four filling ingredients in a small bowl and beat with an electric mixer on low speed until the sugar is absorbed, 15 to 20 seconds. Scrape the bowl with a rubber spatula, turn the mixer to medium-high, and beat until the mixture is light and fluffy, 3 minutes. Stop the mixer twice during the process to scrape the bowl with a rubber spatula.

10. When the cookies are completely cool, turn half of them upside down, and spread each bottom half with a heaping teaspoon of filling. Top them with the remaining cookies.

11. If you plan to eat the cookies the first day, leave them sitting out. If not, store them in an airtight plastic container in the freezer for up to 2 weeks, and bring to room temperature before eating.

Makes about 14 cookie sandwiches

Peanut Butter Sandwiches

❤ ❤ ❤ ❤ ❤ ❤   *crunchy drop cookie*

Time may do its work on me, but I'll never outgrow the thrill of a peanut butter cookie—especially this sandwich version, with its thick crunchy cookies and its layer of peanut butter filling to stick them to-

gether (and to the roof of your mouth). A Girl Scout memory? A triumph for the makers of Skippy? Whatever, these cookies make me sorry I no longer carry a box lunch.

I N G R E D I E N T S

THE COOKIE
¾ cup plus 1 tablespoon all-purpose flour
½ teaspoon baking soda
¼ teaspoon baking powder
½ teaspoon salt
8 tablespoons (1 stick) unsalted butter at room temperature
½ cup smooth or chunky peanut butter
½ cup granulated sugar
½ cup (lightly packed) light brown sugar
½ teaspoon pure vanilla extract
1 large egg
1 cup minus 2 tablespoons quick-cooking oats

THE BUTTERCREAM
1 cup confectioners' sugar
3 tablespoons unsalted butter at room temperature
½ cup smooth peanut butter
2 tablespoons plus 1 teaspoon heavy (whipping) cream

THE GLAZE
2 ounces bittersweet chocolate
2 teaspoons vegetable oil

1. Preheat the oven to 350°F. Line several baking sheets with parchment paper, or lightly grease them with vegetable oil.

2. Sift the flour, baking soda, baking powder, and salt together into a small bowl and set aside.

141

3. Using an electric mixer on medium speed, cream the butter, peanut butter, both sugars, and the vanilla together in a medium-size bowl until light and fluffy, about 1½ minutes. Stop the mixer twice during the process to scrape the sides of the bowl with a rubber spatula.

4. Add the egg and mix on medium-low speed to incorporate it, about 20 seconds.

5. Add the flour mixture and mix on medium-low speed for 10 seconds. Scrape the bowl, then mix until blended, about 5 seconds more. Scrape the bowl again.

6. Add the oats and mix for several seconds on low speed to blend them in.

7. Drop the dough by generously rounded teaspoons about 2 inches apart onto the prepared baking sheets. Using the prongs of a fork (to create a crosshatch pattern), press them down to form ¼-inch-thick cookies about 2 inches in diameter.

8. Bake until the cookies are lightly golden with darker golden edges, about 10 to 12 minutes. Allow them to cool on the baking sheets.

9. Meanwhile, prepare the buttercream filling: Using an electric mixer on low speed, cream the confectioners' sugar, butter, and peanut butter together in a medium-size mixing bowl for 1 minute, stopping the mixer once to scrape the bowl with a rubber spatula.

10. Add the cream and mix until fluffy, 40 seconds, stopping the mixer once to scrape the bowl.

11. When the cookies are completely cool, turn half of them upside down. Spread each bottom half with a rounded teaspoon of filling and top with the remaining cookies.

12. Prepare the glaze: Melt the chocolate in the top of a double boiler placed over simmering water. Remove from the heat. Add the oil and stir until smooth.

13. Drizzle the glaze in a pattern over the top of the sandwiches, and allow to set for 2 to 3 hours (or pop them into the fridge for 1 hour to set quickly).

14. If you plan to eat the cookies the first day, leave them sitting out. If not, store them in an airtight plastic container in the freezer for up to 2 weeks, and bring to room temperature before eating.

Makes about 25 cookie sandwiches

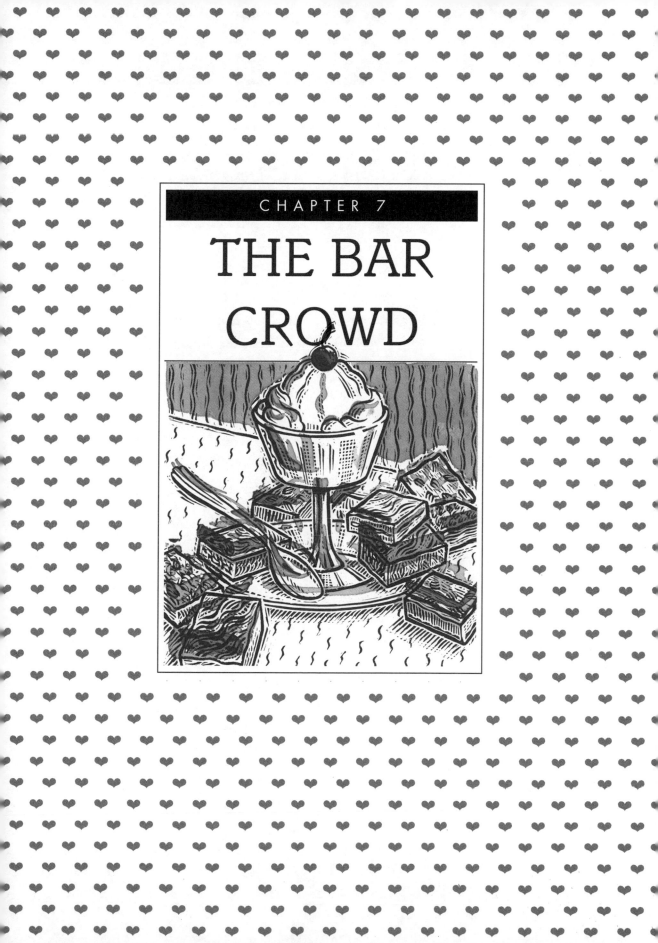

CHAPTER 7

THE BAR CROWD

My New Brownie
Peanut Butter Topped Brownies
Chocolate Raspberry Brownies
New York Cheesecake Brownies
Sour Cherry Cheesecake Brownies
Chocolate Soufflé Brownies
Toasted Pecan Orange Brownies
Chocolate Hazelnut Brownies
Bourbon Brownies
Chocolate Almond Amaretto Brownies
Butterscotch Chocolate Chip Brownies
White Chocolate Macadamia Brownies
Pucker-Your-Lips Apricot Linzer Bars
Blond Linzer Bars
Chocolate Linzer Bars
Hazelnut Cranberry Linzers
Cinnamon Pecan Shortbread Bars
Semolina Shortbread Bars
Noah's Scotch Shortbread Bars
Tosca Bars
Almond Bars
Gooey Butter Bars
Cherry Crumb Bars
Cranberry Crumb Bars
Creamy Cranberry Orange Bars
Cranberry Walnut Squares
Dating Bars
Yummy Cheesecake Bars
Raspberry Cream Cheese Bars
Tropical Macadamia Bars
Caramel Pecan Bars
Pecan Delight Bars
Carrot Cake Cream Cheese Bars
Poppyseed Coffee Cake Bars

There have been moments in the history of Rosie's when I thought we ought to change our name to "Brownies R Us." Our various brownies are major sellers and recipients of numerous awards, and our Chocolate Orgasms featured in *Rosie's Bakery . . . Baking Book*—the fudgy, frosted favorite of family planners and abstention advocates alike—have brought us our share of notoriety. That's not why I created them, though. To me, brownies constitute one of the basic food groups, and these were simply the most luscious to be had.

As American as brownies may now be, they are said to have come to us originally from Holland. Farm wives of yore baked them for their hungry menfolk, who knew a good thing when they saw it. That perhaps was the last time anyone agreed on what a brownie should be. Line up any ten people and ask them about their ideal brownie and I'm willing to bet that you'll get ten, maybe twelve, different opinions: Cakey, fudgy, dense, packed with nuts, cinnamony, unadulterated . . . So many people consider themselves connoisseurs that I've considered setting up brownie tastings. I see them as similar to wine tastings, complete with their own esoteric vocabulary and ratings by year—though I'd vote against limiting samples to a single bite.

In this chapter I tried to create a brownie for every palate, but it seemed a shame to stop there. There are so many other kinds of bars, covering such a spectrum of tastes, textures, and combinations, that nothing would do but to include fruit bars, nut bars, nonchocolate brownies, cheesecake bars, crumbly bars, and bars that refuse categorization, if you please.

What all these bars have in common is the ease with which they're made and the speed with which they're eaten. Just in case I'm proven wrong on the latter, most bars will keep for a week or so in an airtight container and freeze well for a while longer.

As for how and when bars are served, you're limited only by your imagination and your cutting skill. The standard form is a square of generous proportions, but triangles or wedges are also easy to cut and provide a nice change, and long, narrow rectangles, like ingots of gold, make perfect samples for platters of cookies or to accompany ice cream or puddings.

My New Brownie

brownie bar

You wouldn't think there would be anything more for me to discover in my love affair with the basic brownie. I had tested and retested the recipe over the years, and we had settled into a comfortable middle age where companionship and dependability were more important than surprises. Sure, we still had our special moments, but not every day like at the beginning. So imagine my delight when I decided to rekindle that old feeling by trying something new and came up with what I think is absolutely the best brownie ever. Fudgy, bittersweet, simple to make . . . it'll bring a glow to your cheeks and a smile to your lips. Just like the first time.

INGREDIENTS

6 ounces unsweetened chocolate
1 cup (2 sticks) unsalted butter
2 cups sugar
1 teaspoon pure vanilla extract
4 large eggs
1 cup all-purpose flour
½ cup chopped walnuts (optional)

1. Preheat the oven to 350°F. Lightly grease a 9-inch square baking pan with butter or vegetable oil, or line the bottom with parchment paper.

2. Melt the chocolate and butter together in the top of a double boiler placed over simmering water. Let the mixture cool for 5 minutes.

3. Place the sugar in a medium-size mixing bowl, and pour in the chocolate mixture. Using an electric mixer on medium speed, mix until blended, about 25 seconds. Scrape the bowl with a rubber spatula.

4. Add the vanilla. With the mixer on medium-low speed, add the eggs one at a time, blending after each addition until the yolk is broken and dispersed, about 10 seconds. Then scrape the bowl and blend until the mixture is velvety, about 15 seconds more. Scrape the bowl.

5. Add the flour on low speed, and mix for 20 seconds, stopping the mixer once to scrape the bowl. Finish the mixing by hand, being certain to incorporate any flour at the bottom of the bowl. Stir in the nuts, if using.

6. Spread the batter evenly in the prepared pan.

7. Bake the brownies on the middle rack of the oven just until the center has risen to the level of the sides and a tester inserted in the center comes out with moist crumbs, about 35 minutes.

8. Remove the pan from the oven and place it on a rack to cool for 1 hour before cutting the brownies into 2¼-inch squares with a sharp knife.

9. Leave the brownies in the pan, at room temperature, covered, for up to 2 days. After that, layer them in an airtight plastic container with plastic wrap, parchment, or waxed paper between the layers, and store for another 2 days in the refrigerator or in the freezer for up to 2 weeks. They are delicious cold or at room temperature.

Makes 16 brownies

Pan Size Alert

Many of the recipes in this chapter call for a 9-inch square baking pan. If you have trouble finding one (Williams-Sonoma has one), bake the brownies in an 8-inch pan, reducing the heat in most cases by 25°F and adding 10 to 15 minutes to the cooking time.

Peanut Butter Topped Brownies

♥ ♥ ♥ ♥ ♥ ♥ ♥ ♥ ♥   *brownie bar*

In homage to the Reese's Peanut Butter Cup, I've combined a layer of peanut butter buttercream with a layer of brownie and then topped all of that with a bittersweet chocolate glaze. Rich enough, do you think? I recommend very small bites.

INGREDIENTS

1 recipe My New Brownie (facing page)

THE BUTTERCREAM
½ cup plus 2 tablespoons peanut butter (smooth or crunchy)
1 cup confectioners' sugar
2½ tablespoons unsalted butter at room temperature
½ teaspoon pure vanilla extract

THE GLAZE
5 ounces bittersweet chocolate
2 teaspoons light corn syrup
½ cup chopped unsalted peanuts (optional)

1. Prepare the brownies and let them cool completely (you can place the pan in the refrigerator or freezer to speed up the process).

2. Prepare the buttercream: Place all the ingredients in a food processor and process until smooth, 60 seconds, stopping the processor once to scrape the bowl with a rubber spatula. (Or use an electric hand mixer and beat on medium-high speed in a small mixing bowl until smooth.)

3. Using a spatula, spread the buttercream evenly over the brownie, and freeze for 1 hour.

4. When the hour is almost up, prepare the glaze: Melt the chocolate in the top of a double boiler placed over simmering water. Remove the pan from the heat and stir in the corn syrup.

5. Allow the glaze to cool to the point where it is no longer hot but is still loose and spreadable, 8 to 10 minutes. Using a frosting spatula, spread the glaze over the buttercream. Sprinkle the peanuts, if using, over the glaze. Refrigerate the pan and allow the chocolate to harden, 30 minutes.

6. Cut the brownies into 2¼-inch squares with a sharp thin knife, dipping it in hot water and drying it before each cut.

7. When cool, refrigerate the bars in the pan, covered with plastic wrap, for up to 2 days. After that, layer them in an airtight plastic container with plastic wrap, parchment, or waxed paper between the layers, and store for another 2 days in the refrigerator or in the freezer for up to 2 weeks. They are delicious either cold or at room temperature.

Makes 16 brownies

Chocolate Raspberry Brownies

❤ ❤ ❤ ❤ ❤ ❤ ❤ ❤ ❤ ❤ *brownie bar*

The divine combination of chocolate and raspberries is layered in this unforgettable taste experience. For a sophisticated dessert, serve small pieces garnished with whipped cream and fresh raspberries.

INGREDIENTS

1 cup fresh raspberries or thawed, drained frozen unsweetened raspberries
¼ cup raspberry preserves
1 recipe My New Brownie (page 146), sugar reduced by 1 tablespoon

1. Preheat the oven to 350°F. Lightly grease a 9-inch square baking pan with butter or vegetable oil, or line the bottom with parchment paper.

2. Using a spoon or fork, mix the raspberries and the preserves together in a small bowl until the mixture has a pourable consistency. Set it aside.

3. Prepare the batter for the brownies. Scoop half of it into the prepared pan. Shake the pan gently to distribute the batter evenly.

4. Pour or spoon the raspberry mixture over the batter, and spread it out very gently, leaving ¾ inch uncovered around the edges.

5. Spoon or pour the remaining batter in long ribbon-like strips over the filling and spread it gently with a spatula. (Your goal is for the three layers to remain separate.) Shake the pan gently back and forth to level the batter.

6. Bake on the center rack of the oven until a tester inserted in the center comes out clean or with some moist crumbs, approximately 45 minutes.

7. Allow the brownies to cool in the pan for 1 hour before cutting into 2¼-inch squares with a sharp thin knife.

8. Leave the brownies in the pan, at room temperature, covered with plastic wrap, for up to 2 days. After that, layer them in an airtight plastic container with plastic wrap, parchment, or waxed paper between the layers, and store for another 2 days in the refrigerator or in the freezer for up to 2 weeks. They are delicious either cold or at room temperature.

Makes 16 brownies

New York Cheesecake Brownies

❤ ❤ ❤ ❤ ❤ ❤ ❤ ❤ ❤ ❤ *brownie bar*

What better combo for a gal from New York City who grew up on cheesecake and brownies? A layer of cheesecake and a layer of bittersweet brownie, one creamy, one fudgy, and both utterly divine. Eat at room temperature like a brownie, or chilled just like cheesecake.

I N G R E D I E N T S

THE BROWNIE
3½ ounces unsweetened chocolate
10 tablespoons (1¼ sticks) unsalted butter
1 cup sugar
3 whole large eggs
½ cup all-purpose flour

THE CHEESECAKE
1 pound cream cheese, cold
½ cup sugar
1 whole large egg
1 large egg yolk
1½ teaspoons fresh lemon juice

1. Preheat the oven to 300°F. Lightly grease a 9-inch square baking pan with butter or vegetable oil, or line the bottom with parchment paper.

2. Prepare the brownie: Melt the chocolate and butter together in the top of a double boiler placed over simmering water. Let the mixture cool for 5 minutes.

3. Place the sugar and the eggs in a medium-size mixing bowl, and using an electric mixer, beat on medium-high speed until pale yellow, 2 minutes. Scrape the bowl with a rubber spatula.

4. Add the flour on low speed and mix for 5 seconds. Scrape the bowl.

5. Add the cooled chocolate mixture on low speed and blend until mixed, 15 seconds, stopping the mixer once to scrape the bowl.

6. Spread the batter evenly in the prepared pan, and place the pan in the freezer for 10 minutes.

7. Meanwhile prepare the cheesecake topping: Place all the cheesecake ingredients in a food processor and process until smooth, 1 minute. Stop the machine once during the process to scrape the bowl.

8. Remove the pan from the freezer. Carefully spoon the cheesecake mixture over the brownie layer, and using a spatula, spread it over the brownie so as not to mix the two together.

9. Bake on the center rack of the oven until the top is set and the center is just about level with the edges, 1 hour and 5 to 10 minutes.

10. Cool the brownies in the pan for 30 minutes. Using a sharp thin knife, cut into 2¼-inch squares, dipping the knife in hot water and wiping it off after each cut.

11. When cut, refrigerate the bars in the pan, covered with plastic wrap, for up to 2 days. After that, layer them in an airtight plastic container with plastic wrap, parchment, or waxed paper between the layers, and store for another 2 days in the refrigerator or in the freezer for up to 2 weeks. They are delicious either cold or at room temperature.

Makes 16 brownies

Sour Cherry Cheesecake Brownies

♥ ♥ ♥ ♥ ♥ ♥ ♥ ♥ ♥   *brownie bar*

The tartness of the sour cherries cuts the sweetness of the chocolate and the cheesecake, sending a rush of contrasting flavors to your tongue. It's unusual to combine all three elements in one brownie, but I figured, why not? I tried it out and found the results to be sensational.

INGREDIENTS

THE FILLING
8 ounces cream cheese at room temperature
¼ cup sugar
1 tablespoon sour cream
2 large egg yolks

THE BROWNIE
3½ ounces unsweetened chocolate
12 tablespoons (1½ sticks) unsalted butter
1½ cups sugar
2 whole large eggs
¾ cup all-purpose flour
¾ cup canned sour cherries, drained

1. Preheat the oven to 325°F. Lightly grease a 9-inch square baking pan with butter or vegetable oil, or line the bottom with parchment paper.

2. Make the filling: Place the cream cheese, sugar, and sour cream in a medium-size bowl and beat on medium-high speed until blended, 30 seconds. Scrape the bowl with a rubber spatula.

3. Add the egg yolks and mix until blended, 20 seconds. Set aside.

4. Prepare the brownie batter: Melt the chocolate and butter together in the top of a double boiler placed over simmering water. Remove the chocolate mixture from the heat and let it cool for 5 minutes.

5. Place the sugar in a medium-size bowl, and pour in the chocolate mixture. Using an electric mixer on medium speed, mix until blended, about 25 seconds. Scrape the bowl.

6. With the mixer on medium-low speed, add the eggs one at a time, blending after each addition until the yolk is broken and dispersed, about 10 seconds. Then scrape the bowl and blend until velvety, about 15 seconds.

7. Add the flour on low speed and mix for 20 seconds. Finish the mixing with a rubber spatula, being certain to incorporate any flour at the bottom of the bowl.

8. Pour half of the batter into the prepared pan, and spread it evenly. Using a rubber spatula, scoop the cream cheese mixture onto the brownie batter and gently spread it evenly over the surface.

9. Distribute the cherries over the filling, and use your fingers to press them down gently into the cream cheese.

10. Drop the rest of the batter over the filling by large spoonfuls. Then, using a spatula, spread it as gently as possible over the surface (do not worry if the cream cheese shows in places).

11. Bake the brownies on the center rack of the oven until a tester inserted in the center comes out clean or with

moist crumbs, about 50 minutes. Allow the brownies to cool for 30 minutes in the pan. Then cut them into 2¼-inch squares with a sharp thin knife.

12. Refrigerate the bars in the pan, covered with plastic wrap, for up to 2 days. After that, layer them in an airtight plastic container, with plastic wrap, parchment, or waxed paper between the layers, and store for another 2 days in the refrigerator or in the freezer for up to 2 weeks. They are delicious either cold or at room temperature.

Makes 16 brownies

Chocolate Soufflé Brownies

❤ ❤ ❤ ❤ ❤ ❤ ❤ ❤ ❤   *brownie bar*

This fudgy brownie with a thick layer of baked mousse is one of the richest, most luxurious chocolate desserts known to humankind, if I do say so myself. Cut them small or you'll be flying for hours after you eat one. They're delicious cold, at room temperature, or warmed up, topped with vanilla ice cream or whipped cream.

I N G R E D I E N T S

THE BROWNIE

3½ ounces unsweetened chocolate

10 tablespoons (1¼ sticks) unsalted butter

1 cup sugar

½ teaspoon pure vanilla extract

3 large eggs

½ cup all-purpose flour

THE TOPPING

¾ cup heavy (whipping) cream

2 ounces unsweetened chocolate

*4 ounces (¾ cup) semisweet chocolate
    chips*

3 large eggs

5 tablespoons sugar

1. Preheat the oven to 325°F. Lightly grease a 9-inch square baking pan with butter or vegetable oil, or line the bottom with parchment paper.

2. Make the brownie batter: Melt the chocolate and butter together in the top of a double boiler placed over simmering water. Let the mixture cool for 5 minutes.

3. Place the sugar in a medium-size mixing bowl and pour in the chocolate mixture. Using an electric mixer on medium speed, mix until blended, about 25 seconds. Scrape the bowl with a rubber spatula.

4. Add the vanilla. With the mixer on medium-low speed, add the eggs one at a time, blending after each addition until the yolk is broken and dispersed, about 10 seconds. Then scrape the bowl and blend until the mixture is velvety, about 15 seconds.

5. Add the flour on low speed and mix for 20 seconds. Finish the mixing by hand, being certain to incorporate any flour at the bottom of the bowl.

6. Spread the batter evenly in the prepared pan, and set it aside.

7. Make the topping: Heat the cream in a medium-size saucepan over low heat until hot. Add the chocolate and the chocolate chips, stir, and remove the pan from the heat. Cover the pan to melt the chocolate. Meanwhile, with the electric mixer on medium-high speed, beat the eggs and sugar together in a medium-size bowl until pale and foamy, about 3 minutes.

8. Stir the chocolate mixture with a whisk until smooth. Then add the chocolate mixture to the egg mixture and mix at medium-low speed until well blended.

9. Pour the topping over the batter, and tip the pan gently from side to side so that it spreads evenly.

10. Bake the brownies on the center rack of the oven until the top is set, 40 to 45 minutes. (The center of the brownies should never quite rise to the height of the edges.)

11. Remove the pan from the oven and place it on a rack to cool for 1 hour before cutting the brownies into 1½-inch squares with a sharp thin knife.

12. Leave the brownies in the pan, at room temperature, covered with plastic wrap, for up to 1 day. After that, layer them in an airtight plastic container with plastic wrap, parchment, or waxed paper between the layers, and store for another 2 days in the refrigerator or in the freezer for up to 2 weeks. They are delicious either cold or at room temperature.

Makes 36 brownies

Toasted Pecan Orange Brownies

♥ ♥ ♥ ♥ ♥ ♥ ♥ ♥ ♥ ♥ *brownie bar*

I believe it was Maida Heatter's Mandarin Chocolate Cake that first put me in touch with the wonderful combination of chocolate and orange. This brownie takes that perfect union a couple of steps further by adding candied orange slices and pecans.

INGREDIENTS

THE CANDIED ORANGE
1 large orange, thinly sliced
½ cup water
⅔ cup sugar

THE BROWNIE
3 ounces unsweetened chocolate
12 tablespoons (1½ sticks) unsalted butter at room temperature
1 cup minus 1 tablespoon all-purpose flour
3 tablespoons unsweetened cocoa powder
1½ cups sugar
3 large eggs
¾ teaspoon pure vanilla extract
2¼ cups chopped pecans, toasted (page 89)

THE GLAZE
3 ounces semisweet chocolate
1 ounce unsweetened chocolate
2 tablespoons unsalted butter

1. Make the candied orange: Place the orange slices and water in a small heavy saucepan over medium heat. Bring to a boil and simmer gently for 3 minutes.

2. Add the sugar and continue stirring until the mixture is slightly thickened and shiny, 5 to 10 minutes. Remove the saucepan from the heat and allow to cool for 15 to 20 minutes.

3. When the mixture has cooled, drain it, reserving the syrup (there should be approximately ⅓ cup). Chop the drained orange slices coarsely in a food processor (there will be about ⅔ cup), and set aside.

4. Preheat the oven to 325°F. Lightly grease a 9-inch square baking pan with butter or vegetable oil, or line the bottom with parchment paper.

5. Prepare the brownie batter: Melt the chocolate and butter together in the top of a double boiler placed over simmering water. Remove the pan from the heat and allow to cool slightly.

6. Sift the flour and cocoa powder into a small bowl and set aside.

7. Place the sugar and eggs in a medium-size mixing bowl, and using an electric mixer on medium speed, beat until the mixture is thick and pale, 2 to 3 minutes. Stop the mixer once during the process to scrape the bowl.

8. Add the vanilla and mix for several seconds on medium speed.

9. Add the flour mixture and mix until blended, 15 seconds, stopping the mixer once to scrape the bowl.

10. Turn the mixer to low speed and gradually add the chocolate mixture. Mix until blended, 15 seconds, stopping the mixer once to scrape the bowl.

11. Fold in the nuts and the chopped candied orange. Spread the batter evenly in the pan, and bake on the center rack of the oven until a tester inserted in the center comes out with moist crumbs, 25 to 30 minutes.

12. Transfer the pan to a cooling rack and prepare the glaze: Melt both chocolates and butter together in the top of a double boiler placed over simmering water. Using a whisk, vigorously stir in 2 tablespoons of the reserved orange syrup until the glaze is smooth and

shiny. If it is too stiff, add more syrup until it reaches glaze consistency. Spread over the warm brownies.

13. Allow the brownies to set for 4 to 6 hours in the pan before cutting them; or to speed the process, chill them for 1 to 2 hours in the refrigerator and then cut them into 2¼-inch squares, with a sharp thin knife.

14. Refrigerate the bars in the pan, covered with plastic wrap, for up to 2 days. After that, layer them in an airtight plastic container with plastic wrap, parchment, or waxed paper between the layers, and store for another 2 days in the refrigerator or in the freezer for up to 2 weeks. They are delicious either cold or at room temperature.

Makes 16 brownies

Chocolate Hazelnut Brownies

❤ ❤ ❤ ❤ ❤ ❤ ❤ ❤ ❤   *brownie bar*

Here's a news flash: America's favorite flavor is hazelnut. (As of today, that is. Who knows about tomorrow?) Far be it from me to let the moment pass without contributing this light, delicate brownie made with ground hazelnuts and accented with Frangelico liqueur. The liqueur is optional, but with or without it, these brownies are lovely served in small pieces with a cappuccino.

INGREDIENTS

2 ounces unsweetened chocolate
5 ounces semisweet chocolate
2 tablespoons all-purpose flour
2 tablespoons cornstarch
10 tablespoons (1¼ sticks) unsalted butter
    at room temperature
14 tablespoons sugar
½ teaspoon pure vanilla extract
5 large eggs, separated
1½ teaspoons instant coffee or espresso
    powder
2 tablespoons Frangelico liqueur plus 2
    tablespoons water, or ¼ cup water
½ cup hazelnuts, toasted (page 89), and
    finely ground
¼ teaspoon salt

1. Preheat the oven to 325°F. Lightly grease a 9-inch square baking pan with butter or vegetable oil, or line the bottom with parchment paper.

2. Melt both chocolates in the top of a double boiler placed over simmering water. Remove from the heat and allow to cool.

3. Sift the flour and cornstarch together into a small bowl and set aside.

4. Using an electric mixer on medium speed, cream the butter, 11 tablespoons of the sugar, and the vanilla in a medium-size mixing bowl until light and fluffy, 45 seconds. Scrape the bowl.

5. Add the egg yolks and beat on medium speed until blended, 20 seconds. Stop the mixer once to scrape the bowl. Add the chocolate and beat on low speed until blended, 5 seconds. Scrape the bowl again.

6. Dissolve the coffee powder in the Frangelico mixture, and add this to the butter mixture.

7. Add the flour mixture and the ground nuts, and beat on low speed for 10 seconds, stopping the mixer once to scrape the bowl.

8. Using an electric mixer on medium-low speed, beat the egg whites with the salt in a medium-size bowl until frothy, about 30 seconds. Increase the speed to medium-high and gradually add the remaining 3 tablespoons sugar. Beat until soft peaks form, about 30 seconds.

9. Using a wooden spoon, stir one third of the whites into the batter to loosen the mixture. Fold in the remaining whites with a rubber spatula.

10. Spread the batter evenly in the baking pan, and bake the brownies on the center rack of the oven until they are just set and a tester comes out with moist crumbs, 30 to 35 minutes. Let the brownies cool in the pan for 1 to 2 hours before cutting them into 2¼- or 1½-inch squares with a sharp thin knife.

11. Leave the brownies in the pan, at room temperature, covered with plastic wrap, for up to 2 days. After that, layer them in an airtight plastic container with plastic wrap, parchment, or waxed paper between the layers, and store for another 2 days in the refrigerator or in the freezer for up to 2 weeks. They are delicious either cold or at room temperature.

Makes 16 large or 36 small brownies

Bourbon Brownies

❤ ❤ ❤ ❤ ❤ ❤ ❤ ❤ ❤ *brownie bar*

As a rule I like my chocolate unadulterated, but bourbon provides a wonderful accent that complements, rather than disguises, the chocolate taste of these brownies. They're rich and fudgy, so you'll probably want to cut them into small pieces. You may also want to brush the bourbon onto the baked brownie more sparingly than I do; try the recipe once to see.

INGREDIENTS

THE BROWNIE
5 ounces unsweetened chocolate
12 tablespoons (1½ sticks) unsalted butter
2 cups sugar
1 teaspoon pure vanilla extract
9 tablespoons bourbon
4 large eggs
1 cup all-purpose flour

THE GLAZE
3 tablespoons heavy (whipping) cream
3 ounces bittersweet chocolate, chopped fine or shaved

1. Preheat the oven to 325°F. Lightly grease a 9-inch square baking pan with butter or vegetable oil or line the bottom with parchment paper.

2. Melt the chocolate and butter together in the top of a double boiler placed over simmering water. Remove the mixture from the heat and let it cool for 5 minutes.

3. Place the sugar in a medium-size mixing bowl, and pour in the chocolate mixture. Using an electric mixer on medium speed, mix until blended, about 15 seconds. Scrape the bowl with a rubber spatula.

4. Add the vanilla and 6 tablespoons of the bourbon. With the mixer on medium-low speed, add the eggs one at a time, blending after each addition until the yolk is broken and dispersed, about 10 seconds. Then scrape the bowl and blend until the mixture is velvety, about 15 seconds.

5. Add the flour on low speed, and mix for 20 seconds. Finish the mixing with a rubber spatula, being certain to incorporate any flour at the bottom of the bowl.

6. Spread the batter evenly in the prepared pan. Bake the brownies on the center rack of the oven until a thin crust forms on top and a tester inserted in the center comes out with moist crumbs, 45 to 50 minutes.

7. Transfer the pan to a wire rack, and using a small brush, glaze the surface of the brownies with the remaining 3 tablespoons bourbon. Allow them to cool for at least 1 hour.

8. When the brownies are cool, prepare the glaze: Heat the cream in a small saucepan over low heat just to the boiling point.

9. Remove the pan from the burner, add the chocolate, and cover the pan for 1 to 2 minutes. Then stir the mixture with a small whisk until smooth and shiny.

10. Using a frosting spatula, spread the glaze evenly over the surface of the brownies.

11. Place the pan in the refrigerator for 1 to 2 hours so the glaze will set. Then cut the brownies into 1½-inch squares with a sharp thin knife.

12. Refrigerate the bars in the pan, covered with plastic wrap, for up to 2 days. After that, layer them in an airtight plastic container with plastic wrap, parchment, or waxed paper between the layers, and store for another 2 days in the refrigerator or in the freezer for up to 2 weeks. They are delicious either cold or at room temperature.

Makes 36 brownies

Chocolate Almond Amaretto Brownies

♥ ♥ ♥ ♥ ♥ ♥ ♥ ♥ ♥ ♥   *brownie bar*

Almost flourless, these brownies are so elegant that they require only a single string of pearls to go anywhere. I recommend serving them in small pieces because they're also rich. You can opt not to add the Amaretto and still come out with a superb brownie. They're best made a day ahead so the flavor can settle.

INGREDIENTS

¾ cup plus 2 tablespoons all-purpose flour
½ teaspoon salt
3 ounces (½ cup) semisweet chocolate chips
3½ ounces unsweetened chocolate
1 cup (2 sticks) unsalted butter at room temperature
1½ cups sugar
1 teaspoon pure vanilla extract
1¼ teaspoons almond extract
4 large eggs
2 tablespoons Amaretto liqueur (optional)
1 cup coarsely chopped almonds, lightly toasted (page 89)

1. Preheat the oven to 325°F. Lightly grease a 9-inch square baking pan with butter or vegetable oil or line the bottom with parchment paper.

2. Sift the flour and salt together into a small bowl and set aside.

3. Melt both chocolates and butter together in the top of a double boiler placed over simmering water. Remove the mixture from the heat and let it cool for 5 minutes.

4. Place the sugar, vanilla, and almond extract in a medium-size bowl. Add the chocolate mixture, and using an electric mixer, mix on medium speed until blended, 30 seconds. Scrape the bowl with a rubber spatula.

5. With the mixer on medium-low speed, add the eggs one at a time, blending after each addition until the yolk is broken and dispersed, about 10 seconds. Then scrape the bowl and blend until velvety, about 15 seconds.

6. Add the flour mixture on low speed and mix for 10 seconds. Scrape the bowl with a rubber spatula, and complete the blending by hand with several strokes.

7. Spread the batter evenly in the pan, and sprinkle the Amaretto, if using, over the surface. Tip the pan from side to side to ensure even coverage.

8. Sprinkle the nuts over the surface, and bake the brownies on the center rack of the oven until a thin crust forms on top and a tester inserted in the center comes out with moist crumbs, 45 to 50 minutes.

9. Transfer the pan to a rack to cool for 1 hour. Then cut them into 1½- or 2¼-inch squares with a sharp thin knife. If possible, serve the brownies the next day.

10. Leave the brownies in the pan, at room temperature, covered with plastic wrap, for up to 2 days. After that, layer them in an airtight plastic container with plastic wrap, parchment, or waxed paper between the layers, and store for another 2 days in the refrigerator or in the freezer for up to 2 weeks. They are delicious eaten either cold or at room temperature.

Makes 16 large or 36 small brownies

Butterscotch Chocolate Chip Brownies

brownie bar

These chewy bars offer the consistency of a fudgy brownie and the distinctive taste of butterscotch enhanced with chocolate chips. Though the recipe calls for a 9-inch pan, an 8-inch one works also. With the smaller pan, you'll get thicker bars, so you'll need to bake them a bit longer.

INGREDIENTS

1½ cups minus 1 tablespoon all-purpose
   flour
Generous ½ teaspoon baking powder
½ teaspoon salt
12 tablespoons (1½ sticks) unsalted butter
   at room temperature
1¾ cups plus 1 tablespoon (lightly packed)
   light brown sugar
2 teaspoons pure vanilla extract
3 large eggs
6 ounces (1 cup) semisweet chocolate chips

1. Preheat the oven to 350°F. Lightly grease a 9-inch square baking pan with butter or vegetable oil, or line the bottom with parchment paper.

2. Sift the flour, baking powder, and salt together into a small bowl and set aside.

3. Using an electric mixer on medium speed, cream the butter, brown sugar, and vanilla in a medium-size bowl until light and fluffy, about 1½ minutes. Scrape the bowl with a rubber spatula.

4. Add the eggs one at a time, beating on medium speed after each addition until partially blended, 5 seconds. Scrape the bowl. Then beat until the batter is blended, 20 seconds.

5. With the mixer on low speed, add the flour mixture and beat until almost blended, 15 seconds. Scrape the bowl.

6. Add the chocolate chips and mix on low speed until they are blended in,

about 5 seconds. Stir the batter several times with a rubber spatula, and spread it evenly in the prepared pan.

7. Bake on the center rack of the oven until the top has puffed and is just set, and is a golden color, 30 to 35 minutes. (The top won't spring back when touched; a depression remains.) Transfer the pan to a rack and allow to cool for 1 hour before cutting into 2¼-inch squares with a sharp thin knife.

8. Leave the brownies in the pan, at room temperature, covered with plastic wrap, for up to 2 days. After that, layer them in an airtight plastic container with plastic, parchment, or waxed paper between the layers, and store for another 2 days in the refrigerator or in the freezer for up to 2 weeks. They are delicious either cold or at room temperature.

Makes 16 brownies

White Chocolate Macadamia Brownies

❤ ❤ ❤ ❤ ❤ ❤ ❤ ❤ ❤ ❤ *brownie bar*

Customers at Rosie's clamor for this masterpiece of a bar: a chewy white chocolate base dotted with chunks of white and bittersweet chocolate and toasted macadamia nuts. What a way to gild the lily!

INGREDIENTS

12 ounces white chocolate
4 ounces bittersweet chocolate
1½ cups all-purpose flour
½ teaspoon baking powder
⅛ teaspoon salt
10 tablespoons (1¼ sticks) unsalted butter
¾ cup sugar
3 large eggs
2½ teaspoons pure vanilla extract
¾ cup coarsely chopped macadamia nuts, toasted (page 89)

1. Preheat the oven to 325°F. Lightly grease a 9-inch square baking pan with butter or vegetable oil, or line the bottom with parchment paper.

2. Chop 6 ounces of the white chocolate very fine and set it aside. Chop the remaining 6 ounces white chocolate and the bittersweet chocolate very coarse and set them aside.

3. Sift the flour, baking powder, and salt together into a small bowl and set aside.

4. Melt the butter in a small saucepan over low heat. Do not allow it to bubble. Remove the pan from the heat and add the finely chopped white chocolate, but *do not stir.* Set aside.

5. Using an electric mixer on medium-high speed, beat the sugar, eggs, and vanilla in a medium-size bowl until thick and pale, 5 minutes.

6. With the mixer on low speed, add the butter mixture and mix to blend, 15 to 20 seconds. Scrape the bowl.

7. Add the flour mixture and blend on low speed just to incorporate, 15 seconds. Stop the mixer once during the process to scrape the bowl.

8. Using a rubber spatula, fold in the coarsely chopped white and bittersweet chocolates and the nuts. Spread the batter evenly in the prepared pan.

9. Bake the brownies on the center rack of the oven until they are just set and a tester comes out with moist crumbs, 30 to 35 minutes. Allow them to cool in the pan for 1 hour, and then cut them into 2¼-squares with a sharp thin knife.

10. Leave the brownies in the pan, at room temperature, covered with plastic wrap, for up to 2 days. After that, layer them in an airtight plastic container with plastic wrap, parchment, or waxed paper between the layers, and store for another 2 days in the refrigerator or in the freezer for up to 2 weeks. They are delicious either cold or at room temperature.

Makes 16 brownies

Pucker-Your-Lips Apricot Linzer Bars

♥ ♥ ♥ ♥ ♥ ♥ ♥ ♥   *fine pastry bar*

For me, few fruits can rival the beauty and succulent tartness of apricots, so I created these bars to highlight those attributes. I placed a mixture of dried apricots and apricot preserves over a rich pastry crust, topped it with latticework, and came up with the perfect complement for afternoon tea.

INGREDIENTS

THE DOUGH

2 cups plus 3 tablespoons all-purpose flour
½ cup sugar
¼ teaspoon salt
2½ teaspoons grated lemon zest
15 tablespoons (2 sticks minus 1 table-
spoon) unsalted butter, cold,
cut into 15 pieces
2 large egg yolks
1 large egg white

THE FILLING

1 box (8 ounces) dried apricots, chopped
fine
¾ cup apricot preserves
2 tablespoons fresh lemon juice

1. Preheat the oven to 375°F. Lightly grease a 9-inch square baking pan with butter or vegetable oil, or line the bottom with parchment paper.

2. Place the flour, sugar, salt, and lemon zest in a food processor, and process for 20 seconds. (Or whisk them together by hand in a large bowl.)

3. Distribute the butter evenly over the flour, and process until the mixture resembles coarse meal, 15 to 20 seconds. (Or rub the butter into the flour with your fingertips, or cut it in with a pastry blender.)

4. Whisk the egg yolks together. With the processor running, pour the yolks in a steady stream through the feed tube and process just until the dough comes together, 20 to 30 seconds. (Or sprinkle the yolks over the flour mixture while tossing with a fork.)

5. Divide the dough into two-thirds and one-third portions. Gently press the larger portion evenly in the bottom of the prepared pan and a scant ½ inch up the sides. Using a pastry brush, glaze the dough all over with some of the egg white. (Or pour the egg white over the dough, and tip the pan from side to side so the white spreads completely over the surface. Pour off and save the excess.)

6. Bake on the center rack of the oven until golden, 30 minutes.

7. While the base is baking, prepare the lattice dough: Roll out the remaining dough between two pieces of plastic wrap to form a 9½-inch square. Place this, still sandwiched in the wrap, in the freezer while you prepare the filling.

8. Place the apricots in a small saucepan and add water to cover. Bring to a boil over medium heat. Boil until soft, 2 to 3 minutes. Drain the apricots and pat them dry with paper towels. Place them in a small bowl along with the apricot preserves and lemon juice, and mix together.

9. Remove the pan from the oven, and raise the oven temperature to 400°F.

10. Spread the apricot filling over the baked base.

11. Remove the remaining dough from the freezer and peel off the top piece of plastic wrap. Cut the dough into 12 strips approximately ¾ inch wide.

12. Carefully place 6 of the strips across the filling, about 1 inch apart, with the first and last strip touching the sides of the pan. Repeat the procedure with the remaining 6 strips, placing them perpendicular to the first 6, in a lattice pattern. Press the ends of the strips into the dough border on the edge of the pan. Brush the remaining egg white over the lattice strips with a pastry brush.

13. Bake on the center rack of the oven until the lattice is golden, 40 minutes.

14. Remove the pan from the oven and place it on a rack to cool for at least 2 hours. Then cut into 2¼-inch squares, "sawing" the lattice carefully with the tip of a sharp thin knife.

15. Leave the bars in the pan, at room temperature, covered with plastic wrap, for up to 2 days, or layer the bars in an airtight plastic container with plastic wrap, parchment, or waxed paper between the layers, and store in the refrigerator for 2 or 4 days or in the freezer for up to 2 weeks. Bring the bars to room temperature before eating.

Makes 16 bars

Blond Linzer Bars

♥ ♥ ♥ ♥ ♥ ♥   *linzer pastry bar*

For those of us who are linzer fans, here is another variation on the theme. This light-colored version of that classic dessert—made with a spicy dough and filled with apricot preserves—absolutely maintains its true linzer integrity.

INGREDIENTS

THE DOUGH
1½ cups all-purpose flour
¾ teaspoon baking powder
½ teaspoon salt
10 tablespoons (1¼ sticks) unsalted butter
    at room temperature
¼ cup (lightly packed) light brown sugar
½ cup granulated sugar
¾ teaspoon ground cinnamon
¼ teaspoon ground cloves
1 tablespoon grated lemon zest
1 large egg
½ teaspoon pure vanilla extract
1 cup finely chopped almonds

THE FILLING

¼ cup chopped dried apricots

½ cup plus 1 tablespoon apricot
    preserves

5 teaspoons fresh lemon juice

THE GLAZE

1 large egg white

2 tablespoons finely chopped almonds

1. Lightly grease an 8-inch square baking pan with butter, or line the bottom with parchment paper.

2. Sift the flour, baking powder, and salt together into a small bowl and set aside.

3. Using an electric mixer on low speed, cream the butter, both sugars, cinnamon, cloves, and lemon zest together in a medium-size bowl until just mixed. Scrape the bowl with a rubber spatula. Then mix on medium speed until smooth, 2 to 3 minutes, stopping the mixer twice to scrape the bowl.

4. Stir the egg and vanilla together in a small cup, and add to the butter mixture. Mix on medium speed until incorporated, about 10 seconds. Scrape the bowl.

5. With the mixer on low speed, blend in the flour mixture and the almonds until they are incorporated, 5 to 8 seconds.

6. Divide the dough into two-thirds and one-third portions. Gently press the larger portion into the prepared pan, cover with plastic wrap, and refrigerate it for 2 hours or freeze it for 1 hour.

7. Place the smaller portion of dough between two pieces of plastic wrap, and roll it out to form an 8-inch square. Slip the dough, still sandwiched between the wrap, onto a platter or baking sheet and refrigerate it for 2 hours or freeze it for 1 hour.

8. Preheat the oven to 350°F.

9. Prepare the filling: Place the apricots in a small saucepan, add water to cover, and bring to a boil over medium heat. Boil for 2 to 3 minutes, remove from the heat, and set aside for 10 minutes. Then drain the apricots, combine them with the preserves and lemon juice, and mix well.

10. Remove the pan from the refrigerator. Spread the apricot mixture evenly over the dough in the baking pan, leaving a ¼-inch border on all sides.

11. Remove the remaining dough from the refrigerator. Peel off the top piece of plastic wrap, and cut the dough into 12 strips about ½ inch wide (there will be leftover dough).

12. Carefully place 6 of the strips across the filling, about 1 inch apart, with the first and last strip touching the sides of the pan. Repeat the procedure with the remaining 6 strips, placing them perpendicular to the first 6, in a lattice pattern. Press the ends of the strips into the dough border on the edge of the pan.

13. Using a pastry brush, brush the egg white over the lattice strips. Then sprinkle the 2 tablespoons chopped almonds over the surface.

14. Bake on the center rack of the oven until the top is lightly golden and shiny and the filling is bubbling, about 35 minutes.

15. Remove the pan from the oven and place it on a rack to cool completely. Then cut into 2-inch squares, "sawing" carefully through the lattice with the tip of a sharp thin knife.

16. If you plan to snack on them that day, leave the bars in the pan at room temperature, covered with plastic wrap. At the end of the day, layer them in an airtight plastic container with plastic wrap, parchment, or waxed paper between the layers. They will stay fresh in the refrigerator for up to 3 days or in the freezer for up to 2 weeks. Bring the bars to room temperature before eating.

Makes 16 bars

Chocolate Linzer Bars

♥ ♥ ♥ ♥ ♥ ♥ ♥   *linzer pastry bar*

I'm a big fan of linzer bars and tortes, so I had fun trying out all kinds of variations. I knew that nuts

and chocolate go great together, and that raspberry goes well with chocolate, so when it came to variations on a linzer bar, I figured why not make a terrific trio? I put them all together, and this is the result.

INGREDIENTS

THE DOUGH
1 whole large egg
2 large egg yolks
1½ teaspoons pure vanilla extract
1¼ cups plus 2 tablespoons all-purpose flour
7 tablespoons unsweetened cocoa powder
¼ teaspoon baking powder
⅛ teaspoon salt
¾ cup plus 2 tablespoons sugar
1 cup coarsely ground almonds
14 tablespoons (1¾ sticks) unsalted butter, cold, cut into 14 pieces

THE FILLING
¾ cup raspberry preserves
1 tablespoon fresh lemon juice

THE GLAZE
1 large egg white

1. Preheat the oven to 350°F. Lightly grease a 9-inch square baking pan, or line the bottom with parchment paper.

2. Using a fork, stir the whole egg, egg yolks, and vanilla together in a small cup. Set aside.

3. Place the flour, cocoa powder, baking powder, salt, and sugar in a food processor and process to blend, 5 seconds.

4. Add the almonds and process several seconds to blend.

5. Distribute half the butter over the flour mixture and process until the mixture resembles coarse meal, 15 seconds. Then repeat with the remaining butter and process for 10 seconds.

6. With the machine running, add the egg mixture through the feed tube and process for 3 seconds. Scrape the bowl with a rubber spatula, and then process for another 3 seconds.

7. Divide the dough into two portions, one slightly larger than the other. Gently press the larger portion into the prepared pan. Bake on the center rack of the oven until the dough is firm to the touch, about 20 minutes. Then remove the pan from the oven, but leave the oven on.

8. While the base is baking, roll out the remaining dough between two pieces of plastic wrap to form a square approximately 9½ inches. Slip this dough, still sandwiched between the plastic wrap, onto a platter or baking sheet and refrigerate it for 45 minutes.

9. Stir the raspberry preserves and lemon juice together in a small bowl, and spread the mixture evenly over the baked crust.

10. Remove the chilled dough from the refrigerator, and peel off the top piece of plastic wrap. Cut the dough into 12 strips about ¾ inch wide.

11. Carefully place 6 of the strips across the filling, about 1 inch apart, with the first and last strip touching the sides of the pan. Repeat the procedure with the remaining 6 strips, placing them perpendicular to the first 6, in a lattice pattern. Press the ends of the strips into the dough border on the edge of the pan.

12. Brush the egg white over the lattice strips with a pastry brush.

13. Bake on the center rack of the oven until the lattice strips are firm and the filling is bubbling, 35 to 40 minutes. Let the pan cool completely on a wire rack; then cut carefully into 2¼-inch squares by "sawing" with a sharp thin knife.

14. If you plan to snack on them that day, leave the bars in the pan at room temperature, covered with plastic wrap. At the end of the day, layer them in an airtight plastic container with plastic wrap, parchment, or waxed paper between the layers. They will stay fresh in the refrigerator for up to 3 days or in the freezer for up to 2 weeks. Bring the bars to room temperature before eating.

Makes 16 bars

Hazelnut Cranberry Linzers

♥ ♥ ♥ ♥ ♥ ♥ ♥   *linzer pastry bar*

When you want something a little different, here's a linzer bar with a twist. To the spicy dough that's the calling card of a good Viennese linzertorte, I've added ground hazelnuts and the all-American cranberry.

INGREDIENTS

THE DOUGH
1½ cups all-purpose flour
¼ teaspoon baking powder
¼ teaspoon salt
1 tablespoon unsweetened cocoa powder
1⅛ teaspoons ground cinnamon
¼ teaspoon ground cloves
1 cup (2 sticks) unsalted butter at room temperature
½ cup granulated sugar
¼ cup (lightly packed) light brown sugar
1 tablespoon grated lemon zest
1 whole large egg
1 large egg yolk
⅔ cup finely chopped almonds
⅓ cup finely chopped hazelnuts

THE FILLING
¾ cup raspberry preserves
¾ cup fresh cranberries
1 tablespoon grated orange zest

THE TOPPING
1 large egg white
3 tablespoons chopped or slivered almonds

1. Lightly grease an 8-inch square baking pan with butter, or line the bottom with parchment paper.

2. Sift the flour, baking powder, salt, cocoa powder, cinnamon, and cloves together into a bowl and set aside.

3. Using an electric mixer on low speed, cream the butter, both sugars, and lemon zest together in a medium-size mixing bowl until just mixed. Scrape the bowl with a rubber spatula. Then mix on medium speed until smooth, 2 to 3 minutes, stopping the mixer once or twice to scrape the bowl with a rubber spatula.

4. Add the whole egg and the egg yolk, and mix on medium speed until incorporated, about 10 seconds. Scrape the bowl.

5. With the mixer on low speed, blend in the flour mixture, almonds, and hazelnuts until they are incorporated, 5 to 8 seconds.

6. Divide the dough into slightly uneven halves. Gently press the larger half into the prepared pan, cover with plastic wrap, and refrigerate it for 2 hours or freeze it for 1 hour.

7. Place the remaining dough between 2 pieces of plastic wrap and roll it out to form an 8-inch square. Slip the dough, still sandwiched between the plastic wrap, onto a platter or baking sheet and refrigerate it for 2 hours or freeze it for 1 hour.

8. Preheat the oven to 375°F.

9. Remove the pan from the refrigerator. Stir the filling ingredients together, and spread the mixture evenly over the dough in the baking pan, leaving a ¼-inch border on all sides.

10. Remove the remaining dough from the refrigerator, and peel off the top piece of plastic wrap. Cut the dough into 12 strips about ½ inch wide (there will be leftover dough).

11. Carefully place 6 of the strips across the filling, about 1 inch apart, with the first and last strip touching the sides of the pan. Repeat the procedure with the remaining 6 strips, placing them perpendicular to the first 6, in a lattice pattern. Press the ends of the strips into the dough border on the edge of the pan.

12. Brush the egg white over the lattice strips with a pastry brush. Sprinkle the chopped almonds over the entire surface.

13. Bake on the center rack of the oven until the top is shiny and golden and the filling is bubbling, 35 to 40 minutes.

14. Remove the pan from the oven and cool completely on a wire rack. Then cut the bars very carefully into 2-inch squares by "sawing" with the tip of a sharp thin knife.

15. If you plan to snack on them that day, leave the bars in the pan at room temperature, covered with plastic wrap. At the end of the day, layer them in an airtight plastic container with plastic wrap, parchment, or waxed paper between the layers. They will stay fresh in the refrigerator for up to 3 days or in the freezer for up to 2 weeks. Bring the bars to room temperature before eating.

Makes 16 bars

Cinnamon Pecan Shortbread Bars

♥ ♥ ♥ ♥ ♥ ♥ ♥ ♥   *shortbread bar*

A simple shortbread, flavored with cinnamon—the prince of spices—and covered with pecans.

INGREDIENTS

THE BASE
1 cup plus 1 tablespoon all-purpose flour
½ teaspoon plus ⅛ teaspoon ground cinnamon
⅛ teaspoon baking powder
¼ teaspoon salt
8 tablespoons (1 stick) unsalted butter at room temperature
3 tablespoons (lightly packed) light brown sugar
2 tablespoons granulated sugar

THE TOPPING
1 tablespoon granulated sugar
½ teaspoon ground cinnamon
¼ cup plus 1 tablespoon hand-chopped pecans

1. Preheat the oven to 300°F. Have ready an 8-inch square baking pan.

2. Sift the flour, cinnamon, baking powder, and salt together into a small bowl and set aside.

3. Using an electric mixer on medium speed, cream the butter and both sugars together in a medium-size bowl until light and fluffy, 1 to 1½ minutes. Stop the mixer once or twice during the process to scrape the bowl with a rubber spatula.

4. Add the flour mixture on medium-low speed, and mix for 20 seconds. Scrape the bowl. Then mix on medium-high speed until the batter is light and fluffy again, 2 to 2½ minutes, stopping the mixer three times to scrape the bowl.

5. Press the dough evenly over the bottom of the pan, and prick it all over with the tines of a fork.

6. Make the topping: Mix the sugar with the cinnamon. Sprinkle this mixture over the dough, and then scatter the nuts over the surface.

7. Bake on the center rack of the oven until the shortbread is firm to the touch, 55 to 60 minutes.

8. While the shortbread is still hot, cut it into 4 ×1-inch bars with the point of a sharp thin knife. Allow the bars to cool completely before eating.

9. If you plan to snack on them, store the bars in an airtight plastic container at room temperature for up to 4 days. After that, store the container in the freezer for up to 2 weeks. Bring the bars to room temperature before eating.

Makes 16 bars

Semolina Shortbread Bars

❤ ❤ ❤ ❤ ❤ ❤ ❤ ❤   *shortbread bar*

Semolina is the flour used in pasta; here it gives shortbread a grainy texture to add to its already divinely buttery flavor. This shortbread is thick, so be sure that it's baked through and through.

INGREDIENTS

*1½ cups plus 2 tablespoons all-purpose
    flour*
½ cup plus 3 tablespoons semolina flour
½ cup plus 2 tablespoons sugar
½ teaspoon salt
*1 cup (2 sticks) unsalted butter, cold, cut
    into 10 pieces*

1. Preheat the oven to 325°F. Have ready an 8-inch square baking pan.

2. Place both flours, the sugar, and salt in a food processor and pulse to blend, 5 seconds.

168

3. Distribute the butter over the flour mixture and process just until the dough comes together, 40 to 45 seconds. Stop the processor once during the mixing to scrape the bowl with a rubber spatula.

4. Place the dough on a work surface, and work it gently with your hands to bring it together. Pat the shortbread evenly into the pan. Using the tines of a fork, poke deep holes over the entire surface.

5. Bake the shortbread on the center rack of the oven for 45 minutes. Then lower the heat to 300°F and continue baking until it is crisp, firm, and richly golden, 30 minutes.

6. While the shortbread is still hot, cut it into 4 × 1-inch bars with the point of a sharp thin knife. Then let it cool in the pan.

7. Store the bars in an airtight container at room temperature for 3 to 4 days if you think you will be snacking on them. After that, store the container in the freezer for up to 2 weeks. Bring the shortbread to room temperature before eating.

Makes 16 bars

Noah's Scotch Shortbread Bars

❤ ❤ ❤ ❤ ❤ ❤ ❤ ❤ *shortbread bar*

When my son Noah's second-grade teacher asked the class to bring in easy-to-make ethnic recipes to conclude her section on other cultures, we chose this utterly delicious cookie that will be enjoyed by people of all ages. It's amazing how such a delicious treat can be so easy to prepare!

INGREDIENTS

1½ cups plus 1 tablespoon all-purpose flour
½ teaspoon salt
⅛ teaspoon baking powder
12 tablespoons (1½ sticks) unsalted butter
    at room temperature
7 tablespoons sugar

1. Preheat the oven to 325°F. Have ready an 8-inch square baking pan.

2. Sift the flour, salt, and baking powder together into a small bowl and set aside.

3. Using an electric mixer on medium-high speed, cream the butter and sugar together in a medium-size bowl until light and fluffy, 1 to 1½ minutes. Stop the mixer twice during the process to scrape the bowl with a rubber spatula.

4. Add the flour mixture with the mixer on low speed, and blend for 10 seconds. Scrape the bowl, and then beat at medium-high speed until fluffy, 2 to 2½ minutes, stopping the mixer twice during the process to scrape the bowl.

5. Pat the dough evenly into the pan, and pierce the surface all over with the tines of a fork. Bake until it is crisp and golden, about 45 minutes.

6. While the shortbread is still hot, cut it into 4 × 1-inch bars with the point of a sharp thin knife. Then allow it to cool completely in the pan.

7. Transfer the bars to an airtight container and store at room temperature for 3 to 4 days. After that, store the container in the freezer for up to 2 weeks.

Makes 16 bars

Tosca Bars

♥ ♥ ♥ ♥ ♥ ♥ ♥ ♥ ♥   *shortbread bar*

This crunchy shortbread bar is topped with a thin layer of raspberry preserves and a soft almond paste mixture.

INGREDIENTS

THE BASE
1⅓ cups all-purpose flour
⅓ cup sugar
8 tablespoons (1 stick) unsalted butter, cold, cut into 8 pieces
1 large egg, separated

THE FILLING
1 package (7 ounces) almond paste (not marzipan)
3 tablespoons sugar
9 tablespoons (1 stick plus 1 tablespoon) unsalted butter at room temperature, cut into 9 pieces
2 large eggs
¾ teaspoon pure vanilla extract
3 tablespoons all-purpose flour
¾ teaspoon baking powder
6 tablespoons raspberry preserves

THE TOPPING
3 tablespoons unsalted butter
6 tablespoons sugar
1½ tablespoons milk
1½ tablespoons all-purpose flour
¾ cup sliced almonds

1. Preheat the oven to 350°F. Lightly grease a 7 × 11-inch baking pan with butter, or line the bottom with parchment paper.

2. Place the flour and sugar in a food processor, and process the mixture for 5 seconds.

3. Distribute the butter evenly over the flour mixture, and process until the mixture resembles coarse meal, 15 to 20 seconds.

4. With the processor running, drop the egg yolk through the feed tube and process just until the dough comes together, 20 to 30 seconds.

5. Press the dough evenly over the bottom of the prepared pan and ½ inch up the sides. Using a pastry brush, glaze the dough all over with the egg white. (Or you can pour the egg white over the dough, tilt the pan so the white covers the dough completely, and pour off the excess.)

6. Place the pan on the center rack of the oven and bake until golden, 20 to 25 minutes. Set the pan aside, but leave the oven on.

7. Prepare the filling: Place the almond paste and sugar in a food processor and process until the mixture resembles coarse sand, 20 seconds.

8. Add the butter and process until evenly incorporated, 5 seconds.

9. Add the eggs and vanilla, and process until evenly incorporated, 5 seconds.

10. Add the flour and baking powder, and process 5 seconds more.

11. Spread the raspberry preserves over the baked base. Then gently pour

and spread the almond mixture over that. Return the pan to the center rack of the oven, and bake until the filling is set in the center, about 25 minutes. Remove the pan from the oven and preheat the broiler.

12. Meanwhile, prepare the topping: Melt the butter in a small saucepan over low heat. Add the sugar, milk, and flour, and bring to a simmer. Stir constantly over medium-low heat for about 1½ minutes. Do not boil. Remove the pan from the heat and stir in the almonds.

13. Pour the topping evenly over the filling, and spread it gently with a small spatula or a butter knife.

14. Broil the bars until golden, about 2 minutes. *Watch carefully!* Cool completely in the pan before cutting into 2¾ × 1¾-inch bars with a sharp thin knife.

15. If you plan to snack on them the first day, place the bars on a plate or simply leave them in the pan. After that refrigerate, covered, overnight, or layer the bars in an airtight plastic container with plastic wrap, parchment, or waxed paper between the layers. Store the container in the freezer for up to 2 weeks. Bring the bars to room temperature before eating.

Makes 16 bars

Almond Bars

❤ ❤ ❤ ❤ ❤ ❤ ❤   *shortbread bars*

Here is a first-class recipe from Kathleen Stewart (for her other recipe, Apple Galettes, see Index) of the Downtown Bakery and Creamery in Healdsburg, California. It's a bar made of a rich shortbread base covered with a creamy, buttery almond topping.

INGREDIENTS

THE BASE
1 cup all-purpose flour
1½ tablespoons sugar
¼ teaspoon salt
8 tablespoons (1 stick) unsalted butter,
     cold, cut into 8 pieces
1½ tablespoons cold water

THE TOPPING
1 cup heavy (whipping) cream
1 cup sugar
2 teaspoons Grand Marnier or Amaretto
¾ cup slivered almonds

1. Preheat the oven to 375°F. Lightly grease a 9-inch square baking pan with butter, or line the bottom with parchment paper.

2. Place the flour, sugar, and salt in a food processor, and process for 5 seconds. Scatter the butter over the flour and process until the mixture looks like coarse meal, about 20 seconds.

3. With the machine running, add the cold water through the feed tube and process just until the dough comes together, 10 to 15 seconds.

4. Press the dough evenly over the bottom of the prepared pan (it will be thin). Place the pan on the center rack of the oven and bake until lightly golden, about 20 minutes. Then remove the pan from the oven and raise the heat to 400°F.

5. Let the base cool while you prepare the topping: Place the cream, sugar, and Grand Marnier in a medium-size saucepan and cook over medium-low heat, whisking occasionally, until it comes to a rolling boil, 2 to 3 minutes.

6. Remove the pan from the heat, stir in the almonds, and allow the mixture to sit for 15 minutes.

7. Pour the warm topping mixture over the baked base, making sure that the almonds are evenly distributed.

8. Bake on the center rack of the oven until light golden, 25 to 30 minutes.

9. While the bars are still hot, use the point of a sharp thin knife to free the edges from the sides of the pan. Then allow the bars to sit for 15 to 20 minutes before cutting into 2¼-inch squares. After cutting, allow the bars to cool in the pan.

10. Leave the bars in the pan at room temperature, covered with plastic wrap, for up to 2 days, or layer the bars in an airtight container with plastic wrap, parchment, or waxed paper between the layers, and store in the refrigerator for up to 1 week or in the freezer for up to 2 weeks. Bring to room temperature before eating.

Makes 16 bars

Gooey Butter Bars

shortbread bar

Herein lies a tale—or two tales, to be precise. The first involves my mother-in-law, Barbara, who served us a yellow cake bar soaked through with custard so scrumptious that I couldn't help but talk with my mouth full. I asked for the recipe, only to find that she had used a cake mix, and since I had decided that cake mix would never touch my cookbook, I fought temptation and put the recipe aside. Enter tale two. On my travels, I came across the same treat in St. Louis, Missouri, where, as the story goes, a baker working during World War II mistakenly doubled the sugar in a butter cake. Because sugar was rationed, he was loath to toss the cake out. So he sold it—and to his surprise, got rave reviews. The cake has assuaged the St. Louis sweet tooth ever since. I decided to come up with my own, made-from-scratch version,

which has a cakey bottom with a very sweet vanilla custard topping that sinks partway into the base.

INGREDIENTS

THE BASE
1 cup all-purpose flour
½ teaspoon salt
¼ teaspoon baking soda
8 tablespoons (1 stick) unsalted butter
    at room temperature
½ cup sugar
1 teaspoon pure vanilla extract
1 large egg

THE FILLING
12 tablespoons (1½ sticks) unsalted butter
    at room temperature
Pinch of salt
½ teaspoon pure vanilla extract
6 tablespoons sweetened condensed milk
⅓ cup light corn syrup
1 large egg
⅓ cup all-purpose flour

1. Preheat the oven to 350°F. Lightly grease a 9-inch square baking pan with butter, or line the bottom with parchment paper.

2. Sift the flour, salt, and baking soda together into a small bowl, and set aside.

3. Using an electric mixer on medium speed, cream the butter, sugar, and vanilla together in a medium-size bowl until light and fluffy, about 1 minute. Scrape the bowl with a rubber spatula.

4. Add the egg and beat until smooth, 10 seconds. Scrape the bowl.

5. Add the flour mixture and beat on low speed until blended, 10 seconds, stopping the mixer once to scrape the bowl.

6. Using floured fingertips or a spatula, spread the dough evenly over the bottom of the prepared pan. Set it aside.

7. Prepare the filling: With the mixer on medium speed, cream the butter, salt, and vanilla together until light and fluffy, about 1 minute. Scrape the bowl with a rubber spatula.

8. Add the condensed milk and beat on low speed until blended, 15 seconds. Scrape the bowl, then add the corn syrup and mix until blended, 10 seconds.

9. Add the egg and beat for 1½ minutes on medium-high speed until the mixture is light and fluffy again. Scrape the bowl.

10. With the mixer on medium-low speed, add the flour and beat until mixed, 30 seconds.

11. Pour the filling evenly over the base, and bake on the center rack of the oven until the edges appear set but the center is still jiggly, 25 to 27 minutes. Cool to room temperature; then refrigerate until set, about 4 hours. Cut into 2¼ × 1½-inch bars with a sharp thin knife, dipping it in hot water and wiping it clean before each new cut.

12. If you plan to snack on them the first day, place the bars on a plate or simply leave them in the pan. After that, refrigerate, covered with plastic wrap, overnight, or layer the bars in an airtight plastic container with plastic wrap, parchment, or waxed paper between the layers. Store the container in the freezer for up to 2 weeks. Bring the bars to room temperature before eating.

Makes 24 small bars

Cherry Crumb Bars

♥ ♥ ♥ ♥ ♥ ♥ ♥ ♥ *shortbread bar*

Just what the world has been clamoring for: a portable cherry crumb pie. Okay, maybe not clamoring, but this sure beats those commercial snack pies. It's built on a shortbread base, which is layered with a tart cherry filling, then finished off with a crunchy crumb topping.

INGREDIENTS

THE BASE
1 cup plus 2 tablespoons all-purpose flour
¼ cup granulated sugar
¼ teaspoon salt
8 tablespoons (1 stick) unsalted butter,
    cold, cut into 8 pieces
1 large egg white

THE FILLING

2¼ cups canned sour cherries, drained,
but 1 cup juice reserved
3 tablespoons cornstarch
¾ cup granulated sugar
¼ teaspoon salt

THE TOPPING

5 tablespoons all-purpose flour
1 tablespoon granulated sugar
2 tablespoons (lightly packed) light brown
sugar
6 tablespoons quick-cooking oats
Pinch of salt
3 tablespoons unsalted butter, cold, cut
into 4 pieces

1. Preheat the oven to 350°F. Lightly grease an 8-inch square baking pan with butter, or line the bottom with parchment paper.

2. Place the flour, sugar, and salt in a food processor, and process for 5 seconds. Scatter the butter over the flour mixture, and process just until the dough comes together, 20 to 30 seconds.

3. Press the dough gently over the bottom of the prepared pan. Using a pastry brush, glaze the dough all over with the egg white. (Or you can pour the egg white over the dough, tilt the pan so the white covers the dough completely, and pour off the excess.)

4. Bake the base on the center rack of the oven until golden brown, 25 to 30 minutes.

5. While the base is baking prepare the filling: Place the drained cherries in a small bowl and set aside. Combine

¼ cup of the reserved juice with the cornstarch in a small bowl, and set aside.

6. Combine the remaining ¾ cup juice, the sugar, and salt in a small saucepan and bring to a boil over medium-low heat.

7. Pour the cornstarch mixture slowly into the boiling juice, whisking vigorously. Reduce the heat to low and continue whisking vigorously until the mixture turns clear, about 4 minutes.

8. Add the mixture to the cherries and set aside.

9. Prepare the topping: Place the flour, both sugars, the oats, and salt in a food processor and pulse briefly 4 times.

10. Add the butter and pulse 8 to 10 times, until it is incorporated evenly. Scrape the bowl.

11. Remove the base from the oven, and raise the oven temperature to 425°F. Spread the cherry filling evenly over the base, and sprinkle the topping evenly over the cherries.

12. Bake until the topping is lightly golden and crispy, about 25 minutes. Then preheat the broiler. Broil until the topping is a slightly deeper gold, 1 to 2 minutes. Watch the bars the entire time they are under the broiler.

13. Cool completely in the pan on a wire rack. Then cut into 2-inch squares.

14. Leave the bars in the pan, at room temperature, covered with plastic wrap, for up to 2 days, or layer the bars in an airtight plastic container with plastic wrap, parchment, or waxed paper between the layers, and store in the refrigerator for 3 to 4 days or in the freezer for up to 2 weeks. If frozen, the fruit may get a little wet in the thawing process, but the bars will still taste delicious.

Makes 16 bars

Cranberry Crumb Bars

♥ ♥ ♥ ♥ ♥ ♥ ♥ *crumb pastry bar*

If you love cranberries, then you'll enjoy making these bars during the fall and winter, when cranberries are at their peak. Two layers of a crunchy oatmeal crumb cookie are held together by a tart cranberry/raspberry mixture.

INGREDIENTS

THE DOUGH
½ cup whole wheat flour
1 cup all-purpose flour
½ teaspoon salt
½ cup plus 2 tablespoons (lightly packed) light brown sugar
1½ cups quick-cooking oats
½ cup walnuts, chopped small
12 tablespoons (1½ sticks) unsalted butter, melted
1 tablespoon hot water

THE FILLING
¾ cup raspberry preserves
2¼ cups fresh cranberries

1. Preheat the oven to 375°F. Lightly grease a 9-inch square baking pan with butter, or line the bottom with parchment paper.

2. Make the dough: Place all the dry ingredients in a medium-size bowl, and stir with a spoon to mix (or toss with your hands).

3. Add the melted butter and toss with the dry ingredients to distribute the butter evenly.

4. Take a little more than half of the dough and press it evenly into the prepared pan. Bake on the middle rack of the oven until lightly golden, about 14 minutes. Then remove the pan from the oven but leave the oven on.

5. Meanwhile, add the hot water to the remaining dough, and toss with a fork to distribute. Set aside.

6. Prepare the filling: Mix the preserves and cranberries in a medium-size bowl until the berries are evenly distributed.

7. Distribute the berry mixture over the baked base, and using a frosting spatula or the back of a spoon, spread it so that it covers the whole base evenly. Crumble the remaining dough over the filling.

8. Return the pan to the oven and bake until the top is golden and the filling is bubbling, about 45 minutes. Cool completely in the pan on a wire rack before cutting into 2¼-inch squares.

9. Leave the bars in the pan, at room temperature, covered with plastic wrap, for up to 2 days, or layer the bars in an airtight plastic container with plastic wrap, parchment, or waxed paper between the layers, and store in the refrigerator for 3 to 4 days or in the freezer for up to 2 weeks. Bring the bars to room temperature before eating. If frozen, the fruit may get a little wet in the thawing process, but the bars will still taste delicious.

Makes 16 bars

Creamy Cranberry Orange Bars

♥ ♥ ♥ ♥ ♥ ♥ ♥ *shortbread bar*

Start with a layer of crunchy short-bread, smooth it over with a creamy cheesecake mixture flavored with orange, and stud it with fresh cranberries for a deliciously sweet-tart treat.

INGREDIENTS

THE BASE
1 cup all-purpose flour
¼ cup confectioners' sugar
8 tablespoons (1 stick) unsalted butter,
    cold, cut into 8 pieces
1 large egg white

THE TOPPING
10 ounces cream cheese at room
    temperature
2 tablespoons granulated sugar
2 tablespoons sour cream
2 large eggs
1 teaspoon pure vanilla extract
5 tablespoons orange marmalade
½ cup plus 2 tablespoons fresh cranberries
2 tablespoons finely chopped orange zest

1. Preheat the oven to 350°F. Lightly grease an 8-inch square baking pan with butter, or line the bottom with parchment paper.

2. Place the flour and confectioners' sugar in a food processor, and process for 5 seconds. Scatter the butter over the flour mixture, and process until the dough comes together, 20 to 30 seconds.

3. Press the dough gently over the bottom of the prepared pan and about 1 inch up the side. Using a pastry brush, glaze the dough all over with the egg white. (Or you can pour the egg white over the dough, and tip the pan from side to side so the white spreads completely over the surface. Pour off the excess.)

4. Bake the base on the center rack of the oven until golden, about 25 minutes. Transfer the pan to the refrigerator to cool completely, 15 minutes. Keep the oven on.

5. Meanwhile, prepare the topping: Using an electric mixer on medium-high speed, cream the cream cheese and granulated sugar together in a medium-size bowl until light and fluffy, 2 to 3 minutes. Stop the mixer once or twice during the process to scrape the bowl with a rubber spatula.

6. Add the sour cream and beat the mixture on medium-high speed until smooth, about 1 minute. Scrape the bowl.

7. Add the eggs and vanilla and beat on medium-high speed until smooth and creamy, about 10 seconds.

8. Add the marmalade and beat on low speed until blended, 5 seconds. Then fold in the cranberries and orange zest by hand with a rubber spatula.

9. Pour the cream cheese mixture over the cooled base, and jiggle the pan to distribute it evenly.

10. Bake on the center rack of the oven until the top is slightly golden around the edges and a tester inserted in the center comes out dry, 35 to 40 minutes. If the topping bubbles up during baking, prick the bubbles with a toothpick or a thin knife.

11. Allow to cool completely in the pan on a rack. Then cut into 2-inch squares with the point of a thin sharp knife, dipping it in hot water and wiping it dry before each cut.

12. When cool, refrigerate the bars in the pan, uncovered, for the first day. At the end of the day, cover them. They will remain fresh in the refrigerator for 3 to 4 days. To freeze, chill the bars in the refrigerator first, then layer them in an airtight plastic container with plastic wrap, parchment, or waxed paper between the layers. Store in the freezer for up to 2 weeks. Bring the bars to room temperature before eating.

Makes 16 bars

Cranberry Walnut Squares

♥ ♥ ♥ ♥ ♥ ♥ ♥   *shortbread bar*

Patti Chase, an experienced Boston chef, passed the recipe for these squares on to me: a crunchy shortbread base that supports a sweet and gooey mix chock-full of walnuts and tart cranberries. They are a tribute to her talent.

INGREDIENTS

THE BASE
1 cup plus 2 tablespoons all-purpose flour
¼ teaspoon salt
5 tablespoons confectioners' sugar
8 tablespoons (1 stick) unsalted butter,
    cold, cut into 8 pieces
1 large egg white

THE TOPPING

2 cups fresh cranberries
½ cup light corn syrup
½ cup sugar
2 whole large eggs
2 tablespoons unsalted butter, melted
¾ teaspoon pure vanilla extract
1 tablespoon all-purpose flour
½ cup chopped walnuts

1. Preheat the oven to 350°F. Lightly grease an 8-inch square baking pan with butter, or line the bottom with parchment paper.

2. Place the flour, salt, and confectioners' sugar in a food processor, and process for 5 seconds. Scatter the butter over the flour mixture and process until the dough comes together, 20 to 30 seconds.

3. Press the dough gently over the bottom of the prepared pan. Using a pastry brush, glaze the dough all over with the egg white. (Or you can pour the egg white over the dough, and tip the pan from side to side so the white spreads completely over the surface. Pour off the excess.)

4. Bake on the center rack of the oven until golden, about 25 minutes.

5. Meanwhile, prepare the topping: Place the cranberries in a food processor and process for 3 seconds. Set aside.

6. Place the remaining topping ingredients, except the nuts, in a medium-size bowl and stir vigorously with a whisk to blend. Add the cranberries and the nuts, and stir well.

7. Pour the topping over the hot base, and return the pan to the oven. Bake until the topping is set, 40 to 45 minutes.

8. Cool in the pan on a wire rack. Then cut carefully into 2-inch squares, "sawing" with the tip of a long thin knife.

9. If you plan to snack on them, place the bars on a plate or simply leave them in the baking pan, covered, for up to 2 days, or layer the cut bars in an airtight container, with plastic wrap, parchment, or waxed paper between the layers, and place in the refrigerator for up to 4 days or the freezer for up to 2 weeks. If frozen, the fruit may get a little wet in the thawing process, but the bars will still taste delicious.

Makes 16 bars

Dating Bars

❤ ❤ ❤ ❤ ❤ ❤   *crumb pastry bar*

In my younger, sillier years, when Rosie's had just begun, I named this bar. My co-workers and I had a good chuckle, and the name has stuck around all these years. You'll find some version of these bars in nearly every American cookbook—which goes to show, I suppose, that dating never goes out of fashion. Two hearty, crunchy oatmeal layers with a gooey date filling in between.

INGREDIENTS

THE FILLING
1½ cups finely chopped dates
6 tablespoons (lightly packed) light brown
    sugar
¾ cup water
1½ teaspoons pure vanilla extract
½ teaspoon grated lemon zest

THE DOUGH
1½ cups plus 2 tablespoons all-purpose
    flour
5 tablespoons whole wheat flour
1¼ cups quick-cooking oats
½ cup plus 2 tablespoons rolled oats
½ teaspoon baking soda
¼ teaspoon salt
½ cup minus ½ tablespoon (lightly packed)
    light brown sugar
2½ tablespoons granulated sugar
12½ tablespoons (1½ sticks plus ½ table-
    spoon) unsalted butter, melted

1. Preheat the oven to 350°F. Lightly grease an 8-inch square baking pan with butter, or line the bottom with parchment paper.

2. Make the filling: Combine the dates, brown sugar, and water in a small saucepan and bring to a boil over medium heat. Reduce the heat to low and simmer until the mixture has thickened, 5 minutes.

3. Remove the pan from the heat, and stir in the vanilla and lemon zest. Set aside.

4. Make the dough: Combine all the ingredients in a medium-size bowl, and toss to mix.

5. Press half of the dough evenly over the bottom of the prepared baking pan. Spread the date mixture over this, and then sprinkle the remaining dough evenly on top, pressing it down lightly into the dates.

6. Bake on the center rack of the oven until the top is crunchy and golden, about 40 minutes.

7. Cool in the pan on a rack for 30 minutes, and then cut into 2-inch squares with a sharp thin knife.

8. Leave the bars in the pan, at room temperature, covered with plastic wrap, for up to 2 days, or layer the bars in an airtight plastic container with plastic wrap, parchment, or waxed paper between the layers, and store in the refrigerator for 3 to 4 days or in the freezer for up to 2 weeks. Bring the bars to room temperature before eating.

Makes 16 bars

Yummy Cheesecake Bars

❤ ❤ ❤ ❤ ❤ ❤ *crumb pastry bar*

And yummy they are. I've sandwiched two soft crumb layers with a cream cheese and golden raisin mixture. These taste equally good served cold or at room temperature. They will turn a bit soggy after a couple of days in the fridge, but they are absolutely delicious that way too.

INGREDIENTS

THE DOUGH

1½ cups all-purpose flour
6 tablespoons confectioners' sugar
12 tablespoons (1½ sticks) unsalted
    butter at room temperature,
    cut into several pieces
2 tablespoons (lightly packed) light
    brown sugar

THE FILLING

8 ounces cream cheese at room
    temperature
3 tablespoons sour cream
2 tablespoons fresh lemon juice
¼ cup granulated sugar
1 large egg
1 teaspoon pure vanilla extract
1½ teaspoons grated lemon zest
¼ cup golden raisins

1. Preheat the oven to 350°F. Lightly grease an 8-inch square baking pan with butter, or line the bottom with parchment paper.

2. Place the flour and confectioners' sugar in a food processor, and process for 5 seconds.

3. Add the butter and pulse 8 times, until the mixture forms coarse crumbs.

4. Remove 1 cup of the mixture, add the brown sugar to it, and toss it with a fork to incorporate. Set it aside.

5. With floured fingertips, press the remaining dough firmly over the bottom of the pan and 1 inch up the sides of the pan.

6. Bake on the center rack of the oven until lightly golden, 20 minutes. Then remove the pan from the oven, leaving the oven on, and allow the base to cool to room temperature. Wash and dry the food processor bowl and blade for the next step.

7. While the base cools, make the filling: Place all the ingredients except the raisins in the food processor and process until smooth, 15 to 20 seconds. Stir in the raisins by hand.

8. Pour the filling over the cooled base, and top it with the reserved crumb mixture. Return it to the oven and bake until the crumbs are just beginning to turn golden and the bars are set, 45 minutes.

9. Allow to cool in the pan on a wire rack for 1 hour. Then cut into 2-inch squares with a sharp thin knife.

10. When cool, refrigerate the bars in the pan, uncovered, for the first day. At the end of the day, cover them. They will remain fresh in the refrigerator for 2 days. To freeze, layer the bars in an airtight plastic container with plastic wrap, parchment, or waxed paper between the layers. Store in the freezer for up to 2 weeks. Serve cold or at room temperature.

Makes 16 bars

Raspberry Cream Cheese Bars

❤ ❤ ❤ ❤ ❤ ❤ ❤ ❤ ❤ *shortbread bar*

Here raspberry preserves separate a shortbread base from a layer of cheesecake, which is topped with glazed fresh raspberries. When you cut these bars, try to slice between the berries so they don't get bruised.

INGREDIENTS

THE BASE
1 cup all-purpose flour
¼ teaspoon salt
½ cup minus 1 tablespoon sugar
6 tablespoons (¾ stick) unsalted butter,
   cold, cut into 6 pieces
1 large egg yolk
¼ teaspoon pure vanilla extract
1 tablespoon milk, half-and-half, or
   heavy (whipping) cream
1 large egg white

THE TOPPING
11 ounces cream cheese at room
   temperature
5 tablespoons sugar
1 teaspoon cornstarch
1 whole large egg
1 large egg yolk
¼ teaspoon grated lemon zest
¾ cup sour cream

TO FINISH
¾ cup raspberry preserves
1 pint fresh raspberries
⅓ cup red currant jelly

1. Preheat the oven to 350°F. Lightly grease an 8-inch square baking pan with butter, or line the bottom with parchment paper.

2. Place the flour, salt, and sugar in a food processor and process for 5 seconds. Scatter the butter over the flour and process until the mixture resembles coarse meal, 20 seconds.

3. Stir the egg yolk, vanilla, and milk together in a small cup. With the machine running, pour this mixture through the feed tube and process just until it is mixed in and the dough is starting to come together, 1 minute.

4. Press the dough gently over the bottom of the prepared pan. Using a pastry brush, glaze the dough all over with the egg white. (Or you can pour the egg white over the dough, tilt the pan so the white covers the dough completely, and pour off the excess.) Bake on the center rack of the oven until golden, about 30 minutes. Set the pan on a wire rack to cool slightly. Leave the oven on.

5. Meanwhile, prepare the topping: Place the cream cheese, sugar, cornstarch, egg and yolk, lemon zest, and sour cream in a food processor and process just until blended, 15 seconds. Stop the processor once during the process to scrape the bowl.

6. Using a frosting spatula, spread the raspberry preserves over the base. Then pour the cream cheese topping over the preserves and spread it gently.

7. Bake on the center rack of the oven until set, about 1 hour. Transfer the pan to the refrigerator and chill for 1 hour.

8. Top the cooled bars with the fresh raspberries, arranging them in rows (see step 11).

9. Heat the jelly in the top of a double boiler placed over simmering water until liquefied. Glaze the berries by brushing the jelly over them with a pastry brush. Chill for at least 1 hour in the refrigerator so the glaze can set.

10. Cut the bars into 2-inch squares with the tip of a sharp thin knife, dipping it in hot water and wiping it dry before each cut.

11. Once you put the raspberries on top of these luscious bars, they can only be stored in the pan or on a plate. No stacking, please. If you want to make the bars a couple of days before serving, don't dress them with the berries. Complete the bars through step 7. When cooled, cover with plastic wrap and store in the refrigerator until the day they are to be served, then add the berries.

Makes 16 bars

Tropical Macadamia Bars

♥ ♥ ♥ ♥ ♥ ♥ ♥ ♥   *shortbread bar*

H awaii's answer to the dream bar—that traditional shortbread-based bar topped with a gooey coconut mixture that's found in every classic American dessert book. This one is chock-full of toasted macadamias as well as coconut, and it's accented with rum.

INGREDIENTS

THE BASE
1 cup all-purpose flour
½ cup plus 1 tablespoon (lightly packed) light brown sugar
8 tablespoons (1 stick) unsalted butter at room temperature

THE TOPPING
¾ cup plus 2 tablespoons (lightly packed) light brown sugar
¼ cup light corn syrup
1½ teaspoons pure vanilla extract
2 tablespoons rum
3 tablespoons unsalted butter, melted
2 large eggs
3 tablespoons all-purpose flour
½ teaspoon baking powder
¼ teaspoon salt
1 cup macadamia nuts, toasted (page 89) and coarsely chopped
½ cup plus 2 tablespoons shredded coconut

1. Preheat the oven to 350°F. Lightly grease an 8-inch square baking pan with butter, or line the bottom with parchment paper.

2. Place the flour and brown sugar in a food processor and process for 5 seconds. Add the butter and process until the dough comes together, 20 to 30 seconds.

3. Press the dough gently over the bottom of the prepared pan.

4. Bake on the center rack of the oven, until golden around the edges, 20 to 25 minutes.

5. Meanwhile, prepare the topping: Using a whisk, beat the brown sugar, corn syrup, vanilla, rum, melted butter, eggs, flour, baking powder, and salt in a medium-size bowl until blended. Stir in the nuts and coconut with a rubber spatula.

6. Spread the topping evenly over the baked base.

7. Bake on the center rack of the oven until the top is golden and set, about 20 minutes. Allow to cool completely in the pan on a wire rack before cutting into 2-inch squares with a sharp thin knife.

8. Leave the bars in the pan at room temperature, covered with plastic wrap, for up to 2 days, or layer the bars in an airtight plastic container, with plastic wrap, parchment, or waxed paper between the layers, and store in the refrig-erator for up to 1 week or in the freezer for up to 2 weeks. Bring to room temperature before eating.

Makes 16 bars

Caramel Pecan Bars

♥ ♥ ♥ ♥ ♥ ♥ ♥ ♥ ♥ *shortbread bar*

I was always crazy about those little Turtle candies that came in pink-and-white-striped bags, so I decided to capture their spirit in a cookie. A layer of shortbread is topped with a chewy caramel that's packed with pecans, and bittersweet chocolate is drizzled over the whole thing. You'll need a good candy thermometer to determine when the caramel is done, but otherwise the method is straight-forward. They're best if you keep them refrigerated until an hour before eating.

INGREDIENTS

THE BASE
1 cup all-purpose flour
½ cup granulated sugar
8 tablespoons (1 stick) unsalted butter, cold, cut into 8 pieces
1¼ cups pecans, very coarsely chopped

184

THE CARAMEL
¾ cup plus 2 tablespoons heavy
     (whipping) cream
⅔ cup light corn syrup
⅔ cup (lightly packed) light brown sugar
6 tablespoons granulated sugar
5½ tablespoons (⅓ cup) unsalted butter
¼ teaspoon salt
1¼ teaspoons pure vanilla

THE GLAZE
1 ounce bittersweet chocolate
1 teaspoon vegetable oil

1. Preheat the oven to 350°F. Lightly grease an 8-inch square baking pan with butter, or line the bottom with parchment paper.

2. Place the flour and sugar in a food processor, and process for 5 seconds. Scatter the butter over the flour mixture and process until the dough comes together, 20 to 30 seconds.

3. Press the dough gently over the bottom of the prepared pan and bake on the center rack of the oven until golden, 25 to 30 minutes. Place the pan in the refrigerator for 15 minutes to cool completely.

4. Sprinkle the nuts evenly over the base, and set it aside at room temperature while you prepare the caramel.

5. Place the cream, corn syrup, both sugars, butter, and salt in that order in a heavy 2½- to 3-quart saucepan fitted with a tight lid. Cook over medium heat without stirring for exactly 5 minutes.

6. Uncover the saucepan, reduce the heat to medium-low, clip a candy thermometer to the side of the pan (but not touching the bottom), and continue to cook, stirring very frequently, until the thermometer reads 238° to 240°F, about 30 minutes.

7. Remove the pan from the heat and allow the mixture to set for 2 minutes. Then stir in the vanilla.

8. Pour the caramel over the base, and allow it to set for about 3 hours at room temperature.

9. After the caramel has set, prepare the glaze: Melt the chocolate in the top of a double boiler placed over simmering water. Remove it from the heat and vigorously stir in the vegetable oil with a small whisk. Drizzle this mixture over the caramel in whatever pattern strikes your fancy, chill in the refrigerator for no more than 15 minutes, and then set out at room temperature for 1 hour. Cut into 2-inch squares with a sharp thin knife.

10. Store the bars in the pan in the refrigerator, covered with plastic wrap, for up to 1 week. To freeze, cut and remove the bars from the pan, and layer them in an airtight plastic container with plastic wrap, parchment, or waxed paper between the layers, and store for up to 2 weeks. Bring the bars to room temperature before eating.

Makes 16 bars

Pecan Delight Bars

♥ ♥ ♥ ♥ ♥ ♥ ♥ ♥ ♥   *shortbread bar*

A perfect ending to a meal when you crave a bite of something sweet. Not overly rich, this shortbread topped with an ever-so-thin coating of brown sugar suffused with pecans hits the spot.

INGREDIENTS

THE SHORTBREAD
1½ cups all-purpose flour
6 tablespoons sugar
12 tablespoons (1½ sticks) unsalted butter,
*   cold, cut into 12 pieces*
1 large egg white

THE TOPPING
1¼ cups plus 2 tablespoons (lightly packed)
*   light brown sugar*
3 tablespoons all-purpose flour
½ teaspoon salt
2 tablespoons pure maple syrup
3 tablespoons unsalted butter, melted
3 large eggs
1½ cups finely chopped pecans
Confectioners' sugar for sprinkling
*   (optional)*

1. Preheat the oven to 350°F. Lightly grease a 9-inch square baking pan with butter, or line the bottom with parchment paper.

2. Place the flour and sugar in a food processor, and process for 5 seconds. Scatter the butter over the flour mix-

ture and process until the dough comes together, 20 to 30 seconds.

3. Press the dough gently over the bottom of the prepared pan. Using a pastry brush, glaze the dough all over with the egg white. (Or you can pour the egg white over the dough, tilt the pan so the white covers the dough completely, and pour off the excess.)

4. Bake on the center rack of the oven until lightly golden, 35 minutes. Remove from the oven, but leave the oven on.

5. Meanwhile, prepare the topping: Using a hand-held whisk, beat the brown sugar, flour, salt, maple syrup, melted butter, and eggs together in a medium-size bowl until blended. Stir in the chopped pecans. Spread the topping evenly over the baked base.

6. Bake the bars on the center rack of the oven until golden and set, 40 minutes. Allow them to cool in the pan just to room temperature; then cut them into 2¼-inch squares with a sharp thin knife. Using a small strainer, sprinkle confectioners' sugar over the surface if desired.

7. Leave the bars in the pan at room temperature, covered with plastic wrap, for up to 2 days, or layer the bars in an airtight plastic container with plastic wrap, parchment, or waxed paper between the layers, and store in the refrigerator for up to 1 week or in the freezer for up to 2 weeks. Bring to room temperature before eating.

Makes 16 bars

Carrot Cake Cream Cheese Bars

♥ ♥ ♥ ♥ ♥ ♥ ♥ ♥ ♥ ♥   *cake bar*

Okay, it's true: carrot cake is passé. So what's a little passé among friends? Besides, this bar is so light and moist, and the layers of cream cheese so luscious, that I wouldn't be surprised if it ushered in a carrot cake renaissance all by itself.

I N G R E D I E N T S

THE TOPPING
½ cup chopped walnuts
1 teaspoon ground cinnamon
2 tablespoons granulated sugar

THE FILLING
8 ounces cream cheese at room
    temperature
1 large egg
¼ cup granulated sugar
2 tablespoons unsalted butter at room
    temperature
1 tablespoon cornstarch
½ teaspoon pure vanilla extract
1 can (8 ounces) crushed pineapple,
    drained

THE CAKE
⅔ cup puréed cooked carrots (3 or 4
    carrots; see Note)
⅓ cup grated raw carrot
1⅓ cups all-purpose flour
¾ teaspoon baking powder
¼ teaspoon baking soda
¾ teaspoon salt
1¾ teaspoons ground cinnamon
¾ teaspoon ground allspice
5½ tablespoons (⅓ cup) unsalted butter
    at room temperature
⅓ cup vegetable oil
1 cup (lightly packed) light brown sugar
1½ teaspoons pure vanilla extract
2 teaspoons fresh lemon juice
1 tablespoon plus 1 teaspoon fresh
    orange juice
2 large eggs
½ cup raisins

1. Preheat the oven to 350°F. Lightly grease a 13 × 9-inch square baking pan with butter, or line the bottom with parchment paper.

2. Toss all the topping ingredients together in a small bowl, and set aside.

3. Make the filling: Place all the filling ingredients except the crushed pineapple in a food processor and process until smooth, 10 seconds. Stir in the pineapple by hand and set aside.

4. Make the cake: Place the puréed and grated carrots in a small bowl, stir, and set aside. Sift the flour, baking powder, baking soda, salt, cinnamon, and allspice together into a small bowl, and set aside.

5. Using an electric mixer on

medium speed, cream the butter, oil, brown sugar, and vanilla together in a medium-size bowl until well blended, 1 minute. Stop the mixer once during the process to scrape the bowl with a rubber spatula. Add the lemon juice and orange juice, and blend for a couple of seconds.

6. Add the eggs one at a time, mixing on medium speed after each addition until blended, 10 seconds. Scrape the bowl each time.

7. Add the flour mixture and beat on low speed for 5 seconds. Scrape the bowl. Then mix the batter by hand until the dry ingredients are incorporated.

8. Blend in the carrot mixture with several turns of the mixer at low speed. Then add the raisins and blend for several seconds.

9. Spread approximately two thirds of the carrot cake batter in the prepared pan. Then pour the cream cheese mixture gently over the batter, and using a frosting spatula, spread it evenly over the batter.

10. Drop the rest of the cake batter by spoonfuls all over the filling and use a frosting spatula to gently spread the batter. The batter will not thoroughly cover the filling—(it's fine for the cream cheese to show here and there).

11. Sprinkle the topping mixture over the surface, and bake on the center rack of the oven until golden and set, about 35 minutes.

12. Cool in the pan on a rack, and then cut into 3¼ × 2¼-inch bars with a sharp thin knife.

13. If you plan to snack on them the first day, place the bars on a plate or simply leave them in the pan. After that, refrigerate, covered with plastic wrap, overnight, or layer the cut bars in an airtight plastic container with plastic wrap, parchment, or waxed paper between the layers. Store the container in the freezer for up to 2 weeks. Bring the bars to room temperature before eating.

Makes 16 bars

Note: To purée carrots, cut them into 1-inch chunks and steam them until tender, about 10 minutes. Then purée them in a food processor, 10 to 15 seconds.

Poppyseed Coffee Cake Bars

♥ ♥ ♥ ♥ ♥ ♥ ♥ ♥ ♥ ♥ *cake bar*

With these bars, you get two layers of yeasted butter dough surrounding a thick layer of poppyseed filling studded with golden raisins. I originally intended them to be breakfast food, but my friend Wendy Berenson, who tested the recipe, quickly told me that I was selling them short. "Morning, nothing," she announced. "It was 11 P.M. and there I was sitting in bed, the covers up to my chin, while I finished the whole pan!" I'll take her word for it and recommend them as a dessert and mid-afternoon snack too.

INGREDIENTS

THE FILLING
1½ cups canned poppyseed filling
¼ cup golden raisins

THE TOPPING
1 tablespoon (lightly packed) light brown
    sugar
1 tablespoon granulated sugar
2 tablespoon all-purpose flour
½ teaspoon ground cinnamon
1 tablespoon unsalted butter, cold

THE DOUGH
2 teaspoons dry yeast
¼ cup warm water
2 cups plus 2 tablespoons all-purpose
    flour
2 teaspoons granulated sugar
½ teaspoon salt
1 teaspoon grated orange or lemon zest
1 cup (2 sticks) unsalted butter at room
    temperature, cut into 16 pieces
2 large eggs
3½ tablespoons sour cream

THE GLAZE
1½ teaspoons unsalted butter, melted
1½ teaspoons milk
¼ teaspoon pure vanilla extract
6 tablespoons confectioners' sugar

1. Make the filling: Fold the raisins into the poppyseed mixture in a small bowl, and set aside.

2. Make the topping: Place both sugars, the flour, and cinnamon in a small bowl and stir with a whisk. Using your fingers, rub the butter into the dry ingredients until the mixture resembles coarse meal. Place the bowl in the refrigerator.

3. Preheat the oven to 250°F. Lightly grease a 9-inch square baking pan with butter, or line the bottom with parchment paper.

4. Make the dough: Sprinkle the yeast over the warm water in a small bowl. Stir with a spoon, and allow the mixture to sit for several minutes until it appears foamy.

5. Meanwhile, place the flour, sugar, salt, and zest in a food processor and process for 5 seconds.

6. Scatter the butter over the surface of the dry ingredients, and pulse until the mixture resembles coarse meal, 10 seconds.

7. Using a whisk, stir the eggs and sour cream together in a small bowl until blended.

8. Stir the yeast mixture into the egg mixture, and pour this over the flour mixture. Pulse 3 times, and scrape the bowl. Then pulse 4 more times, until the dough just comes together.

9. Spread half the dough evenly over the bottom of the prepared pan, using your fingers or a frosting spatula. Then distribute the poppyseed filling in spoonfuls over the surface of the dough, and spread it very gently with a frosting spatula.

10. Place the rest of the dough over the filling, and spread it very gently with a frosting spatula to distribute it evenly.

11. Sprinkle the topping over the dough. Then wet and wring out a clean kitchen towel, and stretch it over the top of the pan (don't allow it to touch the topping). Place the pan in the oven, turn the oven off, and leave the pan

there for 1 hour. Then remove the pan from the oven.

12. Preheat the oven to 350°F.

13. Bake the bars on the center rack until they are golden on top, about 45 minutes. Cool them in the pan on a wire rack for 45 minutes.

14. Stir together all the glaze ingredients, and drizzle the glaze over the cooled bars. Cut them into 2¼-inch squares using a sharp thin knife.

15. Leave the bars in the pan, at room temperature, covered with plastic wrap, for up to 2 days, or layer the cut bars in an airtight plastic container with plastic wrap, parchment, or waxed paper between the layers, and store in the refrigerator for 3 to 4 days or in the freezer for up to 2 weeks. Bring the bars to room temperature before eating.

Makes 16 bars

190

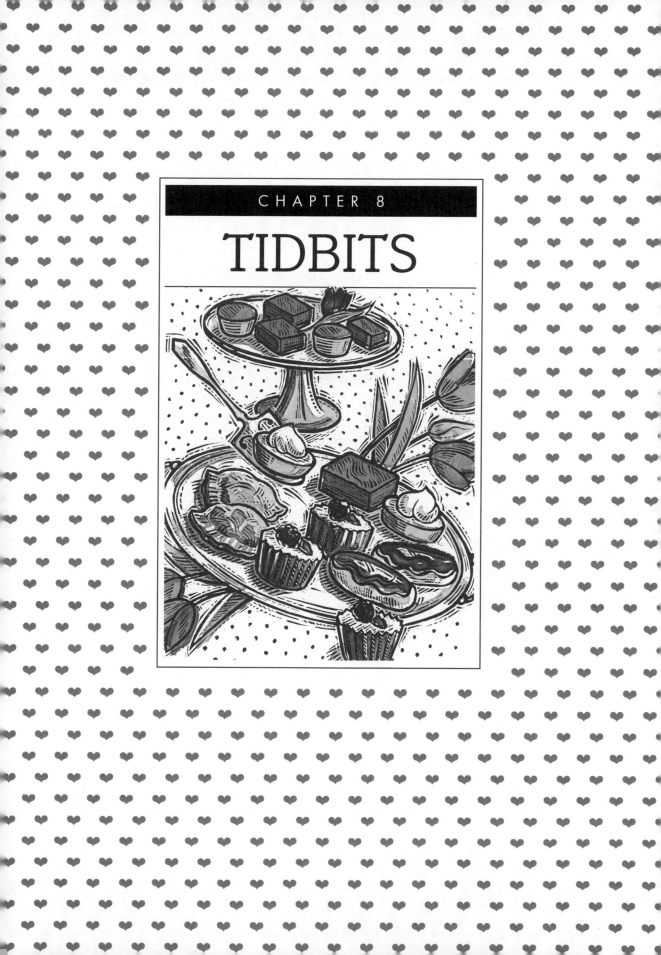

CHAPTER 8

TIDBITS

Whenever I go out to dinner, I can never decide which dessert to order. I am forever tempted by chocolate, yet who can pass up a fruit tart or creamy cheesecake? The only solution for me is to make sure to dine with as many friends as possible. Then, when choosing, I try to convince everyone to order something different  and to share bites. From my dessert indecision, was born the idea of tidbits.

Almost any cake, pie, tart, muffin, turnover, or strudel can be made in miniature form. Somehow, these mini pleasures seem less sinful and more inviting than their full-size counterparts, and a platter of them makes a dazzling end to a special occasion dinner. Serve Rosy Cranberry Tartlets and Apple Galettes for a sophisticated but homey winter's eve dinner party, and mini cakes, such as Maya's Little Butter Cupcakes and Coconut Fluff Babycakes for school birthday parties. Mini Eclairs and Lemon Curd Tartlets make an elegant presentation served with Champagne at an anniversary party. Apple Turnovers and Rosie's Blueberry Muffins are luscious for afternoon tea or even a brunch or breakfast. For a dessert party extravaganza, you can serve them all!

Although it's always best to make tidbits on the day you plan to serve them, if you are making more than one or two kinds, you'll probably want to spread the baking out over a period of time. Most tidbits freeze well and can be made in advance. Tidbits that require frosting or glazing, such as Chocolate Babycakes or Almond Raspberry Gems, should be frozen unfrosted or unglazed; do that step on the day of serving. Flaky pastries containing fruit (for example, Apple Turnovers, Apple Galettes, and Rosy Cranberry Tartlets) can be reheated in the oven before serving in order to restore their crispness.

I find these mini dessert favorites so inviting, I keep a stock in the freezer. Then, when the mood to nibble strikes, I'm ready. Once you try them, I bet you'll want a freezer full, too.

Apple Turnovers

❤ ❤ ❤ ❤ ❤ ❤ ❤ ❤ ❤ ❤ ❤ ❤ ❤ ❤

A miniature version of the old standard: rich, flaky pastry filled to bursting with a simple apple mixture. Make sure that you bake these until they're golden so the pastry reaches the right texture.

INGREDIENTS

THE DOUGH
2 cups minus 1 tablespoon all-purpose
    flour
1 tablespoon sugar
¼ teaspoon salt
12 tablespoons (1½ sticks) unsalted butter,
    cold, cut into 12 pieces
4 ounces cream cheese, cold, cut into 8
    pieces
1 large egg yolk, beaten
3 tablespoons fresh orange juice, cold

THE FILLING
4 cups finely diced peeled apples
    (from 2 or 3 large apples)
5 tablespoons sugar

THE GLAZE
1 tablespoon sugar

1. Place the flour, sugar, and salt in a food processor and process to blend, 5 seconds.

2. Scatter the butter and cream cheese over the flour mixture and pulse until the mixture is the size of small peas, 15 to 20 pulses.

3. Beat the egg yolk and orange juice together in a small cup. Pour this in a stream through the feed tube while pulsing quickly 20 to 25 times, until the dough forms large clumps.

4. Place the dough on a work surface and knead it for several seconds. Then divide the dough in half and form it into two disks. Wrap each in plastic wrap and refrigerate them for 20 minutes.

5. Toss the apples with the sugar. Set aside.

6. Remove one of the disks from the refrigerator and roll it out between two pieces of plastic wrap to form a round 12 inches in diameter. Slide the dough, still sandwiched in the plastic wrap, onto a plate and refrigerate it. Repeat this procedure with the second disk.

7. Preheat the oven to 400°F. Line several baking sheets with parchment paper, or grease them lightly with vegetable oil.

8. Remove one portion of dough from the refrigerator and slide it onto a work surface. Peel off the top piece of plastic wrap. Using a 3-inch round cookie cutter, cut out as many rounds as possible (10 to 12). Gather up the dough scraps and reroll them to make as many more rounds as possible.

9. Place a scant teaspoon of apple filling in the center of each round.

Then fold the dough in half to cover the filling, and using the tines of a fork that have been dipped in flour, press the edges to seal them. Poke the top of each turnover with the tines of the fork to create a vent.

10. Repeat steps 8 and 9 with the second portion of dough.

11. Place the turnovers 1 inch apart on the prepared baking sheets. Using a pastry brush, brush each one with water and sprinkle ⅛ teaspoon sugar over the top.

12. Bake the turnovers for 8 minutes. Then rotate the pan and bake until they are a rich golden color, an additional 8 to 10 minutes. Allow the turnovers to cool on the sheets.

13. These are best eaten on day one, when their texture is crispiest. If you have leftovers, place them in an airtight plastic container and refrigerate them for a day or two. To serve, recrisp them in a preheated 400°F oven for 8 to 10 minutes. For longer-term storage, freeze them; recrisp frozen turnovers at 400°F for 10 to 15 minutes.

Makes about 24 turnovers

Apple Galettes

❤ ❤ ❤ ❤ ❤ ❤ ❤ ❤ ❤ ❤ ❤ ❤ ❤ ❤ ❤

Whenever I visit a new place, I seek out the best bakery in town. When my friend Allen Helschein introduced me to the Downtown Bakery and Creamery in the charming town of Healdsburg, in California's wine country, I went wild. After tasting widely, I decided that my favorite was the Apple Galette, a kind of fruit tartlet wrapped in a delicious crust. Kathleen Stewart, who owns and operates this bakery, shared the recipe. Make lots of these and freeze them as soon as they've cooled. Heat them up right from the freezer in a preheated 400°F oven and no one will guess they were anything but freshly baked.

I N G R E D I E N T S

THE DOUGH
2 cups all-purpose flour
3 tablespoons sugar
¼ teaspoon salt
1 cup (2 sticks) unsalted butter, very cold,
*   cut into 16 pieces*
¼ cup ice water

THE FILLING
4 cups diced peeled apples (¼-inch dice,
*   from 2 or 3 large apples)*
¼ cup plus 2 teaspoons sugar
4 tablespoons (½ stick) unsalted butter,
*   melted*

1. Place the flour, sugar, and salt in a food processor and process for 10 seconds.

2. Distribute the butter evenly over the flour and pulse 40 times. Use a spatula to toss the dough so the butter is evenly distributed.

3. Pour the ice water in a steady stream through the feed tube while pulsing 20 more times. Use a spatula to toss the dough so the bottom doesn't stick. Then process for 15 seconds longer.

4. Place the dough on a work surface, and work it slightly to bring it together. Then divide it into four portions. Form each portion into a log approximately 1 to 2 inches in diameter. Wrap each log in plastic wrap, and refrigerate them for at least 2 to 3 hours or overnight.

5. When you are ready to make the galettes, preheat the oven to 400°F. Line several baking sheets with parchment paper, or grease them lightly with vegetable oil.

6. Toss the apples, 3 tablespoons plus 1 teaspoon of the sugar, and the melted butter together in a medium-size bowl. Set aside.

7. Remove one log from the refrigerator and cut it into 5 equal slices. Place each slice between two pieces of plastic wrap, and roll it out to form a round measuring 4¼ to 4½ inches in diameter.

8. Remove the dough rounds from the plastic wrap, and place them on a surface that has been lightly sprinkled with sugar.

9. Place a rounded tablespoon of the apple mixture in the center of each piece of dough, leaving a ¾- to 1-inch border around the edge. Fold the edge of the pastry over the outer edge of the apples, pleating it to make it fit. Then, using your thumb and index finger, pinch each pleat together to ensure that they will hold. The center of the apples should not be covered with dough.

10. Sprinkle a scant ¼ teaspoon of the remaining sugar over the edge of the pastry. Then place the galettes on the prepared baking sheets, leaving 1 inch between them. Repeat with the rest of the pastry and apples. When you have filled up a sheet, place the sheet in the freezer. Let the galettes freeze for 5 minutes before placing them in the oven.

11. Bake the galettes until they are crisp and golden, 30 to 35 minutes. Allow them to cool on the sheets.

12. These are best eaten the day they are made, when their texture is crispiest. If you have leftovers, place them in an airtight plastic container and refrigerate them for a day or two. To serve, recrisp them in a preheated 400°F oven for 8 to 10 minutes. For longer-term storage, freeze them; recrisp frozen galettes at 400°F for 10 to 15 minutes.

Makes 20 galettes

Almond Raspberry Gems

♥ ♥ ♥ ♥ ♥ ♥ ♥ ♥ ♥ ♥ ♥ ♥ ♥ ♥

The dazzle of these moist mini cupcakes earned them their name. They're made with lots of almond paste, filled with raspberry preserves, and crowned with an almond-flavored confectioners' sugar glaze. If you want to really gild the lily, garnish them with almond halves and raspberries.

INGREDIENTS

THE CAKE
¾ cup all-purpose flour
½ teaspoon baking powder
⅛ teaspoon salt
1 package (7 ounces) almond paste
    (not marzipan), cut into 8 pieces
1 cup minus 2 tablespoons sugar
1½ teaspoons grated lemon zest
12 tablespoons (1½ sticks) unsalted butter
    at room temperature, cut into
    12 pieces
½ teaspoon pure vanilla extract
½ teaspoon pure almond extract
4 large eggs at room temperature
Approximately 2 tablespoons raspberry
    preserves

THE GLAZE
¾ cup confectioners' sugar
2 teaspoons pure almond extract
3 tablespoons hot or boiling water

THE GARNISH (OPTIONAL)
18 almond halves
18 fresh raspberries

1. Preheat the oven to 350°F. Line 36 mini muffin cups with paper liners and set them aside.

2. Sift the flour, baking powder, and salt together into a small bowl and set aside.

3. Place the almond paste in a food processor, add ½ cup of the sugar, and process until the mixture looks like coarse sand, 25 seconds.

4. Add the lemon zest and pulse 5 times.

5. Scatter the butter pieces over the almond mixture and process until creamy, 40 seconds. Scrape the bowl with a rubber spatula. Then add the vanilla and almond extracts and process for 10 seconds.

6. Using an electric mixer on high speed, beat the eggs with the remaining 6 tablespoons sugar in a medium-size bowl until thick and pale, 5 to 6 minutes.

7. Sift the flour mixture over the almond paste mixture. Then pour in the egg mixture and pulse 25 quick pulses. Scrape the bowl, and then pulse 5 more times to blend. Do not overmix.

8. Place a slightly rounded teaspoon of batter in each cupcake liner. Center ⅛ teaspoon of raspberry preserves over this batter, and cover that with another slightly rounded teaspoon of batter. (The batter should reach to about ⅛ inch below the top of the cupcake liner.)

9. Bake until the cupcakes have risen and are set, 20 to 25 minutes. Let them cool in the pans.

10. Meanwhile, prepare the glaze: Place the confectioners' sugar, almond extract, and hot water in a small bowl and whisk vigorously until smooth.

11. Dip the tops of 18 cupcakes into the glaze and stand an almond half, if using, pointed end up, in the center of the top.

12. For the remaining cupcakes, use a fork or spoon to drizzle the glaze back and forth over the top. Top each of these with a fresh raspberry, if using. Allow the glaze to set for 2 to 3 hours.

13. Store the cupcakes at room temperature if you plan to eat them on the first or second day (cover them with plastic wrap if you're holding them over for day two). Otherwise refrigerate them (without the garnish) in an airtight plastic container with plastic wrap, parchment, or waxed paper between the layers, for up to 4 days. For longer storage, they can be frozen for up to 3 weeks.

Makes 36 cupcakes

Black-bottoms

❤ ❤ ❤ ❤ ❤ ❤ ❤ ❤ ❤ ❤ ❤ ❤ ❤ ❤ ❤

The first time I heard about Black-bottoms, I was won over by the idea of a cupcake made of chocolate cake, cream cheese filling, and chocolate chips. Too bad that it tasted mediocre. Not so with this recipe, because its cake is moist and deeply chocolate. Blackbottoms are delicious when cooled just to room temperature and the chips are still soft enough to burst in your mouth.

INGREDIENTS

THE FILLING
*8 ounces cream cheese at room
    temperature, cut into 8 pieces*
¼ cup sugar
⅛ teaspoon salt
1 large egg
1 tablespoon all-purpose flour
6 ounces (1 cup) semisweet chocolate chips

THE CAKE
½ cup warm water
½ teaspoon white distilled vinegar
¾ cup all-purpose flour
*3 tablespoons dark unsweetened cocoa
    powder*
¼ teaspoon plus ⅛ teaspoon baking soda
⅛ teaspoon salt
*4½ tablespoons unsalted butter at room
    temperature*
½ cup plus 1 tablespoon sugar
½ teaspoon pure vanilla extract

1. Preheat the oven to 350°F. Line 24 mini muffin cups with paper liners.

2. Make the filling: Place all the filling ingredients except the chocolate chips in a food processor and process until completely smooth and blended, 30 seconds. Stop the processor once during the mixing to scrape the bowl with a rubber spatula.

3. Add the chips and blend by hand with a rubber spatula or wooden spoon. Set aside.

4. Make the cake: Stir the warm water and the vinegar together in a cup and set aside.

5. Sift the flour, cocoa powder, baking soda, and salt together into a small bowl and set aside.

6. Using an electric mixer on medium speed, cream the butter, sugar, and vanilla together in a medium-size bowl until light and fluffy, 1 minute. Scrape the bowl with a rubber spatula.

7. Add half the flour mixture and mix on medium speed until blended, 25 seconds, stopping the mixer once to scrape the bowl. Then scrape the bowl at the end.

8. With the mixer on low speed, add the water mixture in a stream and mix just until blended, 20 seconds, stopping the mixer once to scrape the bowl.

9. Add the remaining flour mixture and mix on low speed just until blended, 20 seconds. Stop the mixer once during the process to scrape the bowl.

10. Drop slightly rounded teaspoons of the batter into the paper cups. Then top them with rounded teaspoons of the cream cheese mixture (the cream cheese mixture should be mounded, not level).

11. Bake the blackbottoms until the tops are set and a tester inserted in the center comes out dry, 22 to 25 minutes. Cool in the pans before serving. Leave the blackbottoms at room temperature if you plan to eat them on the first day. After that, they can be stored in an airtight plastic container in the refrigerator for a day or two (with plastic wrap, parchment, or waxed paper between the layers), or you can freeze them for up to 2 weeks. Bring the blackbottoms to room temperature before serving.

Makes 24 cupcakes

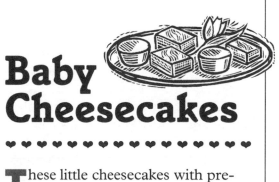

Baby Cheesecakes

❤ ❤ ❤ ❤ ❤ ❤ ❤ ❤ ❤ ❤ ❤ ❤ ❤ ❤

These little cheesecakes with pre-baked graham cracker crusts are made on top of the stove, then put in the refrigerator to set—which means they are a lot easier and quicker to make than the full-grown version. When you trim them with a mélange of berries, they look as stunning as they taste: the perfect ending to a dinner party.

INGREDIENTS

THE CRUST
1 cup minus 2 tablespoons graham cracker crumbs
2 tablespoons sugar
4 tablespoons (½ stick) unsalted butter, melted

THE FILLING
8 ounces cream cheese at room temperature
¼ cup sugar
2 tablespoons sour cream
½ teaspoon pure vanilla extract
2 teaspoons fresh lemon juice
6 tablespoons milk
1 teaspoon unflavored gelatin powder
1 large egg yolk

THE GARNISH
24 fresh berries (strawberries, raspberries, blueberries, blackberries, or a combination)

1. Preheat the oven to 375°F. Line 24 mini muffin cups with paper liners.

2. Place the graham cracker crumbs, sugar, and melted butter in a small bowl and toss together with a fork. The crumbs should be moistened with the butter.

3. Spoon 1 teaspoon of this mixture into each paper liner and press it down with a finger (the mixture will naturally come a bit up the sides when you do this).

4. Place the muffin tins on the center rack of the oven and bake until the shells are crisp and golden, about 8 minutes. Remove from the oven and refrigerate.

5. Prepare the filling: Place the cream cheese, sugar, sour cream, vanilla, and lemon juice in a food processor and process until smooth, 10 seconds. Scrape the sides of the bowl with a rubber spatula.

6. Place the milk in a small saucepan, sprinkle the gelatin over it, and allow it to soften for 3 to 4 minutes, then stir with a whisk. Heat this mixture over medium heat, stirring constantly with a whisk, until it begins to boil, after about 2 minutes.

7. Add the egg yolk, break it with the whisk, and bring to a boil again, continuing to stir constantly.

8. Remove the mixture from the heat and pour it through a small strainer into the cream cheese mixture. Process for 5 seconds to blend.

9. Scoop a generous tablespoon of the cream cheese mixture into each crust-lined cup, and refrigerate until set, about 4 hours.

10. Remove the cheesecakes from the muffin tins, garnish each with a fresh berry, and serve (see step 11).

11. If not serving immediately, refrigerate the cheesecakes (without garnish) in an airtight plastic container with plastic wrap, parchment, or waxed paper between the layers for up to 2 days. For longer storage, they can be frozen for up to 2 weeks. Bring them to room temperature before garnishing and serving.

Makes 24 mini cheesecakes

Maya's Little Butter Cupcakes

♥ ♥ ♥ ♥ ♥ ♥ ♥ ♥ ♥ ♥ ♥

I named these for my daughter because they're as petite, adorable, and perfect as she is.

INGREDIENTS

THE CAKE
1 cup plus 3 tablespoons cake flour
¾ teaspoon baking powder
¼ teaspoon baking soda
¼ teaspoon salt
6 tablespoons buttermilk at room temperature
¼ cup milk at room temperature
7 tablespoons unsalted butter at room temperature
¾ cup plus 2 tablespoons sugar
1½ teaspoons pure vanilla extract
1 large egg at room temperature

THE FROSTING
½ cup heavy (whipping) cream
5 ounces bittersweet chocolate, broken into small chunks
6 tablespoons (¾ stick) unsalted butter at room temperature

1. Preheat the oven to 350°F. Line 24 mini muffin cups with paper liners.

2. Sift the flour, baking powder, baking soda, and salt together in a small bowl and set aside.

3. Stir the buttermilk and milk together in a cup and set aside.

4. With an electric mixer on medium speed, cream the butter, sugar, and vanilla together in a medium-size bowl until light and fluffy, 1 to 1½ minutes. Stop the mixer once during the process to scrape the bowl with a rubber spatula. Then scrape the bowl once again after mixing.

5. Add the egg and mix on medium speed until blended, 10 to 15 seconds. Scrape the bowl.

6. Add half the flour mixture and mix on low speed until partially blended, 10 seconds. Scrape the bowl. Then add half the milk mixture in a stream while the mixer is running on low speed, and mix just until the flour is absorbed, 5 to 10 seconds.

7. Add the remaining flour with the mixer on low speed, and blend just until the flour begins to get absorbed. Scrape the bowl. With the mixer on low speed again, add the rest of the milk mixture in a stream. Mix until smooth and velvety, about 10 seconds, stopping the mixer once to scrape the bowl.

8. Spoon rounded tablespoons of the batter into the prepared muffin cups and bake until the little cakes have risen and are set, 22 to 25 minutes.

9. Remove the cupcakes from the oven and allow them to cool in the pans.

10. If you are planning to serve the cupcakes today, prepare the frosting now (otherwise see step 14): Heat the cream in a small saucepan to the boiling point. Remove from the heat, stir in the chocolate, cover, and set aside for 5 minutes.

11. Transfer the chocolate mixture to a small bowl and refrigerate until set, 30 to 40 minutes.

12. Then add the butter to the chocolate mixture and beat until the mixture is light and fluffy, 2 to 3 minutes. Stop the mixer 3 times during the process to scrape the bowl with a rubber spatula.

13. When the cupcakes are cool, use a butter knife or a small spatula to frost the tops (use about 1½ teaspoons per cupcake); or pipe the frosting onto the cupcakes with a pastry bag fitted with a ½-inch tip. Leave the cupcakes at room temperature until serving.

14. If you do not plan to eat the cupcakes the day they are made, do not frost them. Place them on a baking sheet and cover them tightly with plastic wrap; then frost the next day. If you want to bake them further ahead of time, freeze the unfrosted cupcakes in an airtight container with plastic wrap, parchment, or waxed paper between the layers, for up to 2 weeks. Defrost them overnight before frosting and serving, so they'll be soft.

Makes 24 mini cupcakes

Coconut Fluff Babycakes

❤ ❤ ❤ ❤ ❤ ❤ ❤ ❤ ❤ ❤ ❤ ❤ ❤ ❤ ❤ ❤

When I was applying to colleges, I attended a tea for prospective Wellesley students at a stunning townhouse in New York City. I remember the house, I remember being nervous, and I remember what we were served: white cake with white frosting and coconut. I didn't get into Wellesley, but no matter—that kind of cake is still my weakness. I've transformed it here into cupcakes, which I'm sure will raise all SAT scores by at least 100 points.

INGREDIENTS

THE BATTER

1 cup plus 2 tablespoons cake flour

1½ teaspoons baking powder

½ teaspoon salt

2 tablespoons unsalted butter at room
*   temperature*

2 tablespoons plus 1 teaspoon vegetable oil

¾ cup sugar

1½ teaspoons pure vanilla extract

½ cup milk

2 large egg whites

3 to 4 tablespoons fruit preserves

THE FROSTING

2 large egg whites at room temperature

6 tablespoons sugar

3 tablespoons light corn syrup

½ teaspoon pure vanilla extract

⅓ cup shredded coconut

1. Preheat the oven to 350°F. Line 24 mini muffin cups with paper liners.

2. Sift the flour with the baking powder and salt into a small bowl and set aside.

3. With an electric mixer on medium-high speed, cream the butter, oil, ½ cup of the sugar, and the vanilla in a medium-size bowl until light in color, 10 seconds. Stop the mixer once during the process to scrape the bowl with a rubber spatula.

4. Add one third of the flour mixture by stirring it in lightly with the rubber spatula. Then turn the mixer to low speed and blend partially, 5 seconds. Scrape the bowl.

5. Add half of the milk, and blend it in with several broad strokes of the spatula. Then fold in the remaining flour mixture by hand, followed by the remaining milk. Turn the mixer to low speed and blend until the batter is velvety, 5 to 10 seconds.

6. With the electric mixer on medium-high speed (and clean beaters), beat the egg whites in another bowl until frothy, 20 seconds. Gradually add the remaining ¼ cup sugar and continue beating until soft peaks form, 20 to 30 seconds.

7. Using a rubber spatula, gently fold the whites into the batter.

8. Fill each cupcake liner half full with batter. Then place ⅛ teaspoon of the preserves in the center of the batter, and fill the liner with more batter so that it reaches to ⅛ inch below the top of the liner.

9. Bake the cupcakes until they have risen and are set, 15 minutes. Set them aside to cool in the pan for 20 minutes. Then remove them from the pan and set them on wire racks to cool completely, about 40 minutes.

10. When the cupcakes have cooled, prepare the frosting (or see step 14): Place the egg whites, sugar, and corn syrup in the top of a double boiler placed over rapidly boiling water and beat with a hand-held mixer (electric or rotary) until soft peaks form, about 4 minutes.

11. Transfer the mixture to a medium-size bowl. Add the vanilla and beat with an electric mixer (whisk attachment if possible) on medium-high speed until soft peaks form again, about 30 seconds.

12. Scoop 1 tablespoon of the frosting onto each cupcake, and using a small spatula or a butter knife, spread it over the top of the cupcake.

13. Place the coconut in a small bowl, and dip the top of each cupcake lightly into the coconut. Leave the cupcakes at room temperature until serving.

14. If you do not plan to eat the cupcakes the day they are made, do not frost them. Place them on a baking sheet and cover them tightly with plastic wrap; then frost the next day. If you want to bake them further ahead of time, freeze the unfrosted cupcakes in an airtight container, with plastic wrap, parchment, or waxed paper between the layers, for up to 2 weeks. Defrost them overnight before frosting and serving, so they'll be soft.

Makes 24 cupcakes

Chocolate Babycakes

Because they're practically flourless, these miniature chocolate sensations resemble a soufflé as much as a cookie. Their taste is bittersweet and their appearance lustrous, with a shiny chocolate glaze. I top each with a fresh raspberry in season and arrange them on an antique platter.

INGREDIENTS

THE CAKE
4 ounces unsweetened chocolate
6 tablespoons (¾ stick) unsalted butter
    at room temperature
9 tablespoons sugar
½ teaspoon pure vanilla extract
3 large eggs, separated
2 tablespoons all-purpose flour
6 tablespoons raspberry preserves

THE GLAZE
6 tablespoons heavy (whipping) cream
3 ounces bittersweet chocolate

THE TOPPING
24 fresh raspberries

1. Preheat the oven to 325°F. Grease 24 mini muffin cups with butter.

2. Melt the unsweetened chocolate in the top of a double boiler placed over simmering water. Remove it from the heat and let it cool to room temperature.

3. With an electric mixer on medium-high speed, cream the butter, 5 table-spoons of the sugar, and the vanilla in a medium-size bowl until light and fluffy, 30 seconds. Scrape the bowl with a rubber spatula.

4. Add the egg yolks and beat on medium speed until blended, 30 seconds, stopping the mixer once to scrape the bowl.

5. Add the flour on medium-low speed and blend for 15 seconds, stopping the mixer once to scrape the bowl. Then add the melted chocolate on medium speed and blend for 15 seconds, stopping the mixer once to scrape the bowl.

6. Beat the egg whites in a separate bowl on medium speed until foamy, 20 seconds. Increase the speed to medium-high and gradually add the remaining 4 tablespoons sugar, beating until the whites form firm but not dry peaks, about 45 seconds.

7. Using a rubber spatula, fold one third of the whites into the batter to loosen it. Then gently fold in the remaining whites.

8. Fill each muffin cup two-thirds full with batter. Then place a generous ¼ teaspoon of the preserves in the center of the batter, and spoon enough batter over the preserves to just fill the muffin cup.

9. Bake the babycakes until set, about 15 minutes. Cool them completely in the pan.

10. Meanwhile, prepare the glaze (or see step 12): Heat the cream in a small saucepan to the boiling point. Remove the pan from the heat, add the chocolate, cover, and set aside for 5 minutes. When the chocolate is melted, stir with a whisk until shiny and smooth, about 5 seconds. Transfer the glaze to a small deep bowl.

11. Dip the top of each babycake into the glaze so it is well covered. Place the cakes on wire racks, and garnish the top of each one with a whole raspberry. Allow to set for 3 hours before serving, or place them in the refrigerator for 1½ hours to speed the process.

12. Serve the babycakes that day or store them overnight, uncovered, on a plate in the refrigerator. If you are making them more than 2 days ahead of time, do not frost them; freeze the unfrosted cakes in an airtight plastic container with plastic wrap, parchment, or waxed paper between the layers, for up to 2 weeks. Bring them to room temperature for glazing on serving day or the day before.

Makes about 24 babycakes

M-M-M- Madeleines

So called because they were the exact words uttered by my daughter, Maya, when she tasted these for the first time. I knew she would love them because, like me, she is a lover of basics—in this case a sweet, rich butter flavor accented with vanilla and lemon zest. It's all either of us needs to keep us happy.

INGREDIENTS

6 tablespoons (¾ stick) unsalted butter
½ cup sugar
Pinch of salt
2 large eggs at room temperature
¾ teaspoon pure vanilla extract
1 teaspoon grated lemon zest
½ cup plus 3 tablespoons cake flour,
    sifted

1. Preheat the oven to 375°F. Thoroughly grease 18 madeleine forms with butter, using a paper towel or a piece of plastic wrap to spread the butter into all the little grooves.

2. Melt the 6 tablespoons butter in a small saucepan over medium-low heat. Remove from the heat and allow it to cool to room temperature, 10 to 15 minutes.

3. Meanwhile, using the whisk attachment on an electric mixer, beat the sugar, salt, eggs, vanilla, and lemon zest together in a medium-size bowl until thick and pale, 4 to 5 minutes. Stop the mixer twice during the process to scrape the sides of the bowl with a rubber spatula.

4. Resift half of the flour over the egg mixture, and fold it in gently with the rubber spatula so that it is almost, but not completely, incorporated. Repeat with the remaining flour.

5. Pour the melted butter over the batter in a thin stream, folding it in with gentle strokes.

6. Scoop approximately 2 tablespoons of batter into each madeleine cup, so the batter reaches to about ⅛ inch from the top. Then jiggle the pan slightly to distribute the batter evenly.

7. Place the pans on the center rack of the oven and bake until the cakes are puffed and set, with deep golden edges, 12 to 14 minutes.

8. Cool the madeleines in the pans for 10 minutes. Then use a small spatula or butter knife to gently loosen them, and transfer them to wire racks to cool, flat side down.

9. When the madeleines are cool, place them in an airtight plastic container, layered with plastic wrap, parchment, or waxed paper, and keep them at room temperature for 2 to 3 days. (Their flavor enhances with time.) For longer storage, place the container in the freezer for up to 1 week; bring to room temperature before eating.

Makes 18 madeleines

Rosy Cranberry Tartlets

♥ · ♥ · ♥ · ♥ · ♥ · ♥ · ♥ · ♥ · ♥ · ♥

Tart in shape, tart in taste, these tiny pies hold a cranberry-raisin filling inside a flaky sour cream pastry. Sprinkle them lightly with confectioners' sugar before serving.

INGREDIENTS

THE DOUGH

1⅓ cups all-purpose flour
1½ tablespoons sugar
Scant ½ teaspoon salt
10½ tablespoons (1 stick plus 2½ tablespoons) unsalted butter, cold, cut into 12 pieces
⅓ cup sour cream, cold

THE FILLING

1 tablespoon all-purpose flour
½ cup plus 2 tablespoons sugar
⅛ teaspoon salt
⅓ cup water
1 tablespoon plus 1 teaspoon cornstarch
1½ cups fresh cranberries
½ cup golden or dark raisins
1 teaspoon grated lemon zest
1 tablespoon unsalted butter
2 tablespoons fresh lemon juice

THE TOPPING

1 tablespoon confectioners' sugar

1. Place the flour, sugar, and salt in a food processor and process for 5 seconds.

2. Scatter the butter over the flour mixture, and pulse until the mixture resembles coarse meal, 20 to 30 pulses.

3. Distribute the sour cream evenly over the mixture, and process for 5 seconds. Scrape the bowl with a rubber spatula, then process until the liquid is evenly distributed, 10 seconds. Do not let the dough come together into a ball.

4. Place the dough on a work surface, and divide it in half. Form each half into logs about 1½ inches in diameter. Wrap each log in plastic wrap and refrigerate for 2 to 3 hours or overnight.

5. Make the filling: Combine the flour, sugar, and salt in a medium-size saucepan.

6. In a small cup, stir the water into the cornstarch. Then add this to the flour mixture, stirring it with a whisk.

7. Stir in the cranberries, raisins, and lemon zest. Cook, covered, stirring occasionally, over medium heat until the cranberries start to pop and the liquid is rosy colored and bubbling furiously, 5 minutes.

8. Remove the pan from the heat, and add the butter and lemon juice.

Stir until the butter has melted. Cool the filling in the refrigerator.

9. To make the tarts: Generously grease 24 mini muffin cups with butter. Remove one log of dough from the refrigerator and cut it into 12 equal slices. Place each slice between two pieces of plastic wrap, and roll them out to form rounds about 3¼ inches in diameter.

10. Remove the rounds from the plastic wrap and press them gently into the muffin cups, making sure not to make a hole or tear the dough. Repeat with the second log.

11. Place 1 slightly rounded teaspoon of the filling in each tart. Then fold the excess dough inward to form a ruffly crust around the edges of the cranberry mixture.

12. When all the tartlets have been made, place the pans in the freezer for 10 minutes. Preheat the oven to 425°F.

13. Remove the pans from the freezer and bake on the center rack of the oven until the pastry is a rich golden color, about 35 minutes.

14. Let the pans cool on a wire rack for 10 minutes. Then run a little butter knife around the top edge of each tart, and use the knife to gently lift the tart out of the pan. Cool the tarts completely on the rack. Before serving, sift the confectioners' sugar over the tartlets.

15. These are best eaten on the day they are baked. Otherwise, store them in an airtight plastic container in the refrigerator for a day or two or freeze them for up to 2 weeks. To serve, re-crisp them in a preheated 400°F oven for 8 to 10 minutes, or if frozen, for 10 to 15 minutes.

Makes 24 tartlets

Joyce Miller's Pecan Tartlets

♥ ♥ ♥ ♥ ♥ ♥ ♥ ♥ ♥ ♥ ♥ ♥ ♥ ♥ ♥

My friend Michael Miller swears by his mother's pecan tartlets, and so does his wife, Alisa. So here they are, straight from Joyce's Long Island kitchen—sweet, crunchy, portable perfections designed for pecan pie lovers.

I N G R E D I E N T S

THE DOUGH
1 cup all-purpose flour
2 tablespoons sugar
¼ teaspoon salt
8 tablespoons (1 stick) unsalted butter,
    cold, cut into 8 pieces
3 tablespoons cream cheese, cold

THE FILLING

½ cup (firmly packed) light brown sugar
3 tablespoons dark corn syrup
1 large egg
2 teaspoons pure vanilla extract
⅛ teaspoon salt
2 tablespoons unsalted butter, melted
Generous ¾ cup chopped pecans

1. Place the flour, sugar, and salt in a food processor and process to blend, 5 seconds.

2. Scatter the butter and cream cheese over the flour mixture, and process until the mixture is the size of small peas, 20 pulses. Then process just until the mixture comes together, 15 seconds.

3. Place the dough on a piece of plastic wrap and form it into a mass. Pinch off 24 pieces of dough and roll them into balls with the palms of your hands. Place them on a plate and refrigerate, uncovered, for 30 minutes.

4. Preheat the oven to 375°F. Lightly grease 24 mini muffin cups with butter.

5. Remove the balls from the refrigerator and flatten each one with your fingers. Press them gently into the muffin cups so that the edge of each comes ⅛ inch above the rim. Make sure not to make a hole or tear the dough. Place the pans in the refrigerator or freezer while you prepare the filling.

6. Place the brown sugar, corn syrup, egg, vanilla, salt, and melted butter in a small bowl, and whisk until smooth.

7. Remove the muffin tins from the refrigerator. Place a slightly rounded teaspoon of filling in the bottom of each cup, then spoon a generous teaspoon of nuts over the filling.

8. Bake on the center rack of the oven until the pastry is a rich golden color and the top of the filling has risen and cracked (this will happen before the pastry color is right), 25 to 30 minutes.

9. Cool the tartlets completely in the pan. Run a little butter knife around the top edge of each tart, and use the knife to gently lift the tart out of the pan.

10. These are best eaten on the day they are baked. Otherwise, store them in an airtight plastic container in the refrigerator for up to 1 week or the freezer for up to 2 weeks.

Makes 24 tartlets

Lemon Curd Tartlets

Here's a mouthful of tart lemon curd held in a sweet pastry crust and finished off with a dollop of whipped cream.

INGREDIENTS

THE CRUST
1 cup all-purpose flour
3 tablespoons sugar
⅛ teaspoon salt
6 tablespoons (¾ stick) unsalted butter, very cold, cut into 6 pieces
1 tablespoon cold water
1 large egg yolk

THE CURD
¼ teaspoon unflavored gelatin powder
⅓ cup plus 1 tablespoon fresh lemon juice
4 large egg yolks
½ cup plus 1 tablespoon sugar
1 tablespoon unsalted butter

THE TOPPING
¼ cup heavy (whipping) cream
1 tablespoon confectioners' sugar

1. Place the flour, sugar, and salt in a food processor and process for 20 seconds. (Or whisk them together by hand in a large mixing bowl.)

2. Distribute the butter evenly over the flour, and process until the mixture resembles coarse meal, 15 to 20 seconds. (Or rub the butter into the flour with your fingertips, or cut it in with a pastry blender.)

3. In a small cup, whisk together the cold water and egg yolk. With the processor running, pour the egg mixture in a steady stream through the feed tube and process just until the dough comes together, 20 to 30 seconds. (Or sprinkle the egg mixture over the flour mixture while tossing with a fork.)

4. Place the dough on a lightly floured work surface and knead it several times to bring it together.

5. Shape the dough into a thick disk, wrap it in plastic wrap, and refrigerate it for 2 hours.

6. When you are ready to roll out the dough, generously grease 18 mini muffin cups with vegetable oil.

7. Place the disk between two fresh pieces of plastic wrap and roll it out to form a 12-inch round, a generous ⅛ inch thick.

8. Using a 2½-inch cookie cutter or the rim of a glass that has been dipped in flour, cut out approximately 14 rounds. Gather up the dough scraps and reroll the dough to make an additional 4 rounds.

9. Press each round of dough into a muffin cup so that it rises about ⅛ inch above the rim. Prick the bottom once with the tines of a fork, and place the pans in the freezer for 30 minutes.

10. Meanwhile, preheat the oven to 375°F.

11. Bake the shells until they are a rich golden color with darker golden edges, 18 to 20 minutes. Set them aside while you prepare the curd.

12. Dissolve the gelatin in the lemon juice in a small bowl.

13. Using a whisk, stir the egg yolks

and sugar together in a small bowl until blended.

14. Combine the lemon juice mixture and the egg mixture in a small heavy saucepan and stir with a whisk to blend. Place the pan over medium-low heat, and stirring constantly with the whisk, bring the mixture just to the boiling point.

15. Press the mixture through a strainer into a small bowl, stir in the butter, and let it cool slightly, 15 to 20 minutes.

16. Pour the mixture into the cooled shells, and place the trays in the refrigerator so that the curd can set, about 2 hours.

17. Remove the tartlets from the refrigerator 1 hour before serving. Fifteen minutes before serving, make the topping: Place the cream and the confectioners' sugar in a small bowl, and beat with an electric mixer on medium-high speed until firm peaks form, 1 to 1½ minutes. Garnish each tartlet with a dollop of whipped cream (see step 18).

18. Do not put whipped cream on any tarts that you plan to store. Place these tarts on a plate, cover with plastic wrap, and refrigerate for up to 2 days. For longer storage, place them in an airtight plastic container with plastic wrap, parchment, or waxed paper between the layers and freeze for up to 2 weeks. Defrost the tarts and dollop with whipped cream before serving.

Makes about 18 tartlets

Rosie's Blueberry Muffins

♥ ♥ ♥ ♥ ♥ ♥ ♥

Our full-size blueberry muffins are a favorite at Rosie's. This mini version, chock full of fresh blueberries and accented with lemon zest, are a perfect little snack any time of day and a lovely teatime treat.

INGREDIENTS

THE TOPPING
1 tablespoon all-purpose flour
1 teaspoon quick-cooking oats
1½ teaspoons (lightly packed) light brown sugar
⅛ teaspoon ground cinnamon
2 teaspoons unsalted butter, cold

THE MUFFIN
½ cup plus 2 tablespoons all-purpose flour
½ cup plus 3½ tablespoons cake flour, or another ½ cup plus 2 tablespoons all-purpose flour
1½ teaspoons baking powder
¼ teaspoon salt
4 tablespoons (½ stick) unsalted butter at room temperature
5 tablespoons sugar
1¼ teaspoons pure vanilla extract
¼ teaspoon grated lemon zest
1 large or extra large egg at room temperature
5 tablespoons milk
¾ cup fresh blueberries

1. Make the topping: Place the flour, oats, brown sugar, and cinnamon in a small bowl and stir to mix with a whisk or fork.

2. Place the butter in the bowl, and using a small knife, cut it repeatedly into the dry ingredients until the mixture forms coarse crumbs. Place in the refrigerator while you prepare the muffin batter.

3. Preheat the oven to 375°F. Line 20 mini muffin cups with paper liners or grease them generously with butter or vegetable oil.

4. Sift both flours, the baking powder, and salt together into a medium-size bowl and set aside.

5. Using an electric mixer on medium speed in a medium-size bowl, cream the butter, sugar, vanilla, and lemon zest together until light and fluffy, 45 to 60 seconds.

6. Add the egg and beat for 10 seconds. Scrape the bowl with a rubber spatula. The mixture should be fairly smooth at this point.

7. Add half of the flour mixture and beat on medium-low speed for 10 seconds while adding half the milk in a stream. Scrape the bowl.

8. Repeat step 7 with the remaining flour and milk. Scrape the bowl, then turn the mixer to medium-high speed and beat until smooth, 10 seconds. Scrape the bowl again.

9. Gently fold in the blueberries with the rubber spatula. Then scoop the batter by generously rounded tablespoons into the muffin cups. Pour a little water into each of the unfilled cups in the pan to prevent burning during baking.

10. Sprinkle the topping over the muffins. Place the pans on the middle rack of the oven, and bake until the muffins are firm and lightly golden, about 17 minutes. Cool the muffins in the pan.

11. Leave the muffins at room temperature for the first day. To hold them for the following day, simply cover them with plastic wrap. To store them longer place them in an airtight container in the freezer for up to 2 weeks. Before eating, bring them to room temperature or wrap them in foil and heat them in a 275°F oven for 15 to 20 minutes.

Makes 20 muffins

Mini Eclairs
❤ ❤ ❤ ❤ ❤ ❤ ❤ ❤ ❤ ❤ ❤ ❤ ❤ ❤

Voilà! Here's the solution to the problem of how to eat éclairs so that the filling doesn't spurt out the other end: You make them bite-size and put the whole thing in your mouth at once. These miniatures have all the goodness of full-size éclairs: they're filled with custard and coated with either a bittersweet chocolate glaze or a coffee glaze.

INGREDIENTS

THE CUSTARD
1 whole large egg
1 large egg yolk
⅓ cup sugar
2 tablespoons all-purpose flour
2 tablespoons cornstarch
Pinch of salt
1¼ cups whole milk, scalded
1 tablespoon unsalted butter
½ teaspoon pure vanilla extract

THE ECLAIRS
½ cup plus 1 tablespoon all-purpose flour
½ teaspoon salt
1½ teaspoons sugar
Pinch of baking powder
½ cup water
4 tablespoons (½ stick) unsalted butter
2 large eggs at room temperature

THE CHOCOLATE GLAZE
¼ cup heavy (whipping) cream
1½ teaspoons sugar
1½ teaspoons unsalted butter
*4 ounces bittersweet chocolate, finely
    chopped*

THE COFFEE GLAZE
1¾ cups confectioners' sugar
1½ teaspoons instant coffee powder
2 tablespoons boiling water
1 tablespoon light corn syrup
¼ teaspoon pure vanilla extract

1. Make the custard: Place the whole egg, yolk, sugar, flour, cornstarch, and salt in a blender and blend for 30 seconds.

2. With the motor running, add the scalded milk through the lid hole, and blend for 5 seconds.

3. Pour this mixture into a 1-quart saucepan and bring to a boil over medium heat, stirring constantly. Let boil for 1 minute, continuing to stir.

4. Then, pour the custard mixture into a medium-size bowl, add the butter and vanilla, and stir until the butter has completely melted. Place a piece of plastic wrap directly over the surface of the custard, and refrigerate until it is cold, about 3 hours.

5. When the custard has chilled, make the éclairs: Preheat the oven to 375°F. Line two baking sheets with parchment paper, and fit a pastry bag with a ½-inch tip.

6. Sift the flour, salt, sugar, and baking powder together into a small bowl and set aside.

7. Bring the water to a boil in a medium-size saucepan over medium-high heat. Add the butter and bring to a second rolling boil. Boil for 2 to 3 minutes.

8. Remove the pan from the heat and add the flour mixture, stirring vigorously with a wooden spoon.

9. Return the pan to the stove and cook over medium heat, stirring constantly until the mixture leaves the sides of the pan and forms a ball, 1 to 2 minutes. Cook for 30 to 60 seconds more, until a slight film forms on the bottom of the pan.

10. Let the mixture cool for 1 minute. Then place it in a medium-size bowl, and using an electric mixer on medium speed, beat the dough until the steam stops rising, 1 to 1½ minutes.

11. Add the eggs one at a time, beating until glossy, about 1 minute, after each addition.

12. Transfer the dough to the pastry bag, and pipe 2-inch fingers onto the prepared baking sheets, leaving 1½ inches between éclairs.

13. Bake the éclairs until they are puffed and nicely browned, about 20 minutes. Then open the oven door, pull out the oven rack, and puncture each éclair once to allow the steam to escape (to prevent soggy éclairs). Return the éclairs to the oven for another 3 minutes. Allow them to cool completely on the baking sheets before filling, about 30 minutes.

14. Meanwhile, prepare your choice of glaze: For the chocolate glaze, place the cream, sugar, and butter in a small saucepan and bring to a boil over medium heat, stirring with a wooden spoon, 3 to 4 minutes. Remove from the heat. Add the chocolate, and stir until it has melted and the mixture is smooth and shiny.

15. To make the coffee glaze, sift the confectioners' sugar into a medium-size bowl. Dissolve the coffee powder in the boiling water in a small bowl. Then mix in the corn syrup and vanilla. Pour this mixture into the center of the confec-

tioners' sugar, and whisk vigorously until smooth. If the glaze seems too thick, add an additional teaspoon of hot water until the mixture is a good spreading consistency.

16. Finish the éclairs: Have ready a pastry bag fitted with a ½-inch tip. Spread sheets of parchment or waxed paper on a work surface. Using a sharp serrated knife, cut off the top third of each éclair. Dip these tops in the glaze, and set them aside on the parchment paper to dry.

17. Fill the pastry bag with custard, and pipe a line of custard down the middle of each éclair bottom.

18. Set the dry tops gently on top of the filling. Serve immediately or within several hours for the best results.

Makes 30 éclairs

Note: The glaze should be warm when you dip the éclair tops into it. If it has cooled, place the bowl of glaze in a larger bowl of hot water, and stir to loosen it.

CHAPTER 9

HOLIDAY
COOKIES

Of course I'm partial to holiday baking. After all, were it not for those heart-shaped Valentine's Day sugar cookies so long ago, Rosie's might never have existed. Any holiday is an excuse for me to bake—although *my* personal baking doesn't usually begin until the night before the big day, after I'm freed from a week of hustle and bustle at the bakery.

For many people, holidays are the most fun time of the year for pulling out the baking sheets. It's an important part of the family ritual and joins us all together—moms, dads, sisters, brothers, cousins, aunts, uncles, grandparents—in joyous anticipation of the upcoming day.

There is no cookie that cannot be baked for any holiday (other than Passover, when flour is not permitted), but certain cookies have come to symbolize particular holidays. What is Christmas without gingerbread people,

Valentine's Day without sugar cookies, Purim without hamantaschen? We favor the shapes and flavors that we remember from our childhood, so it is always important to include those in our holiday fare.

Cookies can be wonderful gifts, expressions of our love. What a heartwarming feeling it is when a friend bestows on you a Christmas tin filled with cookies they have made or when a Purim basket filled with fruits and nuts and hamantaschen is left on your doorstep. Have you not cherished a sugar cookie heart given to you by your sweetheart?

So open up your cupboard around holiday time, don your favorite apron, get out your mixing bowls, and pass the spirit of holiday joy on to friends and family.

Molasses Ginger Cookies

❤ ❤ ❤ ❤ ❤ ❤ ❤ ❤ ❤ *drop cookie*

Divinely chewy in the center, crunchy around the edges, dark and gingery with a strong molasses flavor, these are a perfect cookie for the night before Christmas. Just be sure to leave some out for Santa.

INGREDIENTS

2 cups all-purpose flour
1 teaspoon baking soda
1 tablespoon ground ginger
2½ teaspoons ground cinnamon
¾ teaspoon ground nutmeg
¾ teaspoon ground cloves
½ teaspoon ground allspice
¾ teaspoon salt
12 tablespoons (1½ sticks) unsalted butter
*   at room temperature*
1 cup granulated sugar
¼ cup (lightly packed) dark brown sugar
¼ cup dark molasses
1 large egg

1. Preheat the oven to 375°F. Line several baking sheets with parchment paper, or grease them lightly with vegetable oil.

2. Sift the flour, baking soda, all of the spices, and salt together into a small bowl and set aside.

3. Using an electric mixer on medium speed, cream the butter and both sugars together until light and fluffy, 1 minute. Scrape the bowl with a rubber spatula.

4. Add the molasses and mix until blended, 10 seconds. Scrape the bowl. Then add the egg and mix until it is incorporated, 10 seconds.

5. Add the flour mixture and blend on low speed for 15 seconds. Stop the mixer to scrape the bowl, and then blend until the dough is smooth, about 5 seconds more.

6. Drop the dough by heaping tablespoons 2 inches apart onto the prepared baking sheets. Bake the cookies until they are still slightly soft, 15 to 16 minutes. Let them cool completely on the baking sheets.

7. If you plan to snack on them the first day, leave the cookies out on the baking sheet or on a plate. After that, place them in an airtight plastic container with plastic wrap, parchment, or waxed paper between the layers, and store them in the freezer for up to 2 weeks. Bring the cookies to room temperature before eating.

Makes about 16 cookies

Jan Hagels

❤ ❤ ❤ ❤ ❤ ❤ ❤ ❤ ❤ *rolled cookie*

Taste is one of the most evocative senses, and these cookies are among the most evocative I know. They conjure up visions of a wintry Christmas Eve—thin, buttery, and loaded with spices—perfect for snuggling in front of a fire with a mug of hot cider and a plate of these delicacies (and maybe a person to snuggle with, so long as he doesn't eat too many of your cookies).

INGREDIENTS

THE COOKIE
2¼ cups plus 3 tablespoons all-purpose
    flour
¾ teaspoon salt
2¼ teaspoons ground cinnamon
¾ teaspoon ground cloves
1 cup (2 sticks) plus 2 tablespoons unsalted
    butter at room temperature
½ cup plus 1 tablespoon (lightly packed)
    light brown sugar
½ cup plus 1 tablespoon granulated sugar

THE GLAZE
1 large egg white
½ cup slivered almonds, coarsely chopped

1. Sift the flour, salt, and both of the spices together into a bowl and set aside.

2. Using an electric mixer on medium speed, cream the butter and both sugars together in a medium-size bowl until light and fluffy, about 1 minute. Scrape the bowl.

3. Add the flour mixture and mix on low speed for 20 seconds. Scrape the bowl. Then turn the mixer to medium speed and beat just until the dough is blended, about 15 seconds.

4. Turn the dough out onto a work surface and knead it with your hands for several seconds so that it comes together just a bit more.

5. Divide the dough in half, form each half into a slab, and wrap them in plastic wrap. Refrigerate for 2 to 3 hours.

6. Fifteen minutes before baking, preheat the oven to 350°F. Line two baking sheets with parchment paper, or grease them lightly with vegetable oil.

7. Remove the dough from the refrigerator and roll each slab out between two fresh pieces of plastic wrap to form a rough rectangle ⅛ inch thick and approximately 15×10 inches.

8. Remove the plastic wrap and transfer each rectangle to a baking sheet. Using a pastry brush, glaze the rectangles with the egg white, and sprinkle the almonds over the glaze.

9. Bake until golden with darkening edges, about 20 minutes. Remove the baking sheets from the oven, and reduce the oven temperature to 325°F. Cut each rectangle, still on the sheets, into 24 pieces (4 lengthwise slices, then 6 crosswise slices), and return them to the oven. Bake until a deeper golden color, about 15 minutes. Let the cookies cool completely on the baking sheets.

10. Store the cookies in an airtight plastic container for a day or two at room temperature if you think you will be snacking on them. After that, store the container in the freezer for up to 2 weeks. Bring the cookies to room temperature before eating.

Makes 48 cookies

Gingerbread People

♥ ♥ ♥ ♥ ♥ ♥ ♥ ♥ ♥   *rolled cookie*

I t's hard to improve on this classic recipe, or on the classic shape of pudgy little people in their three-button uniforms. My kids love them; they are a part of our holiday ritual each winter. Sometimes we poke little holes in them before we bake them, so they can be displayed as ornaments on a Christmas tree. Despite their name, this dough can be used to cut out all kinds of shapes, depending on the time of year or simply the mood you're in!

INGREDIENTS

THE COOKIE
2 tablespoons dark molasses
1 tablespoon water
1 large whole egg
3¼ cups all-purpose flour
1 teaspoon baking soda
½ teaspoon salt
1½ cups (lightly packed) light brown
    sugar
1½ tablespoons grated orange zest
2 teaspoons ground cinnamon
1 tablespoon ground ginger
½ teaspoon ground cloves
¼ teaspoon ground nutmeg
1 cup (2 sticks) unsalted butter, cold,
    cut into 16 pieces

THE DECORATIONS
Currants
Red-hot cinnamon candies

THE ICING
2¾ cups sifted confectioners' sugar,
    plus 2 tablespoons if needed
2 large egg whites at room
    temperature

1. Using a whisk, vigorously stir the molasses, water, and egg together in a small bowl or cup, and set aside.

2. Place the flour, baking soda, salt, brown sugar, orange zest, and all of the spices in a food processor and process for 10 seconds.

3. Distribute the butter over the flour mixture, and process until the dough resembles coarse meal, about 30 seconds.

4. Pour the molasses mixture over the flour mixture, and process just until the dough comes together, about 35 seconds.

5. Remove the dough from the processor, place it on a work surface, and knead it for several seconds.

6. Divide the dough into two slabs, wrap each in plastic wrap, and refrigerate for 1 to 2 hours.

7. When you're ready to bake the cookies, preheat the oven to 350°F. Line several baking sheets with parchment paper.

8. Remove one slab of dough from the refrigerator and place it between two new pieces of plastic wrap. Roll it out ⅛ inch thick.

9. Remove the top piece of plastic wrap, and using a 5-inch cookie cutter, cut out as many "people" as you can. Using a spatula, place the cookies on a prepared baking sheet, leaving about 1 inch between them. Place currants for the eyes and little cinnamon candies for buttons and the mouth, pressing them down slightly into the dough.

10. Repeat with the second slab. Then reroll the scraps and repeat with that dough.

11. Place the cookies in the oven and bake until firm, 12 to 14 minutes. Cool completely on the baking sheet or on wire racks.

12. While the cookies are cooling, prepare the icing: Place a writing tip on a pastry bag. Set the bag in a tall glass, tip side down, and set it aside. Place the confectioners' sugar and the egg whites in a medium-size bowl, and beat with the paddle attachment on low speed for 30 seconds. Then change to medium-high speed and beat until smooth, 3 minutes. The icing should be stiff enough to pipe. If it's not, add up to 2 tablespoons additional confectioners' sugar.

13. Fill the bag with the icing and pipe decorations, as desired, onto the completely cooled cookies. Allow the icing to set for several hours.

14. Although it's hard to imagine that there would be any gingerbread people left over with kids around, leave the cookies out for a day so the glaze is totally hard, then store them at room temperature for 1 week in an airtight plastic container with plastic wrap, parchment, or waxed paper between the layers. If they are not frosted, the gingerbread people can be stored at room temperature for up to 1 week or frozen for up to 2 weeks.

Makes about fifteen 5-inch-tall gingerbread people

Orange Pecan Ginger Florentines

❤ ❤ ❤ ❤ ❤ ❤ ❤ ❤ ❤ *drop cookie*

Most kids loathe florentines. For starters, they're full of nuts, and then, even if you can pick those out, they still have red and yellow things and bumpy little bits. One of the benefits of adulthood is that you can change your mind, which in this case is a distinct advantage because these lacelike caramel crunch cookies, full of almonds, candied ginger, and orange peel, are as divine as the city they're named after and a perfect festive treat at Christmas. Glaze them with chocolate as the recipe suggests, or eat them unadorned. Either way, you'll be a convert.

INGREDIENTS

THE COOKIE
⅓ cup chopped candied orange peel
    (¼-inch pieces)
1 cup plus 1 tablespoon very finely chopped
    almonds
¼ cup whole almonds, sliced in thirds
⅓ cup chopped crystallized ginger
¼ cup all-purpose flour
3 tablespoons unsalted butter
6 tablespoons plus 2 teaspoons sugar
6 tablespoons plus 2 teaspoons heavy
    (whipping) cream
3 scant tablespoons good-quality honey
¼ cup light corn syrup

THE GLAZE
6 or 12 ounces bittersweet or semisweet
    chocolate (see Note)

1. Preheat the oven to 350°F. Line 3 baking sheets with parchment paper (do not grease).

2. Place the candied orange peel, chopped and sliced almonds, and crystallized ginger in a medium-size bowl.

3. Sift the flour over the fruit-nut mixture, and toss to coat. Set aside.

4. Combine the butter, sugar, cream, honey, and corn syrup in a medium-size heavy saucepan and place over low heat. Stirring constantly, bring the mixture to a boil and boil for 1 minute. Remove from the heat.

5. Add the fruit-nut mixture to the butter mixture, and stir with a wooden spoon just to evenly coat.

6. Drop the batter by rounded teaspoons onto the prepared baking sheets, placing only 5 cookies on each sheet.

7. Dip a fork in water, and use it (redipping as needed) to flatten each cookie so it is 2 inches in diameter.

8. Bake the cookies until they are bubbling all over and golden in color, 11 to 13 minutes.

9. Let the cookies cool slightly on the baking sheets, and then remove the paper and transfer to a wire rack. Allow the cookies to cool completely. Then carefully remove the cookies from the paper by hand. Repeat with the remaining batter.

10. Meanwhile, prepare the glaze: Melt the chocolate in the top of a double boiler placed over simmering water. Remove from the heat and allow to cool to spreading consistency.

11. Using a frosting spatula, spread the bottom of each cookie with ¾ teaspoon of the melted chocolate; then make a fancy design by running the tines of a fork over the chocolate in a zigzag pattern.

12. Set the cookies aside, chocolate side up, on wire racks for the glaze to set, about 3 hours; or place them in the refrigerator or freezer for 1 hour to set quickly.

13. It's really best to eat these the day they're made in order to enjoy them at their peak of crispness. If this isn't possible, layer them in an airtight plastic container with plastic wrap, parchment, or waxed paper between the layers. They will keep this way for 2 days at room temperature and for up to 1 week if frozen.

Makes about 25 cookies

Note: If you prefer less chocolate on your cookie, use only 6 ounces and using a spoon, drizzle the chocolate in a crisscross pattern on the bottom of the cookies.

Almond Chocolate Praline Crisps

❤ ❤ ❤ ❤ ❤ ❤ ❤ ❤ ❤ *drop cookie*

This is a cookie that should be served to you in a fancy restaurant as an accent to a gourmet dinner—on New Year's Eve, perhaps—and yet these lacelike toffee wafers, studded with almonds and sandwiched with chocolate, are surprisingly easy to make. Just watch them carefully while they're baking, because they burn easily.

I N G R E D I E N T S

THE COOKIE
8 tablespoons (1 stick) unsalted butter
1¼ cups chopped almonds
½ cup sugar
2 tablespoons all-purpose flour
3 tablespoons milk
¼ teaspoon pure vanilla extract

THE FILLING
4 ounces bittersweet chocolate, melted

1. Preheat the oven to 400°F. Line several baking sheets with parchment paper (do not grease).

2. Melt the butter in a small saucepan over low heat. Then add the almonds, sugar, flour, milk, and vanilla. Bring the mixture to a simmer and remove from the heat. Allow it to sit for 5 to 10 minutes.

3. Drop the batter by teaspoons onto the prepared baking sheets, spacing them about 4 inches apart. Bake until the cookies are deep golden, 7 to 8 minutes (watch carefully—they burn easily).

4. Remove the cookies from the oven and allow them to cool on the sheets for 1 minute. Then transfer the cookies to wire racks to cool.

5. When they are completely cooled, turn half the cookies upside down and spread the bottoms with ½ teaspoon of chocolate each. Top them with the remaining cookies. Refrigerate until the chocolate is set, about 2 hours.

6. It's really best to eat these the day they're made in order to enjoy them at their peak of crispness. If this isn't possible, layer them in an airtight plastic container with plastic wrap, parchment, or waxed paper between the layers. They will keep this way for 2 days at room temperature and for up to 1 week if frozen.

Makes about 18 cookie sandwiches

Pecan Crescents

♥ ♥ ♥ ♥ ♥ ♥ ♥ ♥ *formed cookie*

Crispy. Crunchy. Buttery. These cookies, made with lots of ground pecans, have all the bases covered. They are wonderful choices to pack in holiday tins. And, oh, did I mention that they melt in your mouth?

INGREDIENTS

THE COOKIE
2 cups all-purpose flour
½ teaspoon salt
½ teaspoon ground cinnamon
1 cup (2 sticks) unsalted butter at room temperature
⅓ cup plus 1 tablespoon sugar
1½ teaspoons pure vanilla extract
1½ cups finely ground pecans

THE COATING
½ cup sugar
1 teaspoon ground cinnamon

1. Preheat the oven to 325°F. Line several baking sheets with parchment paper, or grease them lightly with vegetable oil.

2. Sift the flour, salt, and cinnamon together into a small bowl and set aside.

3. Using an electric mixer on medium speed, cream the butter, sugar, and vanilla in a medium-size bowl until the ingredients are light and fluffy, about 4 minutes. Scrape the bowl with a rubber spatula.

4. Add the flour mixture and the pecans, and beat on medium-low speed for 20 seconds. Scrape the bowl. Then beat until the flour and nuts are completely incorporated, about 15 seconds.

5. Break off generously rounded teaspoons of the dough, and roll them between your palms to form crescents.

6. In a small bowl, stir together the sugar and cinnamon for the coating. Dip the cookies in the coating and place them 2 inches apart on the prepared baking sheets.

7. Bake the cookies until they are lightly golden and firm to the touch, 30 minutes. Cool completely on the sheets.

8. Store these cookies in an airtight plastic container at room temperature for up to 3 days. They become even more delicious as the flavors have a chance to meld. Or freeze for up to 2 weeks.

Makes about 48 cookies

Vanilla Kipfel
♥ ♥ ♥ ♥ ♥ ♥ ♥ ♥ ♥ *formed cookie*

When I was a little girl, my mother knew a German dressmaker named Martha, who made the most unbelievable vanilla kipfel—nutty, buttery crescents rolled in vanilla sugar—and presented them to us every Christmas in a decorative tin. I hoped to get the recipe from her, but learned to my regret that she had passed away. So here is my homage to Martha; my attempt to re-create those childhood treats in honor of a fine dressmaker and a fine baker. These make a wonderful gift for the holidays and store beautifully in an airtight tin, the vanilla sugar flavor permeating the cookies more and more each day.

INGREDIENTS

6 tablespoons granulated sugar
2 vanilla beans, each approximately
    9 inches long
1½ cups whole unblanched almonds
1¼ cups all-purpose flour
1 teaspoon salt
12 tablespoons (1½ sticks) unsalted butter,
    cold, cut into 12 pieces
2 large egg yolks, lightly beaten
1½ cups confectioners' sugar or vanilla
    sugar, sifted (see Note)

1. Preheat the oven to 325°F. Line several baking sheets with parchment paper, or grease them lightly with vegetable oil.

2. Place the granulated sugar in a small bowl. Split the vanilla beans open lengthwise. Using the point of a knife, gently scrape the seeds into the bowl of sugar.

3. Place the almonds in a food processor and process till fine, 45 seconds; do not overprocess. Add the sugar mixture, flour, and salt, and process to mix, 5 seconds.

4. Scatter the butter pieces over the flour mixture and process until the dough resembles coarse meal, 15 seconds.

5. With the processor running, pour the yolks through the feed tube. Stop the processor, then pulse 5 times. Scrape the bowl with a rubber spatula, and then process until the dough comes together, 5 to 10 seconds.

6. Pinch off tablespoons of the dough and form each of them into crescents. Place the crescents 1½ inches apart on the prepared baking sheets, and bake until firm and just beginning to turn golden, 30 minutes. (To test for doneness, remove a cookie from the sheet and cut it in half. The center should not be doughy.)

7. Allow the cookies to cool for 5 to 10 minutes on the baking sheets. Then roll them in the confectioners' sugar, and set them on wire racks to cool completely before eating.

8. Store the cookies in an airtight plastic container at room temperature for a day or two if you think you will be snacking on them. After that, store the container in the freezer for up to 2 weeks. Bring the cookies to room temperature before eating.

Makes about 36 cookies

Note: To make vanilla sugar, place a whole vanilla bean in 3 to 4 cups granulated sugar and let it sit for a minimum of 1 week.

Butter Wreaths

❤ ❤ ❤ ❤ ❤ ❤ ❤ ❤ *rolled cookie*

These little wreaths made of crispy puff pastry literally melt in your mouth. Their flaky texture is best the first day, so if you're planning to serve them for Christmas dinner, prepare the dough up to two days ahead and then bake them on the day you'll be eating them.

INGREDIENTS

THE COOKIE
2 cups all-purpose flour
⅛ teaspoon salt
3 tablespoons sugar
8 tablespoons (1 stick) unsalted butter, cold, cut into 8 pieces
⅓ cup ice water

THE GLAZE
1 large egg, beaten with a fork
½ cup sugar in a small bowl

1. Place the flour, salt, and 3 tablespoons sugar in a food processor and process for 5 seconds.

2. Distribute the butter over the flour mixture, and pulse 25 to 30 times, until the mixture resembles coarse crumbs. Scrape the bowl with a rubber spatula.

3. With the machine running, pour the water in a stream through the feed tube. Then pulse quickly several times just to distribute.

4. Place the dough (it will be crumbly) on a work surface, and press it just enough to form a rough 6-inch square. Wrap it in plastic wrap, and refrigerate for 1 hour.

5. Remove the dough from the refrigerator and leave it at room temperature for 20 to 30 minutes, until it becomes workable. Place it between two fresh pieces of plastic wrap, and roll it out to a 12-inch square. Remove the top piece of plastic wrap.

6. Take the right-hand third of the dough and fold it over the middle third: then take that double thickness and fold it over again onto the remaining third so that you have a 4 × 12-inch rectangle that is three folds deep. Rewrap in plastic and refrigerate for about 3 hours.

7. When you are ready to bake the cookies, remove the dough from the refrigerator and leave it at room temperature for 20 to 30 minutes. Preheat the oven to 450°F. Line several baking sheets with parchment paper, or grease them lightly with vegetable oil.

8. Roll the dough out ⅛ inch thick. Using a 2½- or 2¾-inch cookie cutter with a hole in the center, or a doughnut cutter, cut out the cookies. (If you do not have either of these, use a round cookie cutter to make the cookies, and then use a metal bottle cap to cut out the center hole.) Discard the scraps.

9. Place the cookies 1½ inches apart on the prepared baking sheets, and place the hole cutouts on the sheets too. Cover the baking sheets with plastic wrap, and refrigerate for 15 minutes.

10. Remove one baking sheet from the refrigerator, and using a pastry brush, glaze each cookie wreath and hole with some of the beaten egg. Turn the cookies upside down into the bowl of sugar, and place them back on the sheet, sugar side up. Place the sheet on the center rack of the oven and bake until the cookies are a rich golden color, about 12 minutes. Repeat with the remaining cookies.

11. Cool the cookies completely on the baking sheets.

12. Try to eat these the first day; the delicate flaky texture can't sustain itself much longer than that. If need be, place them in an airtight plastic container and leave them at room temperature for a day or two.

Makes about 30 cookies (wreaths and holes)

Classic Spritzes

❤ ❤ ❤ ❤ ❤ ❤ ❤ ❤ ❤ *piped cookie*

Spritzes are great holiday cookies because they can be squeezed into an endless number of festive shapes. You can also sandwich them with chocolate, or sandwich them with jam and then dip half the cookie in melted chocolate. As I worked on this recipe, I discovered that spritzes made with vegetable shortening hold their shape and thickness best, but that spritzes made with butter taste better, even if they spread and flatten out a little more. For the best results, be sure to cream the butter and sugar so the dough is soft enough to squeeze through the press (use whatever decorative tip you like). If you don't have a press, scoop the batter out by the teaspoonful and flatten them slightly before baking.

INGREDIENTS

1 whole large egg
1 large egg yolk
2¼ cups plus 2 tablespoons all-purpose flour
1¼ teaspoons baking powder
¼ teaspoon salt
1 cup (2 sticks) unsalted butter at room temperature
1 cup confectioners' sugar
¼ cup granulated sugar
2 teaspoons pure vanilla extract
1 teaspoon grated lemon zest

1. Preheat the oven to 350°F. Line several baking sheets with parchment paper, or grease them lightly with vegetable oil.

2. Stir the egg and the yolk together in a cup and set aside.

3. Sift the flour, baking powder, and salt together in a small bowl and set aside.

4. Using an electric mixer on medium speed, cream the butter, both sugars, vanilla, and lemon zest together in a medium-size mixing bowl until fluffy, 1 to 1½ minutes. Scrape the bowl with a rubber spatula.

5. Add the flour mixture and continue to mix on medium speed until thoroughly blended, 3 minutes, stopping the mixer once to scrape the bowl.

6. With the mixer on medium-low speed, add the egg mixture and mix until blended, 30 seconds. Stop the mixer once to scrape the bowl.

7. Feed the dough into the cookie press and press the cookies out onto the prepared baking sheets, leaving 1 inch between them.

8. Bake the cookies for 10 minutes. Then lower the oven temperature to 325°F and bake until they are firm and lightly golden around the bottom edge. The baking time will vary depending on their shape, but the range will probably be 16 to 22 minutes. Cool the cookies on the baking sheets.

9. If you plan to snack on them the first day, leave the cookies out on the baking sheet or on a plate. After that, place them in an airtight plastic container and store them in the freezer for up to 2 weeks. Bring the cookies to room temperature before eating.

Makes 60 to 70 cookies

Dutch Almond Butter Rings

❤ ❤ ❤ ❤ ❤ ❤ ❤ ❤ ❤   *piped cookie*

It seems only appropriate that our word "cookie" comes from the Dutch word *koekje,* since the Dutch have given the world some of its most glorious butter delicacies. The recipe for this crisp piped cookie with its brittle caramel center is an adaptation of a recipe from Corrie Wittenberg, owner of the noteworthy Bakery Butter in Zaandam, who generously shared her knowledge with my recipe tester, Beverly Jones, when she last visited the Netherlands.

INGREDIENTS

THE FILLING
3½ tablespoons unsalted butter at room temperature
6 tablespoons confectioners' sugar
3 tablespoons light corn syrup
½ cup slivered or sliced almonds

THE COOKIE
1 cup plus 1 tablespoon sifted all-purpose flour
1 teaspoon salt
7 tablespoons unsalted butter at room temperature
¾ cup plus 2 tablespoons confectioners' sugar, sifted
¼ cup egg whites (about 2 large eggs)
1 teaspoon pure vanilla extract

THE TOPPING
Generous ½ cup crushed sliced almonds

1. Make the filling: Using an electric mixer on medium speed, cream the butter, confectioners' sugar, and corn syrup together in a small bowl until blended. Add the slivered almonds and blend until they are broken up.

2. Preheat the oven to 350°F. Line several baking sheets with parchment paper, and fit a pastry bag with a ¼-inch tip.

3. Make the cookie dough: Sift the flour and salt together into a small bowl and set aside.

4. Using the mixer on medium-high speed, cream the butter, confectioners' sugar, egg whites, and vanilla in a medium-size bowl until smooth, 30 seconds. Stop the mixer twice during the process to scrape the bowl with a rubber spatula.

5. Sift the flour mixture over the butter mixture and mix on low speed just until blended, 5 seconds. Scrape the bowl, then blend for several seconds. Fill the pastry bag with the dough.

6. Pipe the dough onto the prepared baking sheets, forming 1½-inch-diameter circles 1½ inches apart. Drop ½ teaspoon of the almond filling in the center of each circle, and sprinkle each cookie with ½ teaspoon of the crushed almonds.

7. Bake the cookies on the center rack of the oven until the filling is brown and bubbling and the edges of the cookies are golden brown, 12 to 14 minutes.

8. Allow the cookies to cool on the baking sheets. Then carefully remove them with a spatula.

9. Store the cookies in an airtight plastic container at room temperature for a day or two if you think you will be snacking on them. After that, store the container in the freezer for up to 2 weeks. Bring the cookies to room temperature before eating.

Makes about 50 cookies

Mini Fruit Cakes

❤ ❤ ❤ ❤ ❤ ❤ ❤ ❤ ❤ *tidbit cookie*

These miniature cakes are jammed with rum-soaked fruit, then glazed twice with more rum. Add them to Christmas cookie tins or holiday dessert platters and I guarantee that they'll be appreciated more than their full-size counterparts. If you can, soak the fruit for 3 to 5 days, tossing it occasionally, before preparing the fruitcakes.

INGREDIENTS

THE CAKE

10 ounces assorted dried fruit (raisins, cranberries, apricots, dates, etc.), cut into ¼-inch pieces (about 2 cups)
1 cup rum or brandy
½ cup boiling water
1 cup plus 3 tablespoons all-purpose flour
⅜ teaspoon baking soda
⅜ teaspoon ground cinnamon
⅜ teaspoon ground cloves
⅜ teaspoon ground mace
⅜ teaspoon ground allspice
¼ teaspoon salt
10 tablespoons (1¼ sticks) unsalted butter at room temperature
½ cup granulated sugar
½ cup (lightly packed) light brown sugar
½ teaspoon pure vanilla extract
1½ teaspoons grated lemon or orange zest
2 tablespoons molasses
2 large eggs
½ cup chopped pecans (¼-inch pieces)
½ cup chopped almonds (¼-inch pieces)

THE GLAZE

1 tablespoon plus 1 teaspoon granulated sugar

½ cup rum or brandy

THE FROSTING

¾ cup confectioners' sugar

2 tablespoons plus ¾ teaspoon rum or brandy

1. Combine the dried fruits and the rum in a small bowl, cover, and allow to sit for 8 hours, tossing occasionally. Then add the boiling water, toss, and allow to sit for at least 1½ to 2 days, or up to 5 days.

2. Preheat the oven to 350°F. Generously grease 36 mini muffin cups with butter.

3. Sift the flour, baking soda, all of the spices, and salt together into a small bowl and set aside.

4. With an electric mixer on medium speed, beat the butter, both sugars, vanilla, and zest in a medium-size bowl until light and fluffy, about 1 minute. Scrape the bowl with a rubber spatula.

5. Add the molasses and beat on medium speed until incorporated, 10 seconds.

6. Add the eggs one at a time, mixing on low speed after each addition for 10 seconds. Scrape the bowl each time.

7. Drain the fruits and pat them dry.

8. Add the flour mixture to the butter mixture and mix until blended, 10 seconds. Scrape the bowl, then mix 5 seconds more.

9. Add the dried fruits and both nuts, and blend by hand with a rubber spatula.

10. Spoon the batter into the muffin cups so that it is slightly mounded (see Note). Bake the mini-fruitcakes until puffed and set, 25 to 30 minutes.

11. Allow the fruitcakes to cool in the pan for 20 minutes. Then run a small butter knife around the edge of each muffin to loosen it slightly, and gently remove them from the pan. Place the muffins on a rack or plate.

12. Meanwhile, make the glaze: Place the sugar and the rum in a small bowl, and stir to dissolve the sugar.

13. Using a small pastry brush, paint all sides of the mini cakes with the glaze.

14. Make the frosting: Place the confectioners' sugar and rum in a small bowl, and whisk vigorously until creamy.

15. Turn each fruitcake upside down and dip its top in the frosting. Then turn it right side up and allow to set for 1 hour.

16. Leave the fruitcakes on a plate, uncovered, if you plan on snacking on them the first day. To store longer, layer them in an airtight plastic container with plastic wrap, parchment, or waxed paper between the layers and place in the refrigerator for up to 1 week or the freezer for up to 2 weeks.

Makes about 36 fruitcakes

Note: If you do not have enough batter to fill all the cups, pour a little water into each unused cup to prevent burning during baking.

Chocolate Snowballs

❤ ❤ ❤ ❤ ❤ ❤ ❤ ❤ *formed cookie*

A chocolate version of Mexican wedding cakes—those rich little balls of butter, sugar, flour, and pecans rolled in powdered sugar. I've substituted chocolate for the nuts and rolled them in cocoa.

INGREDIENTS

2 cups sifted all-purpose flour
½ cup plus 1 tablespoon granulated sugar
½ cup plus 2 tablespoons unsweetened cocoa powder
1 teaspoon instant coffee powder
14 tablespoons (1¾ sticks) unsalted butter at room temperature, cut into 10 pieces
1 large egg yolk
3 ounces (½ cup) semisweet chocolate chips
5 tablespoons confectioners' sugar

1. Preheat the oven to 350°F. Line several baking sheets with parchment paper, or grease them lightly with vegetable oil.

2. Place the flour, granulated sugar, ¼ cup of the cocoa, and the coffee powder in a food processor and process for 10 seconds.

3. Scatter the butter over the flour mixture and process until the mixture resembles coarse crumbs, 15 seconds.

4. While the machine is running, add the egg yolk through the feed tube. Then pulse 15 times until it is incorporated. Scrape the bowl with a rubber spatula.

5. Add the chips and process 5 seconds more.

6. Measure out rounded teaspoons of the dough, and roll them into balls with your hands. Place them 2 inches apart on the prepared baking sheets.

7. Bake the cookies until they are firm to the touch, about 24 minutes. Allow them to cool on the baking sheets.

8. Meanwhile, sift the remaining ¼ cup plus 2 tablespoons cocoa and the confectioners' sugar together into a small bowl. Then transfer to a plastic bag.

9. Place 2 or 3 cookies at a time in the bag and shake the bag gently to coat them with the mixture.

10. If you plan to snack on them the first day, leave the cookies out on the baking sheet or on a plate. After that, place them in an airtight plastic container with plastic wrap, parchment, or waxed paper between the layers, and store them in the freezer for up to 2 weeks. Bring the cookies to room temperature before eating.

Makes about 60 cookies

Oatmeal Thumbprints

❤ ❤ ❤ ❤ ❤ ❤ ❤ ❤ ❤ *formed cookie*

Prominent among cookie classics are these small butter cookies with their red jam centers—a festive holiday treat for Valentine's Day or Christmas. For this version I've kept that bright dollop of color and taste but added oats to the batter, which makes the cookies just a little bit heartier. Have no fear, though: they have the same melt-in-your-mouth quality as the originals.

INGREDIENTS

1 cup (2 sticks) unsalted butter at room temperature
½ cup plus 2 tablespoons sugar
2 teaspoons pure vanilla extract
1 cup plus 2 tablespoons all-purpose flour
¼ teaspoon salt
1¼ cups quick-cooking oats
½ cup raspberry or apricot jam

1. Preheat the oven to 350°F, and line several baking sheets with parchment paper.

2. Using an electric mixer on medium-high speed, cream the butter, sugar, and vanilla together in a medium-size bowl until light and fluffy, about 2 minutes. Stop the mixer twice during the process to scrape the bowl with a rubber spatula.

3. Add the flour and salt, and mix on low speed for several seconds. Scrape the bowl. Then turn the mixer to high speed and beat until the batter is light and fluffy, about 1 minute. Add the oats and beat on low speed for 20 seconds, stopping the mixer once to scrape the bowl.

4. Measure out rounded teaspoons of dough, and roll them into balls with your hands.

5. Place the balls about 1½ inches apart on the prepared baking sheets. Then make a firm indentation in the center of each cookie with your thumb or index finger.

6. Bake the cookies until lightly golden, 20 minutes. Remove the baking sheets from the oven, place ½ teaspoon of the jam in the center of each cookie, and return the sheets to the oven.

7. Bake the cookies just until the jam melts and spreads slightly, about 10 minutes. Allow the cookies to cool on the sheets.

8. If you will be snacking on them, store the cookies in an airtight plastic container at room temperature for a day or two. After that, store the container in the freezer for up to 2 weeks. Bring the cookies to room temperature before eating.

Makes about 50 cookies

Classic Sugar Cookies

❤ ❤ ❤ ❤ ❤ ❤ ❤ ❤ *rolled cookie*

Let's hear it for the plain old sugar cookie. It has a special place in my heart and on my palate, partly because it tastes great, partly because it played a big part in Rosie's history, and partly because it's so versatile. Sugar cookies are what got me into the baking biz to begin with, and sugar cookies are what keep me creative. You can adorn them with colored sugars and frosting, send them as Valentines with endearing messages written on top,

throw a decorating party for the kids on your block, deliver them as gifts in satin-lined boxes, or use them as Christmas tree ornaments by forming small holes in them before baking. The sky's the limit!

INGREDIENTS

THE COOKIE

2¼ cups all-purpose flour

½ cup granulated sugar

½ cup confectioners' sugar

⅛ teaspoon baking soda

⅛ teaspoon cream of tartar

½ teaspoon salt

12½ tablespoons (1½ sticks plus ½ table- spoon) unsalted butter, cold, cut into 12 pieces

1 large egg

1 tablespoon pure vanilla extract

THE GLAZE

1 cup minus 2 tablespoons confectioners' sugar

¼ cup heavy (whipping) cream

Food coloring (optional)

THE DECORATIONS

Colored sugars

Sugar confetti

Tiny candies

1. Place the flour, both sugars, the baking soda, cream of tartar, and salt in a food processor and process for 5 seconds.

2. Distribute the butter over the flour mixture, and process until the dough resembles coarse meal, about 30 seconds. Scrape the bowl with a rubber spatula once during the process to make certain the butter is evenly distributed.

3. Stir the egg and vanilla together in a cup. With the processor running, pour this mixture through the feed tube and process until the dough comes together, about 35 seconds.

4. Remove the dough from the processor, place it on a work surface, and knead it for several seconds.

5. Divide the dough into two slabs, wrap each in plastic wrap, and refrigerate for 1 to 2 hours.

6. When you're ready to bake the cookies, preheat the oven to 375°F. Line several baking sheets with parchment paper.

7. Remove one slab of dough from the refrigerator and place it between two fresh pieces of plastic wrap. Roll it out ⅛ inch thick.

8. Remove the top piece of plastic wrap, and using the cookie cutter of your choice, cut out as many cookies as you can. Using a spatula, place the cookies on a prepared baking sheet, leaving about 1 inch between cookies. Gather up the scraps and refrigerate them for rerolling. Repeat with the second slab: then reroll and cut out the scraps.

9. Bake the cookies until firm with lightly golden edges, 15 to 20 minutes depending on their size. Cool them on the sheets.

10. Meanwhile make the glaze: Place the confectioners' sugar and the cream in a medium-size bowl and whisk vigorously until smooth and creamy. If you are using food coloring, divide the glaze among as many bowls as you have colors, and whisk in a drop at a time to get the desired color.

11. With the cookies still on the baking sheets, use a spoon to drizzle the glaze, or a small butter knife or paintbrush to spread it on the cookies. Then sprinkle colored sugar, sugar confetti, or candies on the glaze (see step 12).

12. Place the baking sheets in the refrigerator to speed up the setting of the glaze, or allow the cookies to set for 4 to 6 hours at room temperature.

13. Unfrosted sugar cookies should be stored in an airtight plastic container at room temperature for up to 3 days or in the freezer for up to 3 weeks. When glazed or frosted, it's best to store them in the container, with plastic wrap, parchment, or waxed paper between the layers.

Makes 15 large or 25 small cookies

Poppyseed Hamantaschen

♥ ♥ ♥ ♥ ♥ ♥ ♥ *formed cookie*

I went through a lot of hamantaschen—a fall favorite, served often in celebration of the Jewish holiday of Purim—before I came up with this one. The rejects were dry or tasteless, their dough was impossible to work with, or they called for incongruous ingredients like ginger ale or orange juice. This one is simple to make, rich in taste, and filled with a poppyseed mixture, which you should be able to find in the baking section of major supermarkets (it's made by Solo). If poppyseeds aren't to your taste, use any thick preserves for the filling.

INGREDIENTS

THE DOUGH

2 cups plus 3 tablespoons all-purpose flour
½ cup sugar
⅛ teaspoon baking powder
1 teaspoon grated lemon or orange zest
¾ teaspoon salt
¾ cup (1½ sticks) unsalted butter at room
*   temperature, cut into 12 pieces*
2 tablespoons cold water
2 large egg yolks

THE FILLING

1¼ cups poppyseed filling (see headnote)

1. Place the flour, sugar, baking powder, zest, and salt in a food processor and process for 20 seconds. (Or whisk them together by hand in a large mixing bowl.)

2. Distribute the butter evenly over the flour and process until the mixture resembles coarse meal, 15 to 20 seconds. (Or rub the butter into the flour with your fingertips, or cut it in with a pastry blender.)

3. In a small cup, whisk together the cold water and egg yolks. With the processor running, pour the egg mixture in a steady stream through the

feed tube and process just until the dough comes together, 20 to 30 seconds. (Or sprinkle the egg mixture over the flour mixture while tossing with a fork.)

4. Place the dough on a lightly floured work surface, and knead it several times to bring it together.

5. Shape the dough into two thick disks, wrap each one in plastic wrap, and refrigerate them for 1 hour.

6. Line several baking sheets with parchment paper, or grease them lightly with vegetable oil.

7. Remove one disk from the refrigerator and roll it out to form a round approximately 12 inches in diameter and a generous ⅛ inch thick.

8. Using a 2½-inch cookie cutter, cut out as many rounds as possible. Place them ¼ inch apart on the prepared baking sheets. Repeat with the second disk.

9. Place 1 rounded teaspoon of filling in the center of each round. Then fold the edges of the dough toward the center to form a triangle, leaving a bit of the filling showing in the center. Pinch the edges in three places to seal them. Place the baking sheets in the refrigerator for 30 minutes, or in the freezer for 15 minutes, to chill the triangles.

10. Fifteen minutes before baking, preheat the oven to 375°F.

11. Bake the hamantaschen until they are crisp, firm to the touch, and golden around the edges, 20 minutes. Let them cool completely on the baking sheets.

12. If you plan on snacking on them on the first day, leave the hamantaschen on a plate, uncovered, at room temperature. After that, layer them in an airtight plastic container with plastic wrap, parchment, or waxed paper between the layers and place in the refrigerator for up to 3 days or the freezer for up to 2 weeks.

Makes about 40 hamantaschen

Cream Cheese Rugalach

♥ ♥ ♥ ♥ ♥ ♥ ♥ ♥ ♥   *rolled cookie*

Rugalach and I first met in my childhood, when my mother used to bring it home with her after visiting my grandmother in Queens. Determined to make it more readily available, I've sold it at Rosie's for twenty years, and it has never lost its appeal. That may be because it is perfect served at the end of almost any meal—holiday or not. Making rugalach isn't a simple undertaking, but the dough in this recipe is easier to work with than many I've come across, and the result is certainly

worth the effort. Just remember that you can keep refrigerating the dough intermittently while you're working with it, which makes the whole enterprise less daunting. Also, the filling can be made with fruit-juice-sweetened jam if you're avoiding sugar.

INGREDIENTS

THE DOUGH
1¼ cups all-purpose flour
⅛ teaspoon salt
8 tablespoons (1 stick) unsalted butter at room temperature
4 ounces cream cheese at room temperature

THE FILLING
¾ cup apricot or raspberry preserves
½ cup chopped pecans or walnuts
½ cup golden or dark raisins

THE GLAZE
1 large egg
1 tablespoon sugar
¼ teaspoon ground cinnamon

1. Sift the flour and salt together in a small bowl and set aside.

2. Using an electric mixer on medium speed, cream the butter and cream cheese together in a medium-size bowl until light and fluffy, 1½ to 2 minutes. Stop the mixer once or twice during the process to scrape the bowl with a rubber spatula.

3. Add the flour mixture and mix until blended, about 20 seconds, stopping the mixer once to scrape the bowl. Place the dough on a work surface and work it with your hands until it comes together.

4. Shape the dough into two thick rectangles, wrap each one in plastic wrap, and refrigerate them for 3 hours.

5. Remove one dough rectangle from the refrigerator, and roll it out between two fresh pieces of plastic wrap to form a rectangle about 14 × 8 inches.

6. Peel off the top piece of plastic wrap and turn the dough so one long side is facing you. Spread 6 table-spoons of the preserves evenly over the dough, leaving uncovered a ½-inch strip along the long edge farthest away from you.

7. Sprinkle ¼ cup of the nuts and ¼ cup of the raisins over the preserves.

8. Loosen the filled long edge of the dough from the plastic wrap with a knife or spatula, and roll it toward the uncovered edge like a jelly roll, peeling off the plastic wrap as you roll. The seam should be on the underside. Wrap the roll in fresh plastic and refrigerate it. Repeat the process with the other dough rectangle. Keep the filled rolls refrigerated for 2 hours.

9. Fifteen minutes before baking, preheat the oven to 375°F. Line two baking sheets with parchment paper, or lightly grease them with vegetable oil.

10. For the glaze, lightly beat the egg with a fork. Stir the sugar and cinna-mon together in a small cup. Using a pastry brush, brush the egg over the

outside of both rolls. Then sprinkle the cinnamon-sugar mixture over the rolls.

11. Using a thin sharp knife, carefully cut the rolls into pieces about 1 inch thick. Place the rugalach, seam side down, about 1 inch apart on the pre-pared baking sheets.

12. Bake until the rugalach are golden, 18 to 20 minutes. (Some of the jam will ooze out and start to darken.) Use a spatula to immediately transfer the rugalach to wire racks to cool.

13. Layer the rugalach in an airtight plastic container with plastic wrap, parchment, or waxed paper between the layers and store at room tempera-ture for 1 day before serving. Their fla-vor and consistency will be enhanced by the day of rest. The rugalach can re-main at room temperature for up to 3 days. After that place the container in the freezer for up to 2 weeks.

Makes about 26 rugalach

Sour Cream Rugalach

❤ ❤ ❤ ❤ ❤ ❤ ❤ ❤ ❤ ❤   *rolled cookie*

This recipe is slightly different from the Cream Cheese Rugalach: You form the dough into little crescents rather than long rolls, and you use sour cream to create a light and flaky dough. As my daughter, Maya, would say, "Awesome!"

INGREDIENTS

THE DOUGH
1 large egg yolk
¾ cup sour cream
2 cups all-purpose flour
½ teaspoon salt
1 cup (2 sticks) unsalted
    butter, cold, cut into 12 pieces

THE FILLING
4½ tablespoons sugar
1½ teaspoons ground cinnamon
1 cup raspberry or apricot preserves
Scant 1 cup chopped walnuts
    or pecans
Scant 1 cup golden or dark raisins

1. Stir the egg yolk and sour cream together in a small bowl.

2. Place the flour and salt in a food processor and process for 5 seconds.

3. Distribute the butter over the flour mixture, and process until the mixture resembles coarse cornmeal, 15 seconds.

4. With the machine running, pour the sour cream mixture through the feed tube. Stop the processor, then pulse 12 times. Scrape the bowl, then pulse another 20 times.

5. Place the dough on a work surface and knead it several times.

6. Divide the dough into four disks, wrap each one in plastic wrap, and refrigerate them for 6 to 8 hours or overnight.

7. Remove one disk from the refrigerator and roll it between two fresh pieces of plastic wrap to form a round 9 inches in diameter and approximately ⅛ inch thick. Trim the edges to make a perfect circle. Place the dough, still sandwiched in the plastic wrap, on a plate and refrigerate it for 1 hour. Repeat with the remaining disks.

8. In a small bowl, stir together the sugar and the cinnamon. Set aside.

9. Line several baking sheets with parchment paper, or grease them lightly with vegetable oil.

10. After the dough has chilled, remove one round from the refrigerator. Peel off the top piece of plastic wrap. Spread ¼ cup of the preserves over the dough. Then sprinkle it with approximately 4 teaspoons of the cinnamon-sugar mixture, 3 tablespoons of the raisins, and 3 tablespoons of the nuts.

11. Using the point of a sharp thin knife, cut the disk into 12 wedges. Carefully lift the wide end of each wedge, roll up the triangle toward the tip, and with the point on the bottom, curve in the sides to form a crescent shape. Place the rugalach 1½ inches apart on the baking sheet. Refrigerate for 30 minutes before baking. Repeat with the remaining dough and filling.

12. Fifteen minutes before baking, preheat the oven to 375°F.

13. Bake the rugalach until they are crisp and golden, 18 to 20 minutes.

14. Cool the rugalach for several minutes on the sheets. Then using a spatula, carefully transfer each rugalach to a wire rack (do this before any jam that has seeped out starts to harden). Cool the rugalach completely before eating.

15. Layer the rugalach in an airtight plastic container with plastic wrap, parchment, or waxed paper between the layers and store at room temperature for 1 day before serving. Their flavor and consistency will be enhanced by the day of rest. The rugalach can remain at room temperature for up to 3 days. After that, place the container in the freezer for up to 2 weeks.

Makes 48 rugalach

Buttermilk Doughnut Holes

❤ ❤ ❤ ❤ ❤ ❤ ❤ ❤ ❤ ❤ ❤ ❤ ❤ ❤ ❤

I bow to no one in my love of doughnuts. Not the fancy-schmancy ones, mind you, but your basic, old-fashioned doughnutty doughnut that's crunchy on the outside and soft on the inside—like these doughnut holes. My family devours them in bulk at Chanukah, when tradition calls for doughnuts (for any fried food, actually) to commemorate the oil that miraculously kept the Temple's sacred light burning for eight days and nights. Even divine intervention wouldn't keep these doughnut holes around my house that long, so it's a good thing that they're quick to prepare.

INGREDIENTS

1½ quarts pure vegetable oil

THE COATINGS
1 cup sifted confectioners' sugar
1 cup granulated sugar
2 tablespoons ground cinnamon

THE BATTER
1 cup all-purpose flour
⅔ cup cake flour
½ teaspoon baking soda
1 teaspoon baking powder
½ teaspoon salt
½ teaspoon ground nutmeg
1 large egg
½ cup sugar
1 tablespoon unsalted butter, melted
½ teaspoon pure vanilla extract
½ cup buttermilk at room temperature

1. Attach a candy thermometer to the side of a 4- or 5-quart saucepan placed over medium heat. Pour in the oil (it should be 3 to 4 inches deep) and heat until the oil reaches 375° to 380°F.

2. Prepare one or both coatings: Place the confectioners' sugar in a plastic bag. Place the granulated sugar and the cinnamon in another plastic bag, and shake (with the bag tightly closed) to mix thoroughly. Set the bags aside.

3. Sift both flours, baking soda, baking powder, salt, and nutmeg together into a small bowl and set aside.

4. Using a whisk, blend the egg and sugar together in a medium-size bowl. Stir in the melted butter, vanilla, and buttermilk.

5. Resift the flour mixture over the egg mixture, and using a rubber spatula, fold gently until mixed.

6. Using a 1½-inch diameter ice cream scoop, drop five level scoops of the batter, one at a time, into the oil and cook until they are crunchy and deep golden, 4 to 5 minutes.

7. Using a slotted spoon, remove a doughnut hole from the oil and cut it in half. If the center seems gooey, the doughnut holes need to cook for another minute or two. Remove the doughnuts with the slotted spoon and place them on paper towels to drain. Continue frying the remaining batter in this fashion.

8. To coat the doughnut holes in the cinnamon-sugar mixture: About 1 minute after removing them from the oil, place one doughnut at a time in the bag and toss to coat. Return it to the paper towel to cool.

9. To coat with the confectioners' sugar, allow the doughnut holes to cool completely. Then place them one by one in the bag and toss to coat.

10. These doughnuts should be eaten as soon as possible.

Makes about 20 doughnut holes

Variation: *Cider Doughnuts*

Substitute ½ cup cider for the buttermilk, and add 1 tablespoon ground cinnamon, ¾ teaspoon ground cardamom, and ¾ cup finely chopped peeled apples to the batter.

The Marks's Matzoh Crunch

❤ ❤ ❤ ❤ ❤ ❤ ❤ ❤ ❤ ❤ ❤ ❤

This recipe was plucked from the pages of the self-published *Father and Son Cookbook*, a delightful book by the talented father-and-son team of my good friends Roger and Gabriel Marks. The crunch created a sensation at Rosie's and became a staple at Passover, even for those who don't celebrate the holiday. I'm honored to add it to my repertoire and thank Roger and Gabriel again.

INGREDIENTS

6 boards plain matzoh
1¼ cups (2½ sticks) unsalted butter
1¼ cups (firmly packed) light brown sugar
6 ounces (1 cup) semisweet chocolate chips
   or chopped semisweet chocolate

1. Preheat the oven to 350°F. Lightly grease a rimmed baking sheet with butter.

2. Line the baking sheet with the matzoh, breaking the pieces where necessary to fill in all the spaces.

3. Combine the butter and brown sugar in a medium-size saucepan over medium heat. Stir constantly with a wooden spoon until the mixture boils, 5 minutes. Then continue to cook 3 minutes more, stirring constantly.

4. Remove the butter mixture from the heat, and pour it evenly over the matzoh.

5. Bake until the matzoh is deep golden in color, 10 to 12 minutes. (After the first 8 minutes, check every 2 minutes to make sure it doesn't burn.)

6. Remove the pan from the oven and sprinkle the chocolate over the matzoh. Allow it to melt. Then use a frosting spatula to spread the chocolate over the matzoh. Place the pan in the refrigerator for the chocolate to set, 1 to 2 hours.

7. When the matzoh is completely chilled, break it into pieces.

Makes 6 boards of matzoh crunch

C

D

E

F

G

Low-fat:
   almond biscotti, 79-80
   chocolate chocolate chip
      meringues, 41-42

M

Macadamia:
   bars, tropical, 183-84
   toasted coconut shortbread,
      93-94
   white chocolate brownies,
      159-60
Macaroons:
   chocolate-dipped almond,
      50-51
   hazelnut, 52-53
Mailing cookies, 14-15
Mandelbrot, 79
   Amy's, 83-84
   chocolate chocolate chip, 82-
      83
   orange walnut, 80-81
Maple softies, 109-10
Margarine, 6-7
Marks, Roger and Gabriel,
      241
Marks's matzoh crunch, 241-
      42
Marshmallow, in pumpkin
      whoopee pies, 139-41
Matzoh crunch, Marks's, 241-
      42
Maya's little butter cupcakes,
      201-2
Measuring equipment, 5
Meringues:
   chocolate chocolate chip,
      41-42
   lemon, 85-86
Microwave oven, bringing
      butter to room temp-
      erature in, 7
Microwave-safe dishes, 5
Miller, Joyce, 208
Miniature desserts. See Tidbits
Minteos, chocolate, 120-22
Mixers, electric, 4
Mixing bowls, 5
M-M-M-Madeleines, 206
Molasses:
   cake cookies, glazed, 111-
      12
   ginger cookies, 218
   lemon-glazed hermits, 108-9

Muffins, blueberry, 211-12
My new brownie, 146-47

N

Nastasi, Amy, 63
Neiman Marcus, 44
Nestle's, 37
New York cheesecake brownies,
      149-50
Noah's chocolate chocolatey
      chocolate chips, 34-35
Noah's Scotch shortbread bar,
      169-70
Nut(s), 10
   banana chocolate chunks,
      49-50
   toasting, 89
   see also specific nuts

O

Oat(meal)(s), 9-10
   banana-nut chocolate
      chunks, 49-50
   cherry crumb bars, 174-76
   chocolate chips, 43-44
   chocolate chocolate chip
      cookies, 45-46
   chunky pecan shortbread,
      94-95
   cookies, Rosie's, 42-43
   cranberry crumb bars, 176-
      77
   cranberry orange cookies,
      46-47
   crispy fingers, 134-35
   crumb topping, 211-12
   dating bars, 179-80
   double crispy sandwiches,
      123-24
   freezing doughs with, 12-13
   pecan chips, 44-45
   thumbprints, 233-34
   whole grain earthy chocolate
      chips, 40-41
Orange:
   almond spritzes, 136-37
   chocolate shortbread, 90-91
   cranberry bars, creamy, 177-
      78
   cranberry oatmeal cookies,
      46-47

lemon sour cream cookies,
      105-6
pecan crisps, 73-74
pecan ginger florentines,
      222-23
toasted pecan brownies, 153-
      54
walnut mandelbrot, 80-81

P

Palmiers, très French, 76-78
Parchment paper, 5, 11, 12
Pastries:
   apple galettes, 195-96
   apple turnovers, 194-95
   butter wreaths, 226-27
   Joyce Miller's pecan tartlets,
      208-9
   lemon curd tartlets, 209-11
   rosy cranberry tartlets, 207-8
   très French palmiers, 76-78
Pastry bars:
   blond Linzer, 162-64
   chocolate Linzer, 164-65
   cranberry crumb, 176-77
   dating, 179-80
   general instructions for, 29-
      30
   hazelnut cranberry Linzer,
      166-67
   pucker-your-lips apricot
      Linzer, 161-62
   yummy cheesecake, 180-81
Peanut butter:
   chocolate volcanoes, 48-49
   sandwiches, 141-42
   shortbread cookies, 95-96
   topped brownies, 147-48
Pecan(s):
   banana-nut chocolate
      chunks, 49-50
   caramel bars, 184-85
   chocolate chip mounds, 63
   chocolate chips, 36-37
   chocolate chunkers, 39-40
   cinnamon shortbread bars,
      167-68
   cream cheese rugalach, 237-
      38
   crescents, 224-25
   crisps, 74-75
   dark brown sugar chocolate
      chips, 38

R

S

T

V

W

Y